The Animals Teach Us Everything & Other Short Tails

Lucy Mason Jensen

Copyright © 2019 by Lucy Mason Jensen

All rights reserved. No part of this book may be reproduced or transmitted in any form or by any means, electronic or mechanical, including photocopying, recording, or by any information storage and retrieval system, without permission in writing from the copyright owner.

A note from Lucy –

This is my second compilation of my newspaper columns that were published in the 'South County Newspapers' from 2011 until 2019. In this edition, I am paying more than just a nod to my life's work, my rescue animals and my adorable four legged babies who live with us and thrive in our home called *'Solace'*. It is with all of them in mind – the hearts and souls of those special, innocent creatures whom we rescued and then they rescued us right back – that my compilation of stories and photographs came together.

With this story collection, I wanted to give something back to our local animals, many who are dumped on the side of the road and left to die, or sent to a shelter with little hope of rescue. It was with that in mind that our animal rescue 'South County Animal Rescue' was born. Since we were already doing the work, we felt moved to fill in the gaps and organize our efforts to be able to help more babies and save more lives.

With every book sold, I pledge to make a donation to "South County Animal Rescue", or the suitable acronym "SCAR". Thanks for reading and contributing to rescuing those precious lives that cannot rescue themselves.

Love, bark, hum and meow – not to mention ba and neigh and nicker to your heart's content – just don't spit!

The characters of Solace - Dug, Winston Jr., Tucker, Jaxx, Woodrow, Joey 2, Joey 3, Joey 4, Bone, Mama, Mama Zoe, Max, Harold Malcolm Democracy, Sam, Elvis, Pickle, Pea, Thursday Solo, Turkey and Gilroy – not to mention the fosters that go through our doors and rest for a while until they find their forever homes – and our cherished souls who came and left us too soon. My heart is full to the brim with all of you.

In my humble opinion, the animals *do* teach us everything!

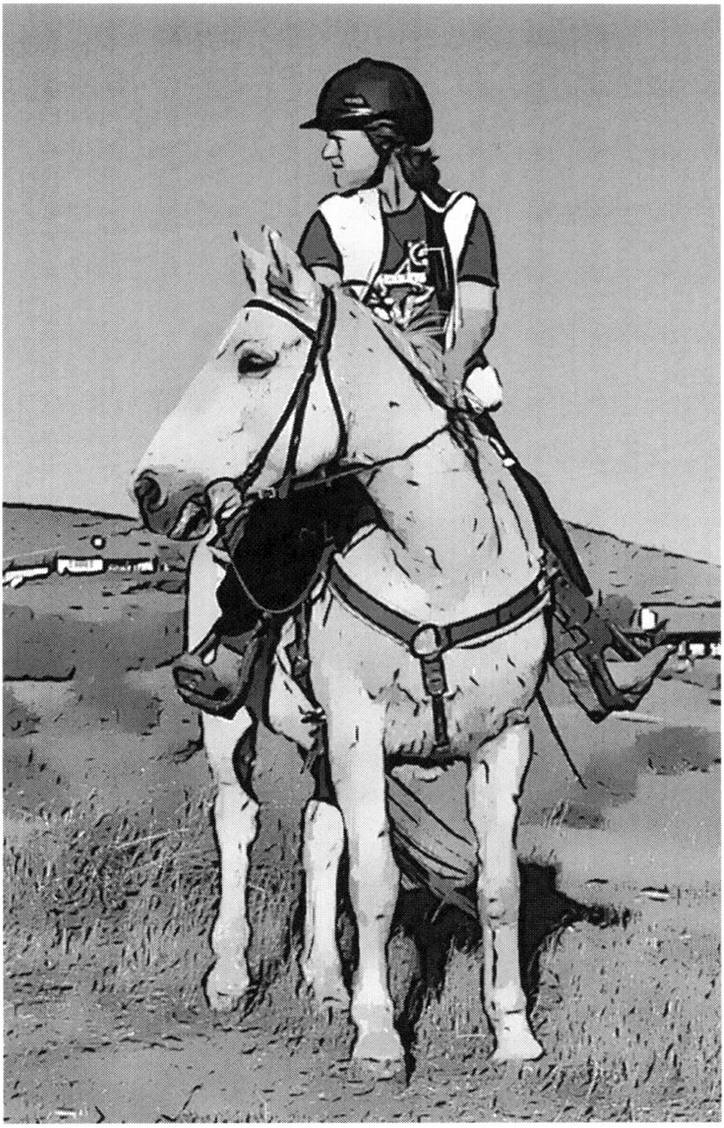

DEDICATED TO THE VERY LARGE & SPECIAL MEMORY OF SIR WINSTON WHITE HORSE, BAXTER, SOPHIE & ROSCOE WHO BECAME FOREVER SOLACE SPIRITS IN 2019.

Lucy

CONTENTS

THE ANIMALS TEACH US: Tolerance, Peace, Magic, Love

16 Years with Mr. Sheet 3
The Fair: This year, a family affair. 7
Bertha and her near escape 13
Call of the wild 18
Comedy of the Teen Years 24
Como se llame 29
Dog people and cat people 34
Gone Fishing 39
It's all in the giving 44
Karma and the Apricot Tree 49
Little House on the Prairie 53
Love and That Crazy Girl 58
Mama Cat in the hood 63
Mothers come in all kinds of bundles 68
Mucking out on a Monday 75
Peace from my horses 80
Penance 84
Rain drops and cow boots 89
Sally, the Champ 92
Saved by the e-kiss 97
Slick and the train he rode in on 101
Someone opened the gate 105
Starring in my own cartoon 112
The box 117
The Crazy Cat Lady 121
The Lousy Pet Sitter 127
The month of the cat 132

The more I know mankind 136
The one-legged bird 141
The peculiar stories of the stolen tomatoes and the clean
colon 144
The War Horse 148
The Wheelbarrow 155
There is something wrong with my feet 159
When the animals speak 164
With every season 170

THE ANIMALS TEACH US: Humor, Joy, Trust, Love

53 and fabulous 177
A marvelous feral called Mama 180
Be still my beating heart 183
Buttering toast for the Chihuahua 188
Carpets & Cowgirls 193
Dogs on a Diet & a trip to the ER 197
Either Madness or Grief 202
Finding Fur-Ever Friends 205
Finding Love in the Mud 208
For the love of a stubborn man 211
Good work is not easy 215
Lizard on a hot tin roof 218
Making a difference 222
My forever girl 225
Puppies and Plane Rides 229
Queen Victoria and the Diet Princesses 232
Sweeping the stable 237
Talking through our phones 242
The Animals Taught Me 246
"The Attack of the Rooster 253
The Boss 257
The Half Date 260
The heart of the animal rescuer 264
The Life of An Animal Rescuer 268

The Llama Games 272
The Nickers of Solace 276
The Pack Horse 281
The story of the wolf and the full moon 287
Throwing out the Garbage... 292
The Winner of the Beauty Contest 295

THE ANIMALS TEACH US: Hope, Courage, Promise, Love

A dog named Spirit 303
A simpler life 307
Always Look On the Bright Side 312
Bacon is a Beast 316
Bricks for Feet.. 320
The Bucket Bruise 324
Changing the Lens 329
Everyone needs at least one animal............................... 333
Fences & Feelings 338
Finding her legs... 343
Happy Birthday, my Beautiful Border Collie.................. 347
Hope springs eternal... 352
Laughing At the Old Man 355
Lucy Saving Lucy... 359
Ode to the Fastest Dog on the ranch............................. 363
Sophie & The Cockroaches 367
The Equitation Safety Guide & Other Cautionary Tales... 372
The Fastest Dog on the Ranch....................................... 375
The Happy Book 378
The Lady Bucket.. 383
The Vineyard Dog... 387
To begin somewhere towards the end........................... 391
Valentine Vacuums 395
Sir Winston White Horse and all the love he gave 399

THE ANIMALS TEACH US:
Tolerance, Peace, Magic, Love

These tales were published in South County Newspapers 2011-2013

16 Years with Mr. Sheet

If you asked my husband how long we have been together, he would honestly have to reply, with an element of panic, "Errrr, I don't know; ask my wife!" That is the same answer you'd receive, if you asked him if he had any money in the bank; but that is quite another issue. He is not good at dates – birthdays, anniversaries etc. just pass him by, they are not his bag. I've warned my daughter that if I float away into oblivion she will have to inherit the banker and calendar crown in the family, or it will be likely that the whole clan, by default, will slip and slide down the greasy slope of poverty, which is what can happen when you just don't remember to pay your bills, or fail to recognize that certain things, in the modern day world, have to be handled by certain dates. By example and without even a glimmer of hyperbole; when I first met my husband, he would wait for his creditors to call him and then pay them their past due bills over the phone. He explained to me, at the time, that this seemed like a much easier option than having to open up the envelopes, write out the checks, buy stamps, mail the letters and so on. They would call him, he would pay them and everyone was happy. He thought. Not surprisingly, once upon a time, his extensive list of late charges far exceeded any of my own previous credit challenges, by far. But again; another story!

We have been together a long time, he is comfortable with me - loves me even - and he doesn't need to ponder over whether we have been together one decade or two or three; that's just mathematics and obviously not his thing. However, he does have the ability to acknowledge when the Hallmark Holidays are coming back around and was, notably, so relieved, prior to this annual season of hearts and flowers, when I told him that I hadn't got him anything for Valentine's Day. "Nothing? Oh that is so great!" he enthused. "So, really nothing? Nothing nothing? And I don't have to get you anything either?" It was like a truce to all the love stuff you can find around that day and it obviously meant a lot to him. My daughter was not so impressed. "What do you mean you are not getting Dad anything for Valentine's Day? Are you guys getting a divorce or something?" (She's seventeen. She can be so dramatic.) "Of course we are not getting a divorce this week!" I staunchly defend our union. "Well, because if you are," she went on. "I'm not going with either one of you! You guys will have to just both move out and I'll be staying here." Ok, so at least we have her position clear in the whole lack of Valentines loot scenario this year!

One of the blessings of living with another human being for a very long time can be the realm of the mundane and the banal. It can also be one of the drawbacks. "I didn't have any of the duvet last night," my Valentine complained, mildly, discussing our divine European goose down filled delight. "Just sheet." I, on the other hand, during that very same night, enjoyed a nice thick chunk of warm soft duvet with lots of feathers and very little sheet on my side of the world. "Well then fix the bed to your liking!" I told him, in no uncertain terms, as you do in the realm of the mundane and the banal. These conversations within a domestic union can also extend to scintillating items such as 'did you buy any more toilet paper or milk? Did you feed the animals?' – and beyond.

It was 4am on Valentine's morning and neither one of us had purchased any Valentine consumer items for the other. The grievance echoed in reconciliatory tone across the shared bed. "Mr. Sheet is asking Ms Feathers for some of her many feathers", he complained. "Yeh, Mr. Sheet is full of sheet!" Ms Feathers scuttle-bucketed back and, at 4.02am, we were both in fits of laughter. And there we had it – our Valentine's gift to each other; the gift of still being able to giggle with each other at the dumbest things at the most random time of the day or night.

The next day – the day of the bright red Valentine, when billions spend billions on chocolates, flowers, diamonds and who knows what, Mr. Sheet and Ms Feathers got to share a hand–made card, illustrating their 4am discussion with one another and how much it made them laugh and love each other all over again at 4:00 am until about 4.04am Western standard time.

Sometimes the rarest gifts are packaged up in the oddest ways and arrive on your doorstep in the strangest parcels. If you have lived with some one - one, two or three decades – who cares, it's only math - and you can still giggle with one another at 4am, the odds are you, really, still, have a good thing going and you will, ultimately, be forgiven if you forget the flowers, eat the chocolates yourself and deal with just the sheet you have been dealt.

Published February 2012

The Fair: This year, a family affair.

I had no idea what to expect. When I was at school, there were no *'Future Farmer'* clubs to join, no fairs or exhibitions to participate in, where you might have the opportunity to sell, at an auction, the animal you had raised. The closest thing we came to raising animals in our school was dissecting a frog in our biology class, or being able to bring in a lady bug in a match box for *'Show and Tell'*. My husband had been a surfer, not a Future Farmer during his school days, so he was no use either. Raising livestock for the fair was uncharted territory in our household.

But my daughter was adamant that she wanted to try it; she wanted to see how it would be to raise a pig to the standards they expect at the County Fair and how well she could do. She was determined to see it through and not get attached to the animal. Or so she said. So many life lessons; so many, I thought to myself, even at the very beginning of our journey. Even last year, when I told her she couldn't do it; she learned something. She would never be able to give up the animal, I told her. But that was last year.

The first lesson was in politics. You have to persuade your parents to allow you to do this thing, because they will also be involved – heavily at times, I noticed. The time expenditure is February to May, so about 3 long months of committed time for your family. Consequently, your parents have to accept, even welcome, the endeavor. Once this exercise in political persuasion is complete, you must tackle the construction part of the journey. You must build a secure home for the animal. It has to be sturdy, practical and kind. It must have shelter, heat and water – the basics of any dwelling – and enough room to be comfortable and interesting. You will need to undergo this exercise with the help of an adult familiar with construction and power tools. This could also be considered part two of your political exam. At the end of this exercise, you will understand that rubber boots are a must in any household and that you will need to inherit your Dad's tool box, if you'll ever have a hope of building almost everything he can. Do not forget, also, that Dad must be bowed down to at every opportunity. If he has to give up at least a full weekend to help you build the pig pen extraordinaire, then you need to thank him accordingly.

In this modern day age of *'eBAY'* and all, most things can be purchased on line. You will learn that even livestock can also be bought online in an *'eBAY'* fashion. You will ultimately learn that many folk are not that familiar with buying online livestock and you could end up with more livestock than you had wanted in the first place, if you are not extremely careful. Case in point, we ended up with four trotters too many. Fortunately for us, a member of the Future Farmer's club had selected a dud from a selection process that was not online and needed our additional four trotters. (And much as we wish her well, we equally hope we didn't give away the Grand Champion!)

Another lesson gleaned is that, once your livestock is in its pen, you need to know exactly how much to feed it every day. You need to check its water twice daily and you need to exercise it. You also need to learn how to control your livestock, as it were. Teach it to walk alongside you with a stick and maneuver it according to your will. You will be in a showmanship arena at the fairgrounds with this animal and the judges will need to know that you have done this before, many times. You will purchase feed for this animal and bedding. You will be required to pay attention to the restocking of this feed and log everything in your log book. Your book will be checked and assessed at weigh-in and shoddy records will not pass the test. You *will* be judged as a future farmer and you had better behave that way out the gate.

You need to make sure your animal is weighed regularly. Whether or not, Sally likes to get on the weigh scale, it must be top of mind that there is a weight limit at the fair and you would hate to be disqualified for carelessness, just because Sally doesn't care to be a player. Whether it takes you and your Ag Advisor an hour or more to coax Sally into the chute, it has to be done and it has to be done at regular intervals. If it takes a full bag of marshmallows or a pint of strawberries to get her situated on that scale, then that is what you need to be armed with to reach your goal. You will learn untold patience and stamina along the way. No amount of education behind your desk at school can teach you that.

Your animal is on track to be shown and auctioned at the fair. You need to prepare yourself. You must purchase the appropriate clothing for your club, or just yourself, if you are showing as an independent exhibitor. You must make sure that you are just as presentable as your animal. Never mind that white clothes are, perhaps, not the best attire, when you are maneuvering livestock into pens and shoveling their droppings; that is the color of the club and that standard must be maintained. There will be a few days when you will need to show yourself just as well as your animal and you must plan for that in addition. At the end of these long days of Fair, you will be exhausted – guaranteed – as will your family. You will have got up very early to take your animal to the fair, (bear in mind, the hours that Sally might need to get loaded up into the trailer!) You will have dealt with the issues of preparation and performance – very tricky at the best of times, even without a pig. You will have tackled the unpredictability of an animal in a crowd – never easy to anticipate. You will have performed in front of your peers – always a challenge and a tad nerve-wracking. You will have made your parents and your grandparents proud. No doubt. And, at the end of the few long-short days of fair, you will have gleaned so many life lessons that your educational cup will be overflowing with accomplishments and pride.

Never mind that you may swear never to eat the meat of the livestock you raised ever again – and maybe you won't – this is how you learn about life's tough journey. We all die. Some of us die for a purpose – livestock – some of us don't – the livestock that was born sickly. At least you now understand a part of the food chain that is the world. You understand how farmers raise animals for market and a piece of what it entails to be a part of that.

During the fair, we will show up and we will participate as we have never done before. We will visit the auction and examine the show pens with the eye of a somewhat-expert we did not possess in the past. This exercise was entirely a family affair, rich with education and knowledge. Prior to our animal husbandry lessons of the past few months, none of us could tell a barrow from gilt; let alone communicate what on earth that meant. Now we can do that and some.

It could be that, after the Salinas Valley Fair, we will mourn the departures of Jeremy and Sally from our ranch. Try as you may, it is almost impossible not to become attached to animals when you are intrinsic animal lovers. But, as the adults, our job is to stand back and ask ourselves if our offspring learned something from this exercise; and even, stand back in amazement, did we? It could be that none of us ever eat that particular meat again. It could be that this slice of education creates a path for the future in some one's life, or, at least, an understanding of many learning curves, as we branch out and onwards. In any case, I will have to say, at the end of it all, that we shall all be very tired. We shall all, no doubt, feel a little overwhelmed and we'll also know a few more things than we knew a bit ago. Now how bad can that be?

Are you ready for the Fair this year? Ready or not, we shall see you there.

Sally surpassed everyone's expectations at the Salinas Valley Fair. She won Grand Champion Reserve and FFA Champion. We so nearly bought her back, we had got so attached. Everyone learned a lot.

Published May 2011

Bertha and her near escape

You just can't run very fast in cowboy boots, even when you are a tad athletic like myself; I can attest to that. It was a hazy morning and I was out in the meadow with my horse, goats and dogs, as I am every morning. It's the way I start my day out right. If everything goes down hill from there, we began at the very pinnacle of a quality existence and sometimes that is all I can ask for. I was grooming Winston, the horse, and trying to persuade Charlie, the goat, that he had his own trough to eat out of and did not need to sit in Winston's hay to feed, when I noticed a couple of guys out at the neighboring lot with their pick up truck. This did not surprise me, since the neighbor's house had gone back to the bank and, any day, we were expecting the bank services to come and clean it up. These particular individuals did seem a bit strange though, so I went over there to talk to them, wishing I had Dug, our Queensland, alongside me to back me up. Dug can be a bit intimidating at the best of times with his ice blue eyes and I am not in the habit of approaching strange men when I know that no one is watching. The men told me they were from the bank and were cleaning up the property; that confirmed my first assumption.

The next thing I know, our large and expensive orange

brush mower 'Bertha' had been hauled up from our land and was in the back of their truck and peeling out from the property. "Stop, you bad people!" I yelled, or words to that effect, as I galloped across the land to try and stop the truck. Yes, well, as I mentioned before; running in cowboy boots is not that efficient, even when you might be young and fast, of which I am neither. I watched to see which way they went on Metz Road and tore into the house to call the emergency services. I did not realize that if you dial '911', as we are wont to do when we are royally upset about something, that the number dialed is automatically to the Highway Patrol, who then connect you with the Sheriff's Department if, in fact, that is what you need. I was a bit upset that it took about 45 minutes for said office to call me back, knowing that the thieves were long gone and out of the area by that time.

I had, however, underestimated our local Sheriff's Department. Deputy Wilson took down all the details and began his investigation. I was surprised when he came to check out the scene of the crime and interview our neighbors. He talked to both my husband and myself, he also contacted the numbers listed at the vacant house and discovered the new residence of the former owner. "Boy, it must be a slow police day," I thought to myself. All of this over a stolen mower? It wasn't just that. I couldn't believe they had got one over me – me, the former city girl, the wise-ass, university grad. I had turned my back and they had ripped me off and that made me so mad.

"You need to calm down about the mower being

stolen," my husband urged as I obsessively tried to recall some details of the perpetrators all morning long. I could remember the pick up truck, but I could not recall much at all of the young man I had asked questions of. Wow, am I that unobservant? You never know in this life, folks, when you are going to be needing details. "Did you get any part of the number plate on the truck?" the deputy asked me. Hmm, when I am running flat out in my cowboy boots and screaming at the top of my voice, I think that little detail escaped me. I called the Home Owners' Association and asked them to check the gate records. I fumed over the lack of cameras and the need for more surveillance at the entrance to our homes. I thought of my own home and how my territorial dogs will be residing inside the property whenever I am not at the property, ready and willing to tear up any one who does not belong there. I began to make all kinds of strategic changes in my life the morning my mower got stolen. And then it went calm. "Don't worry dear," my husband assured me. "The insurance will cover the cost of another mower." That was so not the point. Those crooks had my big orange Bertha and they were going to have their wicked way with her. They would be out there buying lots of 12 packs with the large amount of money they were going to be able to get for her on the black market for slippery brush mowers. There she was, far away from home, on the dark and unfriendly bed of a nasty pick up, not knowing when she would see her peeps again, nor her peaceful pastures green and all that lovely brush she was so good at consuming. I imagined it was real scary out there for her. I had to come to terms with the fact that she had probably already crossed the border or had been disassembled for parts. That was a sad fact of life. There would always be bad folk out there ready to take the possessions of the good folk. Thank goodness for karma, that's what I say and I am not even talking about my kitten of the same name. The next time they came to take advantage of my equipment, they would be received at the jaws of one of my very vicious and hungry dogs.

But Deputy Wilson had not lost a case yet; not even one involving a stolen mower, and he got to the bottom of this one quickly, as he promised us he would. He found the folks that stole our mower – they claimed they were part of the bank crew, which we knew they were not – and he spanked them in a figurative sense, forcing them to bring back Bertha to her homestead under police escort. The only icing to that particular cake would have been a personal apology – bi-lingual accepted – to the girl in the cowboy boots, who had almost broken her ankle trying to catch up with their truck as it sped out of the neighborhood. She could press charges or she could not; she hasn't decided yet, because she is still really angry with the hot-fingered thieves who saw an opportunity and got caught with their hands in the cookie jar.

And the moral of that story is that you should never underestimate me in the early hours of the morning; and definitely never our local sheriffs who lay their lives on the line every minute they are on duty – sometimes in the search of a stolen mower and very often in the pursuit of things a lot trickier.

Lucy is the mother of returned orange runaway DR Brushmower 'Bertha'. Bertha continues to live out her days surrounded by the thick brush she knows and loves.

Published September 2011

Call of the wild

"It's a jungle out there," my friend reminds us, as she appears in her bush hat, looking like some one on their way to an African safari via Hawaii. And for those of us who live in the wild countryside bordering Soledad, she would be right.

I walk through my garage. A black widow hangs off a well-woven web in her shiny black attire. In many parts of the world, that might be considered a lethal species and something to at least run screaming from. For us, it's just part of living in the countryside on the West Coast of America. We pause, take note and move on. Snakes are something we expect every summer in our neighborhood and they never seem to disappoint. Regardless of the fact that some folks – like me – think of the snake as being only really good for not very much; – in these parts they are an important part of the food chain and I really do try and appreciate them for that quality – I honestly do – but deep down, I still despise them and wish this were Hawaii in that respect, where they do not exist. Snakes also scare me – loathing and fear not being a good combination. There's a vision in my mind of my husband trying to find one particular rattle snake, which had fled from our driveway one summer and was rattling in furious fashion in the bushes. My husband had his shovel and the rattler had his poison and I had to run inside, lock all the doors and hide, because I knew the outcome could not possibly be a good one, for my husband especially. We all, fortunately, survived that one intact. (Even the rattle snake, apparently!)

When we adopted pygmy goats, we were warned that they were a Super Food for the mountain lions and coyotes out there in the wilderness. Looking at the swaying healthy bellies on my Elvis and Charlie boys, I can see that they might make a good meal for something very wild and hungry; but having also experienced a horn up the rear from one boisterous Charlie, who was anxiously awaiting his goat granola at the time, I hope that they would not go down without a fight. These days, I eye my fence line more warily. The more attached I get to my naughty goats, the more I realize that others might be keeping their greedy eyes on them too.

It was a gorgeous fall evening. The sun was just kissing the ragged ridge line of the Santa Lucia Mountains, as 3 dogs, 1 horse and I turned for home around the corner of the vineyard. It was calm and still – the fallen leaves were not even dancing to the tune of an autumn breeze. We had had a beautiful ride and run and now the light was quickly fading to dusk. As we turned the corner towards home, we came upon two large coyotes headed in our direction. These animals were not the wily, hungry foxes you might see at a distance, shyly running away from any kind of contact with civilization. These sure-footers had a more wolf-like resemblance, sturdy and confident. My alpha male Baxter loves any kind of animal. Just give him a cat, dog, goat, horse – anything – and he will want to play with it. He is also a little hard of hearing, if something excites him, and, from then on, he doesn't care to hear the human command, however shrill it might be. This has always been an issue with him and now he's about 8 plus years old, there is probably no changing him. Put a rabbit or squirrel in his path and he is gone like the wind. I've never seen a dog catch a squirrel like he can and with such determination. These attributes are not so good, however, when you are face to face, or rather snout to snout with wild animals that would like to rip you up and eat you on the spot.

Here we are eye to eye with two hungry coyotes. I am on my horse, screaming at Baxter to get closer to me. The other two small dogs are at my heels. The horse starts at my scream, scattering the other eight paws, and the two coyotes begin to circle Baxter in stealthy, pack-like manner. I could see what was going to unfold before my very eyes. Baxter, meanwhile, thought they were ready to play chase with him and I knew they were ready to play to the death. But, some how, amidst all the chaos, he must have sensed my frightened tone and, this one time, he heard me. This was about the first time in his life that Baxter has ever been in a play situation and taken the option to listen to Mum and not play on in oblivion. I couldn't believe my surprising good fortune. He was not only listening; he was running towards me. He was not going to be torn to shreds! He was going to be safe inside the fence line with the others. The relief nearly leaped out of my body. I jumped off my horse and put all the animals inside the safe confines of the meadow and then took off after the coyotes, which had already lost interest in our retreating band of possible dinners and were, with keen abandon, fresh on the trail of a scampering bunny.

"Yeh, I showed you!" I thought, wagging my finger at them. That was until today. And there they were again. At my fence line. The same pair. The nerve of it! Had I not yelled at them enough yesterday to move them on down the road, go hang out at my neighbor's house and irritate someone else? If I were *Annie-Get-my-Gun*, I would have been holstering up and chasing after them, probably not on my horse's back, because he's a scaredy-cat too, but still flat out in full pursuit, on a bicycle perhaps. But truthfully, even the pop of a balloon will get me hopping away from the scene of a crime and covering up my delicate ears, so there could be no weapon for me except for the power of my screaming fury issuing forth from healthy lungs, and that should be enough to get most living beasts standing to attention. The coyotes, however, were not impressed. They didn't even flinch. In fact, I could have sworn that one gave me the bird and the other perhaps stuck his tongue out. It's a jungle out there, I tell you. No respect.

Move forward from this near-death experience and we are in fortress-like situation at my place. The fence line has been checked and fortified. The juicy goats moved closer to the house and told not to make such obvious bleating all the time to give predators an easy dinner locator for them. (Anyone out there have a goat gag?) The horse has been put on high alert that his hooves may be needed at a moment's notice and Dug, our resident vigilante Queensland, has been denied his leave and placed on permanent duty outside with his keen eyes fixed on the perimeter of our property, sharpened teeth to the fore. We are armed and we are ready. The dogs are now put in the garage if the horse wants to go out riding in the vineyard. They may not go out into the wilds of the vineyard next door without a security clearance and an escort, more than just me and my fearful steed. Truthfully, we are considering hot wiring the fence line and locking up our prey, until things quieten down out there. We live in the beautiful Californian countryside, but we are currently hostages inside the parameters of our own fence, because we don't want to lose our pets. Prairie living? It's a jungle out there and we are man against beast. Prairie dogs, (also known as coyotes), watch me roar!

    Lucy is a resident of the jungle just outside of Soledad.
Published October 2011

Comedy of the Teen Years

Ask anyone who raises teenagers if they'd like to do it again and they will, most likely, snort at the fact you'd make such a joke. The teen years are quite the journey through hill and valley with some interesting, some funny, some testing and some, frankly, diabolical views along the way. In my house, we hope that we are now raising our last teen; though, bragging not at all, we have got quite good at it over the long years.

It was a weekday evening, nothing special. Our daughter strolls into the kitchen, "Hi Mum, hi Dad!" she says breezily and proceeds to situate herself in front of the pile of dirty dishes in the sink and go to work. My husband and I look at each other dubiously and eyebrows are quietly raised. She finishes her kitchen work and moves on towards the piles of laundry in her bedroom. Once she has the basketfuls undergoing washing and drying, she gets the vacuum out of the cupboard and begins to vacuum her carpet. "Mum, do we have any 'Carpet Fresh'?" she asks, like the house-proud little Miss I know she's not. "Something is going on," my husband noted stonily at this impressive performance. "Time will tell, my dear," I assure him quietly. "In fact, time will probably tell us as late as tomorrow morning!"

And then it was "Goodnight Mum, Good night Dad," and the two of us were practically rolling on the floor with the comedy of it all. That very next morning, as anticipated, the secret was unveiled. "Hi Mum, whatcha doing?" The text arrived in my inbox during Darling's morning break. "Er, working?" I advise cautiously, ready for battle. (She never asks me what I'm doing. Why would she care what I'm doing; she's 16?) Then it was quickly in for the kill. "Mom, can I get a tattoo. I mean nothing dumb, something really cool like a sunflower down my side?" And there it was. Our little Molly Maid wanted to get a tattoo imposed on her pretty white skin before she turned the legal age of 18.

My standard response to anyone over the age of 12 about anything at anytime is, "We'll see." It's a good token response that does not require a real answer, nor coax an argument. It does not say yes and it does not say no. It does not ruin the rest of the day for the party asking the question and has enough encouragement in it to allow for playful banter or bargaining in the future. My present teenager might even be brave enough to claim that a 'we'll see' from her mother as good as constitutes a positive response, but then she does tend to underestimate me just a little.

Situation comedy like this reminds me of life ions ago with our oldest boy, long gone from the nest. He had got himself into trouble. Again. He was about 17 at the time and driving whichever vehicle he had not yet broken. It was either the time that the Watsonville Police called us at 2am and said, "We have Marc," or it was that San Jose incident when he was busted doing something foolish – whenever he did something foolish, he was always busted – and we had to pick him up in San Jose. Or, hang on, maybe it was that time that the truck got towed, or perhaps when he put the car in the ditch. Somehow these memories tend to blend, when you have so many of a similar ilk. In any case, he was in trouble with us again. He also wanted to go away to a special football camp that involved us forking out a chunk of change for him to go out of town with his buddies, have a complete blast and convince himself, yet again, that he had what it takes to be a professional ball player. His dad had told him that he couldn't go, even though he had asked me first – always the better technique, so that I could work on his dad for him. He was now at his wits end, because we - the parental unit - were a pretty united front, as far as he was concerned; having had several sleepless nights and many a towing bill on his behalf, not to mention tickets that needed to be paid. I will never forget it. It was one of those stellar performances that imprints itself on your memory. Almost defeated, he sat down on the stair to our room and put his head in his hands. He was pleading, he was begging, this was his last concerted effort to maneuver us and then his dad choked with the realization. "Oh boy – seriously, you're crying?" His dad chortled with surprise and I do recall thinking that this performer had now also mastered the stage hand's panache of being able to weep on cue. I also remember that he did end up going away on his football camp trip and, no, he never became a professional ball player.

"So what I can I do in five minutes to make 20 dollars?" That was a well remembered line that we still cherish in our family memory book. It also came from the oldest boy. In all the years that my husband had tried to instill a strong work ethic in his boys, somehow work and money never seemed to be connected in their minds when they were teens. Shamefully enough, we sometimes just paid them to go away from us, in order for us not to either lose our minds or simply kill them. The youngest boy never wanted to leave home, let alone take his driving test. At 18, we had to put our united foot down and advise him we would no longer be driving him around. Proof that you never ever know what kind of teenager you're going to get. And now we have the princess in residence. Give me a boy any day.

Parents of teenagers unite; it is a slippery slope that we climb and sometimes the manipulative beasts will get us at our most weak and vulnerable times. We need to be aware and awake at all times; and that is when they are awake and aware. We must always be one step ahead of them and watch out for the next pot hole over which they are hoping we will trip. Be highly cautious any time they say "Mummy" or "Daddy" – that is a dead giveaway. In fact, if they address you directly, or look you in the eye and speak nicely, that is also highly suspect. Watch out for random acts of kindness – doing dishes – or unrequested chores such as cleaning the room, or being independently helpful in any way. There is always an ulterior motive that will be quickly headed towards you and your pocket book.

Call me cynical? Not at all! I am just qualified. As I do remember my mother telling me, "You were awful when you were 16," and she was absolutely right. That is, perhaps, the rite of passage for many a 16-year-old. You can't let them win the battle though and walk all over you, just to have some peace and quiet. Oh no. You just calmly respond in the "We'll see" mode and peacefully go about your business. They will be happy for a little while, confused for a while longer and then, ultimately, they will forget all about it and move on to something else. Ah, the teen years. Fortunately, time moves along at a pace and, before you know it, they will have teens of their own. Pay back, as they say, is a blessing.

Published May 2011

Como se llame

It began with a startling observation, early one morning. We had lived in our little home on the prairie for over a decade and the local coyotes had just learned how to jump over our corral board fence of reasonable height. Over the wooden boards one skipped, without missing a beat, scampered across the meadow and cleared the fence the other side like a show jumper. My dogs, horse, goats and I stood pretty much in unison with our mouths wide open. That was not good. If the coyote was now jumping into the meadow, there was a whole host of my little blessings that could be scooped up into their hungry jaws and whisked away without the beast blinking an eye. I felt strange, I felt vulnerable. I knew what I had just witnessed and it made me shudder. Prior to that moment, Slick the Coyote had taken the chance on peering through my fence to see if there were any snippets to be snatched; he had hung out at the top gate with his mates to see if any fools within the boundary lines might venture forth out into the big wide world of the hungry hunter and their festive round up. But jump inside the boundary? That was a whole other issue. I was in their territory before and now they're in mine.

And then my little white blessing of a cat, Karma, disappeared. I searched for her – I'm still searching for – I called for her; yes, still calling for her too. I cannot give up on the fact that she has to come home again. She has to lie like a baby in my arms once more and let me snuggle with her nose to nose. I can't stand the thought that she is gone for always – never to relax back in my chair again, while the goats, dog and horse continue their busy lives around her. Is she never to visit, cute button nose to muzzle, with the horse again and exchange their peculiar form of dialogue? I hate to think of that. But as the days pass, the likelihood hits me, increasingly powerfully, that she is gone and she's not coming back.

"Llamas protect their flock," the husband stated from his research position of being online and floating around the web. "They will kill coyotes that attack the flock." My ears pricked up. He had previously told me about his friend from Reno who bred llamas and was looking for a good home for a few of the non-breeders, or the few that didn't sport the excessively gorgeous markings necessary to secure the big bucks. "We're going over to Tahoe soon. We can go and get some llamas from Reno," he ventured cautiously.

What started as a fairly ridiculous idea grew from there and sprouted some wings into an actual plan. If we had llamas in our meadow, the coyotes would not come in and kill our babies. We would not have to worry about the goats, cats and dogs while we were gone. We would have llama power, protecting our borders with bayonets ready to strike. The more days that passed with Karma leaving a huge gap in my life, the more the idea began to grow. "Llamas also favor brush and bush over expensive feed," so went on our online researcher. "Raised in the Andes, they can survive on very little but picking at weeds and sticks." Those sounded like my kind of animals. Living in fire country, brush is something you are always battling. We have lots of it ourselves – not to mention the neighboring pastures around us. Maybe we should get some llamas after all.

We just happened to be traveling to Lake Tahoe for the summer celebration of our son's 30th birthday. By good fortune, our llama friend lived in Reno, Nevada, just a hop across the border. We could party in Tahoe and then llama it up in Reno. Sounded so simple! In prep for our mammoth adventure, we had truck and trailer ready and lined up. Off we went, looking like a big rig, as we headed up towards the mountains, empty trailer behind us, containing only our luggage for the weekend, some teenagers and some birthday presents. We had a wonderful surprise birthday party in Tahoe with a few hundred of our son's best friends. We hung around the lake and sampled the mountain air. Our llama mobile stayed firmly parked the whole weekend; unlikely to be able to park the semi again if it was ever to be moved!

Reno was 100 degrees and the llamas had no interest in climbing up into the horse trailer. Though the 'spitting' image of them is somewhat overused and over-exaggerated, they do 'sneeze' rather than spit, with ears back and nose up, when they are perturbed in any way, and this was one of those times. They also weigh about 400lbs each. What a llama don't wanna do, a llama ain't gonna do. You learn that quite quickly in Llama Land. Our election of adopting two llamas had somehow grown into four llamas from the time we had agreed to the adventure and arrived at the pick-up point. Neighbors had wanted some too; then neighbors had changed their collective minds. The llamas had been raised together, they played together. What's an animal lover to do? Four llamas fitted in the trailer; we took the four. Stopping in the 100 plus heats of Sacramento, we parked the llamas in the shade and promised them a better climate at the end of their long and uncomfortable trip, which came eventually.

It was one of those mad adventures that you will never forget. It ended in the cool airs of a Soledad evening and the llamas looking around the meadow and seeming to smile. I could have sworn one of them said to me, jokingly, "so, como se llame?" ("Oh and what's your name?" in translation), as they cantered down the bank and took in the new delights of the running dogs, the skittish goats and the sulky horse. Their run is also blissful to watch.

All continues to be well in llama land – they are quite amazingly beautiful creatures. They chew on the weeds, pull up the stalks of nothing on the prairie lands and scan the horizon for predators threatening our borders. I like that. I feel safer now they are here. They do a flock check every day and I have a feeling they already have the inventory in place of all the munchkins - two and four legged – that they will always protect.

Published July 2011

Dog people and cat people

Growing up there was a clear dividing line. You were either dog people or you were cat people; there was no mixing the two. Maybe it was the fact that we grew up with the cartoon series 'Tom & Jerry', where the bad, bad cat always got the rough end of the stick and nearly died in almost every episode, I'm not really sure; but my family was just not very fond of cats. We were dog people.

If the truth were known, I was actually quite afraid of cats. At about the age of about two, I do somehow recall the terror of reaching out to touch a very large black and white number and it reciprocated with a searing welt down my arm. The horror and the terror, not to mention the pain, ensured that I never went close to cats again. That was until I met up with my husband-to-be and he had four of the pesky creatures, plus a dog, in addition to the two charming teenage boys. This all made for quite the household; but that is a whole other story entirely.

Back to cats! At the time, I was literally forced to at least acknowledge that these sly, four-legged whiskery things had a place in the universe. We had the black and white 'Thumbs' with, yes, an extra digit that looked exactly like a thumb; Fester, who was the slyest female I have just about ever met, woman or feline, and two others who left home shortly after I moved in, either feeling the competition of the other woman, or sensing my non-feline vibe. Who knows. With Fester, she was determined that we were going to be friends and so we became, over time, in the strangest way imaginable. Fester would pop up on the counter while the dishes were waiting to be washed and see what we ate for dinner. That would drive me ballistic, and I'd end up chasing her screaming up the stairs, (the idea of animals up on the counter tops was beyond my level of comprehension!) When we moved to the country, Fester would wait for me patiently at the bottom of the hill. (How did she know when I was coming home from work? And then she would slowly stroll up the hill in front of my car, while I furiously tried not to stall the darn thing or mince her little biosky, which she is what she totally deserved.

When Fester went off to cat heaven or maybe met her fate at the snarly paws of a hungry coyote; we searched for her for some time. We kept expecting her minxy little body to come sleeking up over the valley and demand her wet food, then lie next to her fire and toast her silky black coat. I have to admit to a very sad feeling when I realized that she was never coming home again; and even now I can get a little adoring when I see a photo of the old witch. I have come a very long way from being a cat-loather, I can tell you.

A few cats later, and then along came Joey. Joey was a rescue kitten and bad to the bone from the beginning. When he was just a mere fur ball, he would bounce, as if electrocuted, through the house and attack just the twitch of a toe. We should have known back then what we were in for. If there was something ludicrous to be done, then Joey would find a way to do it. From parking himself on top of the roof and watching the world, while he wondered how he would get down, (he had a broken tail and no sense of balance), to lying in full airing position on the carpet and clawing anyone's arm who dared to think he wanted a belly rub. Joe became a legend in his own time in just a few short years. Though now 'mature', he still has his eccentric ways; his overwhelming yearning for wet food, his adoration for becoming a thick scarf for any unsuspecting visitor to the spare room, his squalling when my daughter is not at home to sleep with, his odd twitches when something gets moved or changed in the home, (such as the annual positioning of the Christmas tree.) Yes, Joe is quite something and we still don't know how he selected our home to rest his thick tabby coat in, except that, perhaps, we are quite eccentric too.

Yet, when my father came to stay – another seemingly non-cat person – I came to realize that animals can have quite magical powers in addition to all their other surprises. "Come here, Tiddles!" I heard through the half-cracked windows; and there were father and Joseph having a little morning chat, which they proceeded to do every morning of his visit. Both sitting there, in their way quite resembling one another, and both liking things how they liked them with little room in between for flexibility. There were even some physical similarities, but we won't go there.

Dog person or cat person? I guess that I can honestly say it is possible to be both. I have two dogs and three cats at the moment, including Joey who doesn't believe he's a cat. They provide a richness and a warmth to life that I highly recommend. Anyone in need of chasing something on a daily basis from the counter top or entertaining the visitors; or even just a companion who'll wait for you at the bottom of the driveway and cause you to stall all the way up the hill; cats are a part of life's amazing layers and, on the whole, a pleasure to behold.

Lucy Mason Jensen

Published December 2013

Gone Fishing

He left. He actually left! Just because I said he could go and not to worry about me; how did he fail to understand that that is female speak for "No, of course, you can't go! What will I do without you? Who will make the coffee in the morning, mow the lawn, fix the garage door, feed the dogs – and a whole long list of other things besides?" I'm still reeling from the fact that, not only did he leave, but also, he is still not back.

They say that absence does make two hearts grow more attached; and, though it's a cliché, I have found it to be true of any relationship worth keeping. (The others not so much!) I think there is almost nothing healthier for devoted couples than periods of time apart. No one said that, when you got married, you had to stay physically connected at the hip and, on the whole, I think it's beneficial for both parties when one person gets full roam of the bed, as it were, for a limited period of time. They get to leave the dishes in the sink longer than the other person would allow and definitely the hair on the face or leg is allowed to sprout just that bit more than would be considered acceptable ordinarily. These are days of a disconnection with the norm, yet a reconnection with what is of ultimate importance and at the core of your lives together. I had a few of these days recently.

Friends of ours offered my husband a few days away in another State. Every time they had talked about traveling to their cabin in this particular place, my husband would 'ooh and aah,' telling them he really wanted to go there some time. He liked the 'great outdoor' concept; he loved the sound of lakes full of fish and real seasons with big wide skies. I, on the other hand, am not used to my husband taking vacations, unless I am personally involved. Ordinarily it is me that gets to pack a bag and leave the nest for a few days. With the shoe on the other foot, things can look a bit different; I tell you!

I really didn't think he'd go, to be honest. I figured he would find all kinds of excuses that he would not be able to go because of work, child, obligations, me even. I did not want to tell him that he couldn't go, he shouldn't go; but I figured he'd find his own excuses in any case. Shock! He didn't. He was going. How was I going to manage? I could not imagine.

First of all, you have the school run. Not only is he the one to rouse the house in the early hours, but he brews the coffee, calls the teen, calls the teen again and, ultimately, gets the teen seriously up and moving towards not being late for the first bell at school. None of this is something that I will see on any given day that he is in residence. My day starts when he kicks the bed – somewhat like the reconstruction of an earthquake – and advises that there is no more coffee and he is leaving. Normally there is, at least, one cup left in the pot; but the threat is enough to get me conscious and in motion. The school run scenario altered this week. In fact, I found myself stone cold awake at 6am, worrying about over sleeping and my child missing the bell. That was not a place I expected to find myself. Then came the various mid-day dramas of needing help with real estate – doing, fixing, changing, showing and all the calamities that can befall a busy agent on any and every day. There are so many scenarios in any given day, where I will call on my trusty partner to help me out, make it happen, fix it, attend to it, make the call. I surely couldn't ask him to pitch in for all of these tasks from the place over yonder with poor cell service; or could I? Maybe he really could make those calls from the lake?

Most of the time, I really do appreciate him, honestly I do. I know all that he does and I value that long list of items immensely. But also what happens when you live with some one for a long time is that your expectations of that person become and stay high. Sometimes they even border the ridiculous. When I knew he was leaving us for a week, and really leaving, my brain started flitting around and alighting on all the tasks that normally he would take care of. I began to cram in a whole bunch of tasks for him to handle before he left the state. Here he was trying to walk out of the door and I was still trying to have him take care of that one last thing that I could see I couldn't handle. And then he was gone. Even his cell phone didn't cooperate very well after he left. There was a huge, vacuous hole where he had previously been.

A few days with Superman gone and the house and

property take on an uncannily untended air. I can only imagine what it would be like after a month. Who knows how to start the mower? I don't and I don't want to know. If he never comes back, I will, either, have to remarry very rapidly, or pay large sums of money for all the work that needs doing around here every week. There is no in between option. The countryside can quickly turn into the jungle in a blink of an eye.

I miss that big old bear. I call him up, sweetly, in his large and peaceful cabin in the middle of some state somewhere close to the middle of our country. "How is everything, honey?" I say adoringly. "Oh, we are off fishing," he replies calmly, not even attempting to lie. I run off to my crazy, cram-filled existence of running a day designed for two working folk, when one is on vacation. At the end of the day he has caught three fish and, the way I see it, I have run a marathon. "How was your day, dear?" I say, somewhat sardonically, but he is in fish bliss and unable to catch my unconcealed tone. "When are you coming home?" I add a little more stonily. "Dunno," he replies. "I could hear the wolves howling next to the cabin last night," (as if that had any bearing on the situation!)

My team also enquired when he was coming home, (he's useful; they miss him too!) "I don't know!" I reply. "You don't know!" they exclaim in unison, as if they have never heard such a thing. "He's gone fishing," I explain, as if that answers everything. And so the case of the missing man goes on. His teenager daughter enquires, as do his dogs and other inquisitive creatures. "When is he coming home?" they ask and we don't actually know. What we do know is that one very vital person leaves a large hole in their home life when they vacate it, even just for a few days, and that there will be a very long list for Superman to accomplish when his fishing trip is over and he saunters back to the homestead fully relaxed, we hope, and ready to take care of everything we let go in his absence.

Published September 2011

It's all in the giving

"I've bought three presents!" the husband announced proudly, from his elongated position in his man cave, feet up and smiling ear-to-ear, as he lounged in front of a brand new wide screen. A 'Plasma or High Definition Television', I believe, was the object right in front of his big grin, and I am not remotely a television person. "Three gifts and two of them are for me!" he bragged, with only a hint of humor in his presentation.

Having dealt with a fuzzy television screen from the mid 90's for several years now, the Lord and Master decided that it was past time for him to have some viewing pleasure after a hard day's work. To his credit, he did ask for permission to chock up some dollars on the smoking old credit card first - instead of forgiveness after – and I could hardly say 'no' after all these years of putting himself last in this family. And boy does he love his early Christmas gift! There were, therefore, many reasons for us to rejoice over the fact that he purchased his own present and that it gave him such pleasure. You would think that that saved us a lot of time and effort in this season of buying and wrapping.

Then came the gift number two - to just himself. You cannot have a supremely clear and sparkly picture, apparently, without wishing to catch up on some of the movies you have missed over the years. 'Blue Ray, baby!" he chortled. "That's the way to go!" Not really knowing what *'Blue Ray'* meant, or whether we actually needed it in our lives, I knew only that it was going to cost me some more money. "Yeh!" he said, with winning spirit, after his enthusiastic visit to a large store full of boy toys. "Now that's what I'm talking about. A Blue Ray player and then you are all set up to buy the Blue Ray DVD's!" No one tells you – the Blue Ray Widow – that things can continue to get really expensive for you, even after the desired 'Plasma' or 'High Def' box enters your home; the chosen boy toy, that you think, in the beginning, is going to be the end of a lot of sighing and moans and groans in front of the fuzzy 1990's number. No, not at all! Be warned – that is just the beginning.

Technology in our modern day era involves continual upgrading and the shoveling of more and more dollars out the door, it seems to me, to try and be up-to-date on your systems – a place you will never find yourself, for sure. No sooner have you purchased the latest wow television, than another wow set is right in your face, telling you that you screwed up and got ripped off by the first one. Take it back and buy this one, they tell you, many times over. These techno folk count on the men folk in our nation to be able to successfully entice them with the latest and greatest; and then lead them by the nose to the cash till. It is not a pretty sight.

So here we are, owners of a brand new sparkly bright large screen and a Blue Ray player that, to date, boasts only one 'Blue Ray' disk. The man seems happy in his man cave with his wide screen, however, and that is an important thing in any happy family. He flicks his remote control and chortles at his shows. "I like my Christmas present!" he yells, very loudly, over a week before Christmas; in case none of us can hear him.

But little wifey here did not know that the Man Folk was going to be purchasing his own presents this year and here we have the 17-year-old doing inventory under the tree. "No fair!" she declares, with a tone. "Dad has got all kinds of presents under the tree, and he was supposed to have already got all his presents!" She spits, pointing aggressively at the 'Blue Ray' and the large screen. I gave her the look. "My sweetness, my love, my reason for living," I tell her, as I always do, (as an attractive option to swotting her rear end!) "Your father will not buy his own socks and under wears. Therefore Santa has to!"

"Ah, yuck – TMI!" (Or 'too much information', if you are over 18 and can't translate!) She squeals. "That is so totally gross!" And there we had it – just a few words from me about a parent's undergarments, and peace once more reigns in our home. I did not need to explain to the teen that I start my Christmas shopping in August every year and, therefore, cannot be to blame if the Man Folk gets a bee in his bonnet on any given year and feels the need to go out and buy his own presents. Forgive me if I had already purchased his treats in advance – not to mention his socks and UW's – and she should not be in there doing inventory under the tree in any case.

Young teen does her own Christmas shopping. "What did you get your father?" I ask knowingly. She nods at the wide screen and smiles. "I thought he had already bought his own presents this year?" I queried and she smiled once again. Sometimes it doesn't matter how many presents one person gets in any given year, it's the giving that counts and the fun that you have along the way. I imagine there will be an additional gift for the Man Folk this year under the tree and it will probably have something to do with the large sparkly box. It will also give him another reason to sing "I love my Christmas present!" (And for us to laugh about it all over again.)

May we all have a wonderful, peaceful Christmas this year and enjoy the jokes about what might be under the tree, more than the items under the tree themselves. May Man Folk be bowled over with our gratitude to him this year, because he's a pretty special person! May young teen be surprised, when she really does the inventory, that she also scored pretty well this year. May our young neighbors down in King City be enjoying their warm jackets this year, may the less fortunate children of Soledad be thrilled by the local toy drive, delivering up until the brink of Christmas. May the hungry be less hungry, thanks to all the local donations from the food bank and may we all be a little kinder, a little more peaceful and a little more loving during the season that should illustrate all of those things and then some.

Merry Christmas my friends! Enjoy your season of giving.

Published December 2011

Karma and the Apricot Tree

You could never call me a particularly religious type of gal. I'm much more likely to be found shoveling manure on any given Sunday, rather than sitting my rear in any type of religious institution – I have my own church per se, if you like. But, if you know me at all, you will know I am a great believer in Karma and her powers to tilt the axis of the universe sometimes in such small ways that if you are traveling too fast through life you might not notice. Karma has been visiting these parts recently and she's been giving us a little wake up call.

When we first moved into our house a mere 12 years ago, my father gave us money to buy trees. Noting that our ranch home looked like something in 'The Little House on the Prairie,' surrounded by corn colored hills and without even a leafless branch in sight, father wanted us to buy trees. One of the first trees we purchased was an apricot. Being very green at the time - and not in a good, green-fingered way - as to the wiles of the Soledad wind, not to mention the various tree eating beasts that might find our new tree-lined homestead, we planted away our 300 dollars worth of trees in happy oblivion to the tree-eating wolves that lay at our door.

For a long time now, the apricot tree has been the last

of that bunch to survive. Not a fact I am proud of. Over the years, she has given us a little fruit here and there. One fire year, she was ablaze with fire colored apricots that led to some extremely yummy jam, we naturally and proudly called 'Fire Jam'. In more recent years, the drip hose to the tree has deteriorated and we have not paid much attention to her at all. She just sat there on her lonesome hoping for a bit more rain than usual of a year and not giving us very much in return to remind her of her solitary presence on the hill.

Husband and I were arranging a bench with some rocks up on the hill near the tree and we both noticed her sad demeanor. "We really should water that poor old tree!" one of us said. "Can't remember the last time she gave us any apricots!" the other noted. And so it was decided that we would work on our tree as a daily project, a pilgrimage - visit our church as it were - and try to make up for all the years she had sat in sheer abandonment, waiting for some one to pay attention so that she could perk up and be amazing again.

It had been a rough start to the year for various reasons in our house and we needed to try and dig up some Karma and make a small settlement with the universe we had apparently been ignoring in our quests to get more work, make more money, pay more bills and so on. Sometimes you have to go back to the basics of what really matters in life and the rest will then follow; all having nothing to do with money or earning a living. First, we gave our apricot tree a good soaking, a rub down and touched her thick, warm trunk. Then we set up watering hoses, so that she would receive the daily drink we had been denying her. We surrounded her with fencing so that the horses, goats and llamas would not pick at her and give her any good reason not to flourish. Every day I visit with her on my way up or down the hill with the hose and admire the way she is coming back to life, blossoming, giving even a hint at a gift of fruit or two. It had not taken that much to get her back on track and our attentions back where they should have been all along; but I kid you not, once the tree was back in our lives and loving life again, Karma gave us a nod and, pretty much, all of a sudden, things started to straighten up in our world, our plateaux began to settle and life began to be a little easier on us both. Our daughter moved back to the area and seemed to be happy and flourishing herself, with a serenity and sweetness we had not seen in a good while. Our work began to pick up and mounting bills began to get paid. Our new puppy found us and gave some puppy into our lives we had forgotten we were missing. Our feral mama gave birth to 5 healthy kittens and was the mama cat we would never have dreamed of. Our ageing mare started to put on the weight I feared she never would and her balding patches healed. The tomatoes and apples were growing beautifully, the roses popped out divine and healthy this spring. Health all seemed to be good, family was good, animals were good, life is good!

Thank you, our apricot tree, for reminding us that sometimes in life you have to go backwards to be able to go forwards again. We are humbled and we are reminded.

We will always be in your debt, you beautiful, patient, elegant thing.

Published 2013

Little House on the Prairie

There's a photo from 12 years ago, the year we bought our home on the foothills of the Gabilan Mountains, that shows a tiny little house on the prairie. No trees, no fencing and very few houses and inhabitants were in our neighborhood back then. It was a peaceful time in some ways, but we had no idea truly where we were living at the time and with what dangers.

Once moved in, we started the process, almost immediately, of turning the wild piece of homestead we had purchased into a home. Luckily I married a carpenter, landscape designer and gardener, among other things, all in one. We planted trees and flowers; put up fences and more fences, then cross-fenced those in addition. We built decks, sheds and stables, front areas with waterfalls and fruit trees, back areas with ponds and patios and wind blocks. We put in a pool and a horse box. We did a lot of things, over a period of time, to turn our little house on the prairie into a beautiful house in a, hopefully, civilized world. What we seemed to forget for a while was that the land around us remains wild; always will be, in all likelihood. And no matter how much we would like to think our beloved animals are safe within the recesses of our property lines; a hungry wild animal knows few boundaries. We were reminded of that recently.

It was a calm, early evening with still plenty of sun to give us before she dipped down over the Santa Lucias and so it was the perfect evening for a mother-daughter ride. Since my daughter has moved back home, I so like to go riding with her. She is by far the superior rider and I love to watch how she handles a horse with a competence and confidence that I could only ever dream of. Even though I am always the gate keeper and some things just never change, do they, we still have a lot of fun together clip-clopping along in the vineyard with our five canines trotting alongside and getting under the horses' hooves, as we yell at the foolhardy pups and laugh and yell some more. It is our time to catch up and visit a bit together.

We are so lucky to live where we do. Our neighbor is a vineyard. We tolerate the midnight machines and the bird cannons as required each season on his side of the fence, he tolerates a clunky old rescue horse or two from next door with their fleet of un-pedigree hounds using his thousand acres as their own back yard. It is a mutual respect society that I entirely appreciate.

And so we went off, as we do quite often, into our neighbor's yard next door and it seemed just like the regular bout of fresh air we treat ourselves to quite often after a long day at work and school. Absolutely nothing was out of the ordinary! However, rounding a corner with the larger dogs in front of us and Sophie Halloween Jensen, our older Pom-Chi cross behind us, with her tiny little legs running a million miles a minute as per usual, my daughter and I both, at the same time, hear a tiny squeal. Sophie is wont to squealing, by the way; being surrounded, as she always is, by a fleet of hunky-chunky brothers who are all, without exception much more in the range of 30-60lbs compared to her delicate and teetering 8, but, despite that, my daughter and I turned to look back at the same time and we witnessed one of those jaw-gaping moments as we eye-spied a coyote running away with little Sophie dangling out of its mouth like a rag doll, hanging down limp on both sides of its mouth. My daughter kicked up her horse and took chase, screaming and crying, with a pack of angry hounds accompanying her. My heart fell into my boots as I kicked up my own steed behind them. My ornery little yellow furry witch would be no more; she had been whisked up and away to be dinner at the coyote table. I couldn't bear it. All our rescuing and nurturing and loving over the years was going to end up like this and there was nothing I could do about it. I had, ultimately, failed to rescue her at all. I screamed inside at the thought of heading home without her and listening to my daughter howling ahead of me. As I took the bend behind them all, imagining that the coyote and Sophie would be long gone, I see little Sophie tearing up the dust in front of us and headed for home. The dogs were all riled up and ready to fight and the wild dog had some how disappeared. My daughter was still yelling and crying because little Sophie would not stop running ahead and we had no idea how badly she was hurt. I take off after the tiny dog, aware that the coyote might try to cut through the vineyard around us and scoop her up at the end of the lane ahead. My daughter turns to see the very same wily beast behind us and trying to lope up to our other smallest dog Roscoe. At this point she leaps off her horse and goes tearing off towards the coyote, losing the reins off her horse as she lost her temper. I swear, if she had had a gun, she would have shot it. Such was her rage. I am ahead, at this point, and hear the thundering of hooves behind me. And here we have a riderless horse in addition to one injured Pom-Chi somewhere ahead, a tiny little terrier mix being stalked by the hungry coyote behind us and the other dogs going absolutely nuts with the drama of it all. My horse, in the meantime, not to be shy about getting involved in the melee that was all around, takes off after the thundering horse with me on his back and we still could not catch the Pom-Chi. You just cannot make up stories like this.

At the end of the day, we were so very grateful to still have 5 dogs to go home with. Our Sophie was pretty beat up and required a day or two of major pampering, turkey and cheese snacklets at regular intervals and some major loving – in addition to plenty of hydrogen peroxide over her nicks and scratches. Our other dogs received awards for their bravery in the form of extra dog cookies and special chew bones for the weekend. My daughter received the highest award I could bestow upon her at the time – the Riverview Cowgirl Award for Bravery and Impressive Reaction Time. Me, on the other hand, I am in recovery from all the drama and pondering how we will ever be able to go out riding in the vineyard with our dogs again, now that we have been reminded that we live in the prairie and we always will. With that beautiful, wild, peaceful countryside can also come along a whole host of danger and possible devastation in your lives. Like a lot of things in life, it's a toss up.

Published March 2013

Love and That Crazy Girl

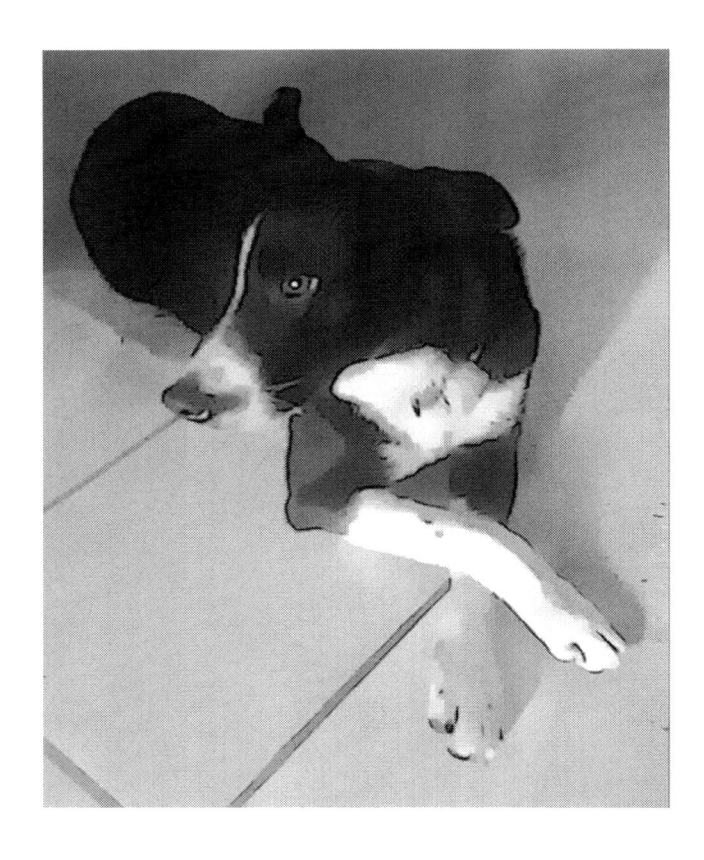

She strolled into my life near on 4 years ago, when she was quite young, and, well, so was I. At the time, I thought she had, at least, some marginal psychological issues – if not a full blown personality disorder, to be honest. It was, seemingly, her way or the highway about most things in life. She was very focused; truthfully almost manic. She had extremely clear views about most things and her mental insistency was powered equally by her fully muscled body and full bolt determination, when she made up her mind about what she was to do and she would then do it.

When we first met, I stayed a little clear of her sharply focused path, knowing how attached she was to her primary owner and how fiercely devoted to that one singular person she appeared to be for eternity. I was sometimes the feeder, sometimes the ball-thrower and sometimes the one that appeared to be only a port in the storm. But our relationship did grow from there.

When her first owner left town and she was unable to go with him, she attached herself like glue to her feeder, which was me. Everywhere I went, she would go – from the bathroom to the outside to the meadow. There was no containing her. She could and would scale a fence to be by my side. It's just how it was. When I was apart from her, I missed her and couldn't wait to be back by her side and ready to do all the things she liked to do. There was a predictability in the opening of the door and knowing that she would have heard the car, the garage door and would sprint to be right there when I opened the door. It was a comfort too, knowing that she waited and she listened so attentively and so caringly. At night she would curve her considerably muscular body in spooning fashion against mine and would sigh the deepest of exhalations, signaling that the day was truly over and we could both finally rest, happy with each other. She slept so well and I loved to hear her deep, deep sleep, snoring like the best of us. I thought it would always be that way; except that, in the back of my mind, I knew that, in reality, she always belonged to An Other and I would only ever be number two. All it would take would be a return to town and she would leave me and our lovely quiet routines in the dust. But as time passed, as she does, I put all of that out of my mind and just enjoyed our time together.

Then the unthinkable happened and he returned to town, missing her and wanting her back. His message drew tears to my eyes, as if I had never imagined that moment. The only reasonable thing I could think of in response was a shared responsibility, a shared custody – like a child with two parents. I could not conceive of her being away forever. She would miss me, I would miss her; it was too dreadful to imagine. But that first week of the 'agreement' and it became clear that the sharing custody concept would not work. First of all, there was the emotional moment I witnessed when we did the exchange and she realized who it was who had come to collect her. I could not believe the feelings I saw. A year and a bit later, she immediately recognized her number one. Always an emotional creature, I saw her true heart on her sleeve in that moment and it affected me deeply. Then there was the inevitable dredge of 'stuff' that comes up when a romantic relationship falls by the wayside and two people are forced to cross paths again. My daughter and my dog's first owner felt the need to exchange opinions about this shared custody that actually involved only me, him and the canine. I felt a responsibility for the situation that I had never willed in the first place. In short, it was easier on all of us – and probably most of all on Allie, that emotional creature – that I give her back to her first owner. Whether he had technically 'abandoned' her in the first place is not my judgment to make. All I know is that I did what I felt was right in the moment, but it still caused me pain. I miss her still, that crazy collie. I think of her body curving into mine at night and her seeking eyes when I opened the door and she was waiting for me, knowing and trusting that all was well. Maybe she will come back to me – who knows – and maybe she won't. But I do know that a special love, such as that, is reserved only for the few and that a corner of my heart has been carved out for her and her only and will remain forever waiting for the possibility that she may, perhaps, return.

Published 2013

Mama Cat in the hood

It started out as two big, wild eyes in the back of the horse box. "How was she getting in? Why was she getting in?" We had a lot of questions at the time. Then wild eyes near my saddle progressed to a snippy snarl in the back of the shed over yonder. She was working her way closer to the house and the realm of the other felines. "Hello. You are not my cat," I told her in no uncertain terms, hoping she would soon find a reason to head home. I live in the countryside where, for some, dumping animals is a daily occupation. Of course, the tabby had no home. I fed her and she still snarled at me. Okay, so it was going to be that kind of a relationship. I've been there before. I heard her howling from the shed in next door's yard and, for a short while, imagined that she belonged to them and they were trying to train her to stay home. The howling stopped. "Good, she's gone," I thought to just myself.

Then one day I went outside and there she was, happily feeding with the other cats and not acting spiteful or feral at all. She let me pick her up and snuggle a bit; right before a dog came over to see what the fuss was about and it was then that Scratch got her official name. I couldn't believe that this was the same animal that had almost spat in my face a few days prior, let me love on her like today and then scratched me in her efforts to escape. "You're still not my cat," I yelled at her, as she legged it away from me. "I already have too many!"

"Oh but she loves to play with Gus! Look at them!" my husband noted, (Gus being the most recent arrival previously; the sweetest black kitten you could imagine, who just walked into our meadow one night.) "They are just like young kittens playing together." But they weren't that young, apparently; just under-nourished. And they were certainly playing; but in more of a procreative way. And there you have it, deep in the heart of springtime, when the sheep are a-lambin' and the cats are a-catting; and unto us a child – or six, if we are very unlucky – is ultimately born.

I am just about the heaviest supporter of spaying and neutering that I know of, plus all my flock are rescue animals, so the 'fixing' per se is not normally even an issue, just about as soon as they step over the threshold. But we missed the boat with Gus and Mama Scratch. And here I am dealing with the results of irresponsible pet-parenting, a place I did not ever expect to find myself and where I am not real proud to be sitting.

"She's getting really fat!" husband observed, not that long after we noted the playing antics of the two mating cats. "I can feel three lumps." And there a lesson in biology ensued, since neither one of us could recall the gestation period of a cat. We quickly discovered it was pretty brief.

"Mama Scratch just had a kitten under your car!" husband observed helpfully. "Well don't even think of leaving the premises before that little thing has been removed!" I responded swiftly, imagining myself army crawling in all my work togs under the low suspension of my car to try and deal with the wrath of Mama Scratch and her needy offspring, before I could speed off down the road to work. Fortunately for him, he did just that and soon Mama S. and her first born were nicely situated in a cardboard box well away from my wheels. "She's having another one!" our pet health reporter of the morning followed up with a breaking news alert. And then I started to feel it a little bit. There was some magic going on in my garage. Life was peeking out and saying hello, the way she does.

As soon as husband left, I snuck out there with my flash light. Mama S was at home in the box, nuzzling one of the kittens, but the other was stone cold away from her, breathing, but damp and chilly. "Mama, you have to love all of your babies," I told her sternly, picking up the tiny cool thing and edging it closer to the warm belly of its mother. I hoped it might work. Mama S. just looked at me coolly and gave me one of her snarly sighs. Oh no, she was going to be one of those mothers with abandonment tendencies, raising a fleet of needy munchkins with early disadvantages.

I tootled around the place, giving her a little time for the maternal instinct to kick in and then crept back, a tin of her favorite wet food in hand. "Mama Scratch", I cooed. "Breakfast time!" All I could see was fur and pieces of what I perceived to be animal bits around the box. Surely not! Horrified, I dashed away and departed the homestead, notifying husband en route that I had witnessed some possible suspect cannibalism in the realm of our two-car garage.

"We have two healthy kittens," our resident pet reporter noted on his arrival back to the homestead later on in the afternoon. "Two?" I retorted, still in recovery from all I had beholden that morning. "Any sign of a crime scene. You know – fur, ears?"

"No". Our resident CSIR - crime scene investigative reporter - noted nothing of any consequence in his report. Maybe Mama S. nursed that little damp cool munchkin back to full kitten purring strength by the end of the day and I was completely imagining all I thought I might have seen in the dirty-dusky garage the morning of their entry to the world. Perhaps I had totally underestimated Mama S., her maternal skills and nature's way to handle all as it should be handled. But what of the fur I thought I saw and the pieces that made me leave in a hurry? Did Mama S. have three kittens and ate one, or did she only have two and I am undermining her integrity? Such a mystery! We may never know.

What I do know is that we have two additional mouths to feed on the ranch. I'm not much of a whizz at mathematics, but five plus two does equal 7 cats and that is about 12 feline paws too many, I think. But who says what is too many and what is enough, when mouths show up needing nutrition and you have the ability to feed and fulfill need where you see it?

Published September 2012

Mothers come in all kinds of bundles

"You should become a foster parent!" my friend noted, as we passed like ships in the night within our shared office space. I think she caught my look of horror at the time. She was onto her second foster child, 'only' having four children of her own and one that she claimed as hers through adoption; therefore a present sum total of a mere five. She may even be able to adopt the present child she is caring for and who knows how many more will pass through her doorway and into her heart over the next several years. It is a gift that some have; and others definitely do not. I cannot imagine dealing with that many children; and willingly so. To me, that honestly smells of nightmare.

When I gave birth to my own daughter, I am not proud to say that I had never even changed a diaper, (or 'nappy,' as they call it in England). I went from childless to child, seemingly, without blinking, if you were to discount my rapidly swelling frame and puffy feet that, towards the end, I couldn't see. From start to finish, near on, I had not a maternal bone in my body and my pregnancy pretty much remained a surprise to me the entire 9.5 months of its duration. It wasn't until I saw her, my baby, that I understood what another friend of mine had previously commented - that 'you have to have at least one'. At the time I thought my friend was crazy, as I observed her dealing with cleaning up continual messes in pants and out of them – vomit, feces, sickness, teething, fever, sleepless nights and worse. I do remember casting a sympathetic eye at her, as she multi-tasked with this squealing, squalling bundle of slimy mess and wondered why on earth any sane human being would want to go there.

Somehow, and not surprisingly, I managed to bypass or probably avoid all the babysitting gigs when I was going through the teenage years. I was much more likely to work as a waitress or shop assistant than go anywhere near the young people. I had grown up with two younger sisters and that had been more than enough of experience with children for me.

I digress. To return to my first paragraph, I think my response to my Foster Queen of a friend went something like, "The more I know people, the more I love my animals," or "I know what I am good at and what I am certainly not." But I am so impressed by mothers, foster mothers, adopting mothers – all types – I just do not belong in that league in my estimation. I count myself in the arena of an animal mother and lover, first and foremost. Give me an animal, any kind, except for snakes and spiders most likely, and I will love them and they will love me right back. It has always been that way. I will take in way more foster creatures than I really should and I make a point to never calculate my feed or vet bills, lest I receive a nasty shock. It's just what I do; it's my life's work, if you like. Just as well my husband is right there with me, or we'd have a mother of a time agreeing on any of the core values in our lives. Most of our animals have showed up at our doorstep in one way or another and stayed. You save their life in a sense and then they rescue you right back. Or that's my take on it in any case.

Mama Scratch – a squawky, awkward looking tabby cat – showed up on our property a while back with supreme feral attitude. The first time I ever tried to pet her she scratched me; hence her name. That's what you get, in the name of love, for feeding a hungry creature! But she stuck around the place, much as I told her she wasn't my cat and needed to go home, and insisted on eating the food I delivered to her at regular intervals and snarled at me when I tried to be marginally friendly. Her first batch of kittens was not her finest moment. She gave birth to three, ate two – no way to soften the blow there – and sort of raised the third who grew up with some social dysfunctions and a broken tail to boot. If you tried to catch Mama S., so that she would never be able to experience mother hood again, she would thwart you at every turn. And then some one dumped a fully-fruited male in our neighborhood and he found Mama S. And you know exactly how that goes. Sometimes it is, sadly, not the most perfect mothers who have the ability to procreate; just look at society. Scratch obviously didn't, apparently, snarl too much at Fruity Male, because, before long, it became vastly apparent that Mama S. was with child, again. 'Oh no', I said to just myself and my expanding pet food bill. But sometimes life will throw you a surprise or two, and I was so pleasantly surprised this time around by Mama S. and her motherhood performance, that she practically blew my mind.

First of all, she religiously fed all of her five babies, only leaving her mother-perch on the top of the garage in the spare cord and battery box for her own water and nutrition and would then return to diligent baby feeding right away. This was not the dirty-stop-out Mama S. that we had witnessed the first time around, the feline that we had to trap and corral into giving her baby the milk she needed. This was a different, more mature, less frenzied and definitely less scratchy Mama.

And then something even more amazing happened.

Another feral mama in the neighborhood decided to have her babies under a bush at the top of our driveway. She had obviously abandoned the first nest that she had made for another safer one close by, but she had left a tiny little baby behind, crying to be rescued. We saw the baby and cushioned it deeper into the nest, hoping that the Mama would realize her mistake and return for her last one. She never came back. The next morning, the baby was out in the middle of the tiled patio, now several feet away from the nest – looking like Mama had gone back and dragged her further away from herself and the rest of the children, as if to say, 'die, loser, die!" The little kitten was quite the tiniest most pathetic little bundle, but still – how could a mother do that? Husband and I couldn't stand the kitten wailing though so, defying nature, we put the weency crying, starving bundle in with Mama Scratch and asked her to be super-nice, (via an extra portion of the wet food that she adores, and a cautious stroke.) After a quick snarl, she licked the baby and then allowed it to feed. The wailing stopped and all was quiet in Nature's kingdom. We checked on the baby several times that day and it was miraculously feeding and resting alongside all the other much larger kittens. Mama S. had become a foster mother and a darn good one at that. Over a week on and they are all doing marvelously well as a family of 6 kids and a single mom. The kittens all lie together like pieces of a large pie and the tiny baby we named Carey, after my cat adoring friend who told me that Solace needed to keep that little bundle of Miracle, is going from strength to strength and is, amazingly, accepted by all.

Wonderful and awe-inspiring things can happen if you open your eyes to see. From my friend – the Foster Queen – who carries so many human children in her heart, it is inconceivable, truly, that she could remember all their birthdays, but she does – to Mama Scratch who came through for a poor lil abandoned kitten and made the world a better place in the minds of those who witnessed the marvel. May your children be loved, wherever they are and whoever they truly belong to! Love is the food and the essence of life. That scrawny, screechy, scratchy feral cat Mama Scratch has made a believer out of me!

This story is dedicated to Precila and all the marvelous foster mothers out there that do their part to make young lives whole.

Lucy Mason Jensen

Published May 2013

Mucking out on a Monday

When you work all weekend, as I am wont to do frequently these days, it is quite often that you will take a sizeable slice of Monday morning to do a little extra mucking out – if, like me, you have two stables that require daily attention - not to mention the soiled contents of my brain that, essentially, need a complete mucking out after a full week in the war zone of the property world. It's amazing where your mind can go when it is surrounded by the most potent piles of horse manure on a Monday morning.

Sometimes, pitch fork in hand, I notice I can veer off in my mind, briefly, towards recent politics – 'Ah, those darn pesky folks at the IRS! What is up with that? …..What about, the cover up, dare I say, that seems to have taken place yonder in Bengazi?……Even, oh heck, don't get me started about some of our local political tomfoolery and the issue of one rogue councilman/school board member who is out there causing all kinds of chaos!' All of that garbage can get you going of, what we'll just call, a Manure Monday, as you reach, scoop, shovel, scrape your way through the piles before you at the very beginning of a new, fresh week and some how the more you pick up, the more there is before you.

But those agitated thoughts are not really a calming start to the new beginning, a poetry in motion of a Monday when, you should be taking the whole darn day off – in lieu of the weekend you just lost – but, actually, most of a Monday Morning is all you can muster for your Manure Maneuvers and that is truly too many 'M's' in one sentence to get you befuddled, before you have even, really, started.

As my mind recently spun around those not-at-all calming topics, I reached for the vinyl and changed the tune. Never a bad idea, I'd say! Some of you may know that I have been attempting to partially restore my vinyl collection, that I lost decades ago somewhere back in London, England, to the possession of my baby sister, and, I have become quite obsessed with it. Recreating the music of your youth is quite a fun pastime to uncover. It can also take you on journeys back through your memory bank to very different times, attitudes and places; some that had got shrouded in gunk and needed to become unshrouded. You can find yourself decades younger even, just by the turn of the table if you go there, as I did.

It was 1980 and we girls were always out. 'Where are you going?" my father would ask. "Out!" I'd reply, as if that should suffice. "Who are you going out with?" he would pursue, knowingly. "Someone!" I'd reply. I remember a glimmer of his smile, as if that was our own personal language, for 'I'm going to ask you where you are going, but I will never expect you to tell me exactly.' 'Out' was a place that the young longed for back then and the older just smiled at. We girls loved to go out, down town London, freedom, danger, all of that good stuff - and listen to the new bands out there in the clubs with their novel, raw energy. That was our thing. We loved the music, the excitement, the vibe, the magic. Maybe we should just call it 'youth' and leave it at that.

A certain band called 'The Reluctant Stereotypes' from the Midlands captured our attention and we would follow them from club to club, mostly in London but sometimes beyond those boundaries. It was in the basement club of 'The Rock Garden' in Covent Garden that we first found them to our liking and held them close. If you are good at mathematics, as I am definitely not, then that computes to a mere 33 years ago from where we are now. Knock me over with a feather! Recently, endeavoring to compile a memory pile of my former vinyl collection I wondered if I could ever, again, find the band's one and only album that we intensely loved and knew inside and out. Could I ever find, again, those feelings, that time, that lost piece of paradise that we never knew we'd miss so much later down the road when we were also quite far down the road? It was 'Online', a place we had not known back in 1980, that I found their vinyl that I thought had been lost forever and had been, amazingly, found in a place it never was in the first place. It made no sense to me either, but I could not have been more delighted to find this treasure from the memory bank, if you had told me I had hit a partial 'Powerball' and stood to earn ga-zillions.

I awaited, expectantly, for this piece of 1980 memorabilia to hit my mail box and it did not disappoint.

The cover was pristine. I observed, with interest, that the cover art work contained images of people smoking. Well, that wouldn't happen nowadays, would it now? It seemed almost primitive. I had never noticed the nuances before. Then I put the coveted vinyl onto the 'Crosley' stereo in my stable and from there, I was moved from one time zone to another. I was back there in the 'Garden', the lights were low in the basement and there was a lot of second hand smoke going on which assisted with the atmosphere. Our band were wearing their signature green scrubs and the lead singer was electric with his theatrics and his sharp good looks, rousing the crowd to love him just a little bit more than they did before. 'Just a Visual Romance,' the song, talked about a TV viewer romancing daily, in his mind, with his news reader on the screen before him and this could still be the case, the dialogue seemingly without age, the emotions still possible, the rhetoric an echo of the past, yet timeless still.

As I muck out on a Monday with the Mullings of times past still Much upon the Mind, I have to give a nod to the portion of the Memory that lets such visuals leap back with a vengeance to give ones history a visual feast through audio and open the drawbridge to so many emotions and such an historic positioning in the lives of us girls. I have to reach back out to my girlfriends who were there with me at that time and feeling those feelings that you never really forget. I have to give great gratitude to the gods of vinyl and those of the internet too for allowing me to have a second chance at all things past and all things vinyl and for making it possible to see life from where we were 33 years ago and also from now. What super views I have enjoyed from my position at the manure pile to the vinyl revisit and beyond!

This story is dedicated to my dear friends Carey and Kate, all the fun we had back then and all the fun and love and laughs we continue to have all these 33 years on and for always.

Peace from my horses

These days, given a choice, I can pretty much be found in the stables, or out in the pasture. Give me a pitch fork and a bale of straw and I can go off into a fantasy world I never imagined. I will go out to 'feed', as I call it; and return two hours later having had a good physical work out mucking out the straw, loading and unloading Lola, (my yellow wheelbarrow), chatting to the llamas and goats, loving on my horses, throwing balls for my manic collie, making up straw beds, filling up water troughs and more.

This chunk of peace in my life gives me more than I can describe. It gives me life, it gives me peace; it makes me feel as if I have truly arrived. When I am outside with my animals, I feel an indescribable peace I can find nowhere else. All my other troubles evaporate.

Recently, our chief llama Harold Malcolm Democracy, has decided that alfalfa cubes are where it's at and he likes them to be hand fed twice a day; more, if available, is acceptable. He will seek me out and tell me that it is time for our connection time and he makes me laugh every time I see him strut up the hill, intent on his mission to engage with me. He will even chase me, on occasion; that can give me quite a rise, considering he is, in some ways, more like a camel than not. It can make a morning; or an evening, even. A day, a life; in actual fact.

My daughter's horse is serenity incarnate. She is older; she is a solid and wise character. She lets you love on her and talk to her. She talks back. She tells you exactly what she wants, in no uncertain terms, and allows a bucket load of snuggling and loving in return. I am on a mission to increase her by the 250lbs they say she needs; she is on a mission to let me do it. When I deliver her evening pail of hot oats, dried apples, barley, molasses and more, we call it her 'muesli'; there is a serenity pact between us that defies any specific definition you could pinpoint. She chortles her happy grumble, I love on her and tell her to gain the weight she needs. I put on her two coats and kiss her and we are as one. To this day, I have never even ridden her.

My own horse is always tuned into my mood and spirit.

We are as one; an incongruous pair. He can tell when my spirits are down and I need some extra soft and insistent muzzling, along with a gentle but firm horse hug. He knows when he can be frisky and funny and when not. He tunes into me every time I appear and that is a magic I can get from nowhere else. Recently when I was going through a tough time and standing out in the meadow at night, looking for answers through the ether and to the planets beyond, he came to me and told me that the answers were actually not to be found out there; they would just become clear to me over time and, perhaps in another place, when I least expected it. That communiqué all came through a nuzzle or three, with sweet hay-scented horse kisses on a moonlit night. It calmed me all the same; it gave me peace and made me look forward to seeing him, all over again, in the morning, so he could teach me some more.

Though I initially rescued him, there have been many, many times I have felt that he has rescued me right back and more over these past short 18 months. Gifts like that can never be sought out or purchased. They are an offering to the soul that humans need to recognize and treasure as one of life's huge and indefinable delights.

Merry Christmas season to all! May all your gifts be as rare and special as mine in the form of the rescued horse soul from a Mexican ranch, who came to me unexpectedly, when I needed him most and gives me all the peace I need, every day of both of our lives.

Published December 2012

Penance

Penance is described in the dictionary as 'an ecclesiastical punishment imposed for sin'. Religious or not, I believe that my husband and I have been suffering penance for a few weeks now; and that, now our penance is, hopefully, complete, we should be poised and free to go on with our lives, heads still bowed, but free of the shame we carried from last month.

There was a brief moment when I realized that life was going to take on a different course; that life was supposed to take on a different course. There was that very bright and illuminated second of my existence. We were in the stands at the auction for the Salinas Valley Fair. Animals were being swiftly raffled on a per pound basis and purchased for mostly meat, some breeding. There were hundreds of them. My daughter had won Reserve Grand Champion AND FFA Champion for Sally, her gleaming black, sleek, prize hog and, we hoped upon hope, that Sally would be bought for a breeding program, gorgeous looker that she was. Today was the day that some one would either take her home to produce more Simons and Sallys, or today would be the day that she would become prize pork chops – the lottery was in the air and no one knew which way it was going to go. The brief moment I am describing was the frozen pause in time when the Reserve Grand Champion and FFA Champion hog could not be located and neither could my daughter. Some how she had mistaken non-communication with wrong communication and had decided to go and take Sally to the regular chute instead of remaining in the pen where she was supposed to remain until summoned, as the Reserve Grand Champion of the event.

Her father and I were sitting, clueless, in the stalls, waiting for her grand entrance, camera on hand, and we knew nothing about any of this chaos until a whisper went around the auction ring that the Reserve Grand Champion had gone missing and was on the verge of being disqualified from the auction, due to her, obvious, non appearance in the ring. I remember a flash of reality hitting me in the head. "Oh good!" my brain spoke to just me. "Now Sally will have to go home again with us, where she should have stayed all along – playing ball with the dogs, in fact chasing the dogs, chatting away to anyone who'd listen and eating strawberries and marshmallows as if her life depended on it." There was a moment there, when I was really happy and really relieved about the apparent outcome. Then my daughter appeared with her pig and the auction of the pig went as planned. And then it ended and a farm had bought the pig. "Mum, I'm so glad that a farm bought her," my daughter told me. "Now I know that Sally will be saved and she will get to live a good life out on the pasture, raising little Sallys." I so wanted to believe her, I still want to believe her; but a part of my cynical adult mind tells me sternly, "not so fast grown one." (I'm talking to myself.) "You had your chance and you blew it." My chance was when my daughter was missing from the ring and I could have made it so she was eternally missing to the point of expulsion from the auction. (We would have to have limped home with our champion hog in tow.) The other chance was my opportunity to bid my way up to being the highest bidder for my daughter's pig, meaning that we would be out of funds for quite some time, or in debt to my kid at least, but that Sally – or O'Mally as my husband liked to call her – would have come home with us to live out her beautiful life in pastures rich with strawberries and balls intended for dogs. None of those things happened. Sally was purchased and we went home ridden with guilt that we had not saved her from who knows what.

Believe it or not, misfortune pursued us after Fate slapped us on the hand and told us we had turned the wrong corner and made the wrong choice at the auction ring that day. Things broke at home – a lot - bank accounts over drew, alarm bells rang, tires needed mysteriously replacing, havoc spewed out of just about every orifice of our struggling lives and, for a time there, all of our natural alignment plates refused to fit into place. My husband would look at me with his 'O'Mally' look and I would know that he knew what I was thinking. We both knew that we were paying and we wondered how long it would last. We will, maybe, always pay in one way or another; but Sally, at least, knows that we cared about her and that we wished her the very best – and that has to, at least, count for something in the universal scheme of things.

Then, for no good reason, we rescued a pair of litter mates – a pair of pygmy goats that needed a home and they found a home with us. Charlie and Elvis, we called them. I had never seen myself as much of a goat herder. I always thought the horns were a bit prohibitive. But Charlie and Elvis came into my life and I melted. They were the sweetest pair of characters I had encountered, since Sally – well, she wasn't exactly sweet per se, but she was a character. We built them a pygmy palace – call it penance if you like, it was a family affair – and we lathered them with love. Charlie always was more like a dog than a goat, but Elvis took a little longer. After about a day of smothering adoration and insistent petting and Elvis was eating out of the hand too. And, in addition, our dogs accepted them, all five of them, as additional members to an increasingly eccentric pack.

And then came the call that I had probably waited for since I was about 7 years old and I got the wooden rocking horse as opposed to the warm flesh and blood horse I had been hoping for. A horse needed a home and would we like him. We wanted him before we even knew him. He needed us, we needed him, Sally would have said, "Sure, cool, bring it on. Can we have a strawberry with that, or maybe a banana?" And there we were - a huge, multi-faceted conglomeration of legs, arms, paws, hooves, horns, teeth and more – all looking over the fences at one another and smiling through the hay in our teeth and saying, "Sally! Really – Sally did all of this?" And the miracle of it all is that we think she may really have played quite a part.

Published June 2011

Rain drops and cow boots

It was 105 down in Lockwood and the air was thick with smoke from fires all around the place. The Lakes, the Mountains, Canyons, Valleys. It seems as if nowhere in our beautiful State has been spared this summer from the ravages of fire, from fear of fire, from smoky airs and the smell of burning wherever you go. Desperate home owners are tired of waiting to hear whether or not they have a home to return to. The waiting is agony. Firefighters are tired of working long hard days on the lines and spending weeks away from their families. I am tired of waking up at night to the smell of smoke and, for a moment, worrying if our property is on fire – only to realize it's the air quality we have been living with for a while now. The first few days of the Soberanes fire, my eyes were red and streaming. I felt as if I had hot ash in them and had to keep applying eye drops that seemed to be in short supply at the drug store. Now I think my body is becoming accustomed to the new air quality we are all dealing with – not happily though. It seems as if most people are very, very tired of this terrible summer of fires.

"It's not even as if we are in fire season yet," she said. I paused. Oh crimeney. She was right. Normally our fire season really takes off in the early fall when the winds and the heat kick it up a notch and the State goes on high fire alert. Oh my goodness me – and what will that be like this year? It honestly doesn't bear thinking about, the way this long summer has been one long blaze after another. What will LA County be like when the Santa Ana winds come to town? LA is already one big burning mess.

It's about this time of year that I start to long for winter – the crunch of the leaves in the vineyard, the solid ground turning to mushy clay as the rain drops soak in and the news men getting excited about the 'storm watch' and just how many inches we might glean during the next wet system. I start to think about my coveted cashmere sweaters and my winter cowboy boots, which have been gathering the dust of summer in dark cupboards. I long to walk on the land which has turned green with the winter rains and watch the Salinas River flow again. I want to stroll through the grasses and not worry about lurking snakes. I want to smell clear airs again and the freshness of a morning after a night of rain.

I want a lot of things to come very soon for all of us; but I think I'm dreaming at this junction of the 8th month in our year and spot bang in the middle of high summer at that. My friend sent me an article from the "London Guardian" about Global warming and whether the obscene amount of fires this year in California could be attributed to another example of extreme global warming. The consensus was that no, it's likely not. Looking at the properties constructed way up high above Big Sur, these are very special, precious homesteads located above the

Pacific Ocean, nestled eye to eye with the condors and the Century plants; but these are also very precarious areas of wilderness that, perhaps, were not supposed to have residences constructed up there. There is a price to pay for living in the glory lands, where few other folk can live. Fires don't care how much you paid for your property or whether or not you have insurance. And now I hear that folk are complaining about the fire breaks around their pieces of paradise, which are scarring the land and leaving unattractive welts around the place. Oh dear me. Mankind; we are never happy, are we. The Native Americans respected fire for its ability to clear the land and make new again. That's the good side of fire, yes.

While my cashmeres remain in the darkened closet and we, all of us, remain on the fire watch instead of the stormy one, let's hope that the winds stay calm, the heats stay down and the brave fire fighters are allowed to perform their difficult work the way they are trained to do. That way, at least, there will be a minimal loss of life during this very difficult fire season. Before we know it, winter will swing into town again and remind us of how much we missed her; how glad we are to welcome her again to our poor charred State that has seen little mercy from Mother Nature this summer.

Published August 2013

Sally, the Champ

You get to the end of some weeks and feel as if you have just climbed a mountain, encountering treacherous but wonderful things along the way, which can make a deep mark or scar on your memory bank. This was one of those weeks. It was the week of the Salinas Valley Fair and I knew it was going to be full on with two kids under our care showing animals. I also knew that, at the end of the week, I would be utterly sleep deprived and exhausted. I was right on both counts – it was just the middle part that contained so many surprises. I am so old that I am always surprised when things surprise me.

I am from England – we do not have fairs where children raise and show animals in this way, and then kindly local folks bid on these animals for serious money and help the kids out with college funds, cars, the long days of summer – you name it. It is quite the concept. I am also a big animal lover, so I knew that it would not be easy to separate myself from the animal, when it came time to say goodbye. I, equally, knew I was in emotionally deep waters when I found myself hand feeding bananas and strawberries to Sally and Jeremy and laughing as they kicked up their heels on our lawn and chased our dogs. All the waifs and strays which show up at my place get to stay, whether they are socially well-adjusted or not. That's just how we are. My husband is a hippy from Santa Cruz County and he is the same as me. People have told me that, when they die, they'd like to come back as one of my animals. I know what they mean.

Wednesday was weigh-in day at the fair. Thanks to friends of ours who schlepped our pigs, plus additional pigs from the high school down to the weigh scales, everything went as planned. (Plan B was for my husband to take them down to fair in our VW van and that would not have been a pretty sight.) Fortunately, Sally, our black pig, had skipped breakfast that morning, because she came in only 4lbs shy of the maximum allowed weight. That was our first skate through the chute! Beginner's luck, you might say; and you'd be right. Thursday I had to work. I had clients flying in from Hawaii to look at properties and that was the only day they had free to go out. Little did I know all that I would miss!

The texts came in rapid fire succession. "Sally made Grand Champion FFA, Jeremy made Blue Ribbon, Sally made Weight Champion. Sally made Reserve Grand Champion …" I couldn't believe what I was hearing, knowing there were some serial and experienced performers out there in our tri-county area with near 400 participants vying for the piggy prize.

But then we'd always said Sally was a Champ. Sleek and black with the perfect pink trotters in front, a straight back and incredible haunches, we knew she was a looker. She also had a great sense of humor and liked to tease our dogs and chat to us. Sally would hear the van returning home and start loudly chatting away to get our attention. She loved marshmallows and liked to play 'find the marshmallow' in her bedding – that was a favorite. As you can see – regardless of telling people that "having livestock is not like having a pet" – I failed at my own competition to raise an animal for the fair and then be able to see it through without tears. I really did fail miserably at that.

Thursday evening, I was done with my clients and waiting for my husband to run home to pick me up and take me down to greet our newest valley champions. I was quite tired out by my day. Sirens were howling. What on earth? There must have been a bad accident on Metz Road – the sirens kept on coming. Our dogs were howling. All of a sudden, my husband came running in, "there's a fire, a fire!" I dashed outside and he was not joking. Yet again, 18 months or so on, we had still more fires burning in the hills behind our houses and they were already roaring down the hill through the dry brush behind the vineyard and towards my neighbor's house. I called 911. "We have a fire here in Riverview Estates", I told the dispatcher. The fire line told me that they had it under control and I told them that I didn't think they did. "The wind has changed," I told them, "and the fire is now headed directly for our houses." Again, lives changed in a flash. None of my neighbors could believe this was happening again. We gazed obsessively at the flames, as you do when a sight is so horrific it captures your psyche to the extent that you are near paralyzed with shock.

We weren't going to be going anywhere that night to celebrate a champion or two – we were going to be fighting to save our home. Or, that was exactly how it felt, as the fire tankers roared overhead and scooped up buckets of water from the river and back to the flames. Thick smoke filled the air and our lungs, our animals howled in discomfort and fear. The wind turned back again and, with it, the mood. "It's turning away!" the assembled group of neighbors said, "It's turning away." Then, the wind would rise up once more and, in her fickle way, play games with us again. Night fell, the chopper left, and we were told that there were crews fighting the fires in the hills from the ground. It was another one of those scary nights you don't care to remember, but always will.

Then it was back to the fair and another surreal day.

Our Champion got to try curly fries for the first time in her life – by the way, she really likes ketchup - and many folks expressed the shock and surprise that accompanies a random accomplishment of that ilk. "Reserve Grand Champion? It's a once in a lifetime thing," a gnarly old rancher told me. "One time!" Well and good that we were only going to be doing this the one time, I thought to myself, and we were going to be leaving the swine arena while we were ahead. Knowing how I can't help falling in love, even with a farmyard pig, I now know enough to know what I can and cannot handle and I cannot handle this. Sally and Jeremy had the sweetest of existences while they were with us in their pig cabana, rich with tiki torches, heat lamps and umbrellas on the south forty with side plates of strawberries and marshmallows and I only hope their next residence is as kind, wherever it may be.

What I am left with is a sunny memory of my first and last journey out with a super-smart pig or two in my life and the deeper respect I have now gained from my few months of encounters with the breed. As for the fires; I hope we are done for the season. I will have no lasting and sunny memory of them, though I deeply respect them. They can stay far, far away forever, as far as I am concerned, and I won't miss them one bit.

Published May 2011

Saved by the e-kiss

The house had gone strangely quiet. There is a peculiar noise of silence when everyone, but you, has left in the morning. It is a noise almost delicious enough to send you right back to sleep. My husband had left for the school run and then briskly maneuvered his way onto the freeway to work in Salinas. He had taken his cell phone; he had taken his daughter. Now, what had he forgotten? Oh yes, it came to me immediately. He had forgotten to kiss me goodbye.

Once a marriage has some age behind it, sometimes the goodbye peck is all you are going to get, by way of emotional engagement, in the course of any given day; so when it is missing, if you are female, you notice and you worry. 15 years down the road and, already, we no longer even peck in the morning like marginally hungry chickens? It was quite worrisome.

In my mind, I could see before me the family meeting; the painful gathering when the two parents sit down with the child in the dark, chilly parlor, only ever used for Christmas Day or difficult conversations, and they tell her that they are going to be splitting up the family unit. They tell her that mummy and daddy can no longer live together, but they will always adore her. She will always be the main thing. They paint colorful pictures of how fabulous it will be for the child in the middle of the two of them to have two homes, two rooms to junk up, the enormous benefit of being able to be spoilt by two parents and be able to successfully play one against the other and, mostly, win, especially in the early days. And all the child in the middle can do is to cry and beg them not to go there. My child always said that if her Dad and I were to split, she wouldn't be able to go with either one of us, because she couldn't choose. That would teach us.

But here my brain is flying away with me, as a woman's brain tends to do, over-analytical beasts that we are. Just because I was a real bear last year to live with, I spent much of the year sickly and on my back – and not in a good way. I couldn't even fulfill my usually useful role of going to work very much, or making much money for the family coffers, so really what was my use? Some cute chick in the bank had caught his eye. She was single and sexy. She still had breasts and hair and, here, he was only a man. And sometimes that's all it takes. All those things pass through the female frontal lobes also, over the extensive examination of the simple missing kiss in the morning. Men just don't get it.

And then it came over the ether. A text from the guilty husband, which read, simply - no introduction needed - '*e-kiss*'. Now I had seen it all! I felt the horror of my mother run back from wherever she'd been and explode with disgust. "Not only do you forget to kiss me goodbye in the morning, but then you think you can make it up with an '*e-kiss*', not even a verbal apology?" I can hear her now, if she ever allowed herself to understand what an *'e-kiss'* might be. My father would probably have had a plate aimed at his head the next time he walked in the door if he had ever dared do such a thing, which he definitely would not. But the times they have a-changed, mother, and some of us have some of our very best conversations over texting. *'E-kiss'*. It tickled my funny bone. I roared with laughter. Never mind my vision of the girl in the bank. She was history. He was immediately forgiven.

People ask me what the key might be to a long and successful marriage, the one I think I have. I think it is pretty simple. You have to be the best of friends and you have to make each other laugh. Just as your working lives are forced to evolve with the times and over time, so your committed relationship has to continue growing in one way, but establish deeper roots in another. It's an interesting combination – a seesaw that is always striving for the perfect balance, just like life itself.

"We should go dancing," the man with the e-kiss technique informed me. This was just days after he hosted a fabulous 'tiki-cabana' party – torches and all - to welcome three FFA pigs to their near palatial quarters at our home. He never used to be the dancing type – let alone be the one to suggest that we host a party. "Oh yes," I responded cryptically. "And where would you like to go and do this dancing?" "Oh, maybe a blues club, something like that," he replied. And maybe we should. Years ago, when we lived in Santa Cruz County, we had often talked about going to listen to music at Moe's Alley, a local blues club. Knee deep in raising kids and working all hours, we never made it. Perhaps now we should not only make it another thing we aim to do, but that we should plan to do it – give it a date, make it happen. Right on the heels of my swimming with dolphins, which was up there on my list and I checked it off the list last year, I'm thinking it's time to acknowledge that the years never go backwards and life is a measured entity; you just never know what kind of measure you are going to get.

Reach out and grab those e-kisses whenever you can, plan to do as many fun things as you are able, and for sure, go out and dance with your partner, if he asks you to dance, whether you are dancing folk or not. It just might help the roots dig a little deeper.

Published March 2011

Slick and the train he rode in on

For want of a better name, we'll just call him 'Slick', as in 'Slick Willie'. Slim and fairly handsome, if you like that kind of thing, he had a swagger to his walk that reminded me of an unsuitable love interest in a romance movie; the kind where The 'Slick' always ends up leaving the broad, probably for another less likeable broad, breaking the hearts this way and that, as he strolls in and out of the long suffering wenches' lives.

When he first swung his legs over my fence, I knew instantly that we were in for trouble. Rumor has it he belonged to a former neighbor who left town and all of their responsibilities behind, when they lost their home. Bad luck or foolhardy judgment in life should not be fodder for bad behavior, but that is a whole other story. Other tales had him belonging to the neighbor home; a home where they either do not care, or cannot imagine the impact an unfixed male can have on the neighborhood in which they have moved themselves and their Slick.

Whatever the truth of the matter, Slick pulled into town and along with himself came a whole trainload of wenches of no fixed abode and dubious moral fiber. All of a sudden there were feral females everywhere screaming and whaling and howling day and night. Whether they were in pain or not, or just trying to attract Slick's attention, we'll never quite know, because we couldn't ever get close enough to them to be able to either rescue or catch them.

We hoped Slick and his entourage would leave town quickly and let us be in peace. Our own felines were pretty fed up with the whole hoo-ra and ready to leave town themselves. They were not supportive of this yowling, howling spring behavior, reminiscent of something that would occur in the big city of Felinity and definitely not here in their chosen place of Neuter-dom; and they proceeded to sit protectively next to their food dishes, hoping it would soon all end and the relative tranquility at Solace would reign once more.

But Slick liked what he found at our place and soon was like the fox in the proverbial hen house, having his way all over town with the floozies, which seemed to show up in droves to witness and subject themselves to his dubious charms at work.

We were in cat crisis. We stopped feeding our own cats in the front of the house, as we had been wont to do for the past several years of home ownership. Our alpha tabby began crying to come into the house in the middle of the night to get away from the melee, ensuring that his grouchy owner would become even grouchier than usual through lack of shut eye. Others, who were formerly front yard cats, overnight, transformed themselves into back yard inhabitants. No problem there. Slick just maneuvered his way over the fence from front to back and ate his meals and caused his chaos back there too, or wherever he willed, frankly. He had no respect for rules or the train she rode in on. He had no qualms or any moral compass to speak of. The cat was among the pigeons, as it were, and habits of a lifetime were disappearing instantaneously among our brood, as the feline Dictator, and not even one of ours, moved into our homestead and Armageddon proceeded to rule rampant in the feline world.

"Trap his wily ass!" said one helpful expert. (He's feral and smart as they come, old Slick. Not as easy as you might think.) 'Call the animal rescue!" said another. (I'm sure my home would be a real priority for those folks, short handed and constantly in crisis mode as they always are, rescuing the truly needy, the injured and the starving. I'd tell them the Slick story and they would, for sure, snicker and advise me to get a trap. See expert number one.)

No, this would take the survival of the fittest, this would take The Husband and his 'smarter than thou' ways, his Boy Scout training, with tools sharpened, to fix our critical issues and restore our homestead to an eventual plain of relative peace. Recalling the war he waged against the gophers and the turmoil they created in our yards, once upon a time, in the form of the 'Gopher Bomb', I'm quite sure that my resident warrior will come up with a plan to catch Slick before he impregnates any more unwitting females, or at least before the rest of our own resident brood leave home. Once Slick has been dealt with, snipped and sent on his way to Pastures Elsewhere, we will then have to deal with the results of his ravenous appetite and try to pick up the ladies of his night and whatever other seeds he may have planted along the way.

It is definitely spring time in our world and it is not as pretty a sight as it should be. If you have any Slicks in your immediate area and they have not been spayed or neutered, please do not wait to make it right. The responsibility for your pets that you bring into your home begins when you take them on and it is not something that can wait until next spring when they will, for sure, be out there causing havoc in some else's front and back yards. Too many humans ignore this simple task and Slick and his kind are the results. This does not make for a happy home!

Published March 2013

Someone opened the gate

We knew she was slowing down. She began tripping a bit when some one was on her back, dragging her stiff back foot behind her. Her feet were sore; she only wanted to walk on really soft ground. It was time to retire her from the ride she loved so much. Then there was the memorable day when she no longer wanted to go down to the meadow with the others. She just stood at the open gate, gazing over down the valley, and then turned her pretty head away to go and graze some more on the lawn by the house. She had always loved going to the meadow to push the llamas around, make the gelding a little nuts with her antics and observe the full and colorful adventures of the resident animal world down there; not to mention roll her body around in the warm earth and sleep in the sun. The day she didn't want to go there was a day of concern. We changed up her arthritis medicine, increased her grain and calorie intake and got both of her blankets ready for winter.

My sister-in-law took one look at her over the Thanksgiving break and told us she wouldn't make it through the winter. I defied that prognosis and started making hot mash to feed her every night full of molasses, oats, sugar, dried apples, beet, senior grain and more – oh and there were always carrots on top, because she adored carrots. When the freezing weather arrived, my husband arose in the early hours of the morning and got a nice oak stove up and blazing near her stable, so she would be warm and toasty with her shelter, her two coats and now her own personal fire. We tried everything we knew how to do and then some.

It was a warm Tuesday afternoon and we had headed home early for a ride. Strangely enough, we were all home early that day and that never happens. I went over to the stable to saddle up the noble steed. It was then that I glanced back and saw the form of Abbey Rhode lying on the ground near her stable. I called for the husband and raced over to her. Her eyes were still open, she was still alive. Husband went to call for the vet. Though her breathing was labored, she was strangely calm with her eyes wide open, as if to say, "I know I'm leaving home. Let's not make a fuss; just let me relax and lie here a while with y'all." My daughter rushed over too and we both loved on her, relating stories from the past – when she had insisted on running up hills with our new riders just because she always had to be first at the gate – when she had refused to get back into the trailer when we were in Watsonville and had the husband running circles around over and over in order to try and get her into the trailer – when she had insisted on always bombing into his lord and master's stable, regardless of his rules about such things and the chaos that then ensued with water troughs kicked over and more, her love of the garden hose – and the stories of the games she played with the gelding's head are a whole story unto themselves. We talked to her, kissed her, loved on her and told her it was okay to let herself go off to the unchartered waters; we had had our blissful times with her. Though we were not ready, she most likely was. The vet arrived and she tried to get her up again, but she was too weak. It was determined that the kindest thing was to let her go in peace, which we did. Three minutes after the long injection and she had passed quietly on. I cried for a day and a half; I shall grieve for much longer. That sweet soul has a permanent lodging in my heart.

What we had completely underestimated was the effect her passing would have on the noble steed. The vet had said that we should probably let him see her lying down where she had passed, to give him some closure, but no amount of strength could get him through the gate that day to see her. He simply couldn't face it and refused to go. The day after she passed and her body was under a tarpaulin, he stood at the gate gazing down the pathway where she lay. Once the body had left, he stood there still. We let him graze around after she had left and visit her stable. He seemed alright at the time.

And then the heavens opened. I decided to take him for a ride. He was like a 2 year old, bucking, bolting and raging. There was no putting even a saddle blanket on this boy. He was huffing and puffing and stressing like he was in pain. We gave up trying to calm him down that day and just let him loose into the meadow. He raced down the hill bucking and kicking, threw himself to the ground, kicked and rolled, jumped up and threw himself down again. We had never seen anything like it. Even the dogs just stood there watching him in awe and without comment. This is a horse who asks permission for a little roll after a ride at the beach and never kicks or bucks under any circumstance, ever! After all these theatrics, he pranced his way again up the hill from the meadow to the gate and looked down again to where she had been lying down the alley. If you strained your eyes, you could still barely see the imprint of her body in the dirt. He whinnied, as if crying. We all looked at each other in disbelief. Guess what: horses grieve too. "Give him some time," friends urged. "Take him to visit another horse and show him he is not the only horse still out there!" "Summon the horse whisperer!" urged another. "How about the horse massager?" There were so many thoughts and concerns and suggestions for this poor a-grieving gelding that I was completely silenced by all the love. All this surge of feeling for one poor old rescue horse who had lost his meadow mate? Let's not forget that when she arrived he couldn't help but remind her who was boss with a nip or two to the rear end. Lest we not remember that he never let her think she was the boss of him, nor was she entitled to any of his real estate in the form of alley or stable time. No, this was not a regular case of love and adoration; but, ultimately, it was a case of grieving for sure. He had loved her in his own way, apparently.

And he was angry with me too; gosh he was angry with me. I'd try to hug on him as is usual for us and his body was like a rock with ears firmly in the back/not-friendly position. I found myself telling him, "I miss her too, you know!" "It wasn't my choice that she had to go!" "It wasn't my fault she needed to leave." He was inconsolable. Apples, marshmallows, cookies and more; nothing seemed to help.

The next morning, we found him grazing out on the lawn just as she had always done, except that his gate was always closed and hers was open. "Some one opened the gate for him last night," I told husband and we both looked at each other knowingly. This had never happened before. Abbey wanted him to feel better, so she opened the gate – as she was wont to do – and let him out, to help him along his way and aide him with his healing.

Then my husband went out and had a little chat with him in the stable. "We had a talk," he said. "I think he's doing a little better." Later, I took my armory of sweets out with me and Winston and I had a little talk too, ending with a rather – on his part - reluctant and conciliatory hug. The next day he was better and the next even more so. Finally about 10 days after the passing of our beautiful Abbey Rhode, we were able to saddle Winston again and ride him just as we used to.

I will never again underestimate the emotional capacity of an animal. We all saw it first hand and it was quite something to witness.

This story is dedicated to the life and legacy of the most beautiful equine soul – Abbey Rhode – whose spirit will live on always in the meadow at 'Solace,' where she passed many, many happy days towards the end of her life.

The Animals Teach Us Everything & Other Short Tails

Starring in my own cartoon

When I was very young, I was a horse fanatic. I would play with hobby horses, farm horses, soft horses, toy horses. I would read books about horses, study their anatomy and watch 'Black Beauty' over and over again. In retrospect, I think I was a bit of a horse addict. There was something about those beasts that just grabbed a hold of my imagination and took me to wonderful places.

My friend at elementary school, Isabel, lived on a farm at the top of our village and her sister had a horse called 'Blackie'. Yes, he was black with a white star. I loved to go to their dairy farm and ride Blackie along the lanes and through the fields around her home. It was always my dream to, one day, have my own horse. In addition, every Sunday, I would go to the local riding stables near our village and we would be allotted certain steeds to mount. When I was quite small, maybe five, my 'steed' was a certain, stubborn Shetland pony called 'Steppie'. Steppie was an obstinate little white munchkin and gave me a run for my money. I didn't care though – I loved them all – Starlight, Gulliver and even Steppie. My mother would often buy me the 'Thelwell' cartoon books about little girls and the feisty steeds they would try and control; mostly to no avail. I must have been a bit of a 'Thelwell' girl myself with my braids, jodhpurs and black hat, my chubby little legs staunchly chasing after reluctant horses and ponies around the green and hedged pastures of the English countryside. I couldn't see it then, but I see it now. With age comes a certain sense of humor that is so intrinsic to the continued enjoyment of life.

We lived in the middle of the village, but there was an adjacent lot to our house I knew my dad was trying to buy, I thought, so that I could finally get my own horse. It had to happen, I sensed it in the air; I knew it was on the cards. I had that certainty that only a child of around 6.75 years old can have.

On the morning of my seventh birthday, I felt sure today was the day. I could already feel my arms wrapped around the warm, furry neck of my own horse, its soft muzzle nuzzling mine. What would I call him or her? With all the farms I had played with over the years, I had a whole theater of characters to choose from. There was Easter, Prince, Johnny, Lady, Starlight and more. I would just have to meet him or her first and then decide. I was so excited that I positively wriggled with anticipation.

In the living room, there sat a wooden rocking horse and he was my birthday present. Though he had the coloring of 'Morning Starlight', also known as 'Horace', a dapple grey show horse from the riding school, he did not have a warm body or the soft muzzle I had been hoping for. He was made of wood and his expression was fixed. I was happy to have him, but still I had to hide my huge disappointment. How could I have been so wrong about such an enormous thing? My dad had not been able to buy the land and that was that. I understood it and I made the best of it. Some evenings I would sneak downstairs and get on my rocking horse's back in the darkness. I would close my eyes, wrap my arms around his neck and imagine that Moonshine came to life as I held onto him and that then, and only then, the magic would begin. Memories like that don't fade very much; no matter how many years ago they were made.

10 years ago we moved to the California countryside and finally had a little bit of space to call our own. There's nothing like that for making you feel like a princess. We got dogs and cats, we got goats and even some turtles, but, years on, I had still never owned my own horse. I had wanted to, but it had not been the right time. It's like planning for a child; there is probably never a good time. And there is probably never a good time to take on a horse; but life has a way of fixing that. I was just waiting for Winston and he was just waiting for me; that's the only way I can describe it. When I found out that he needed a home and that no one else wanted him, I knew he was the one for me. We are both a bit scarred and a bit grey; we've both been through it a bit – him even more than me, since he was rescued from who knows what on a ranch in Mexico. He has bite marks all over his body and a split in his hoof. He has weird habits that you know came from somewhere closely related to hell and yet, in spite of all that, he is the sweetest soul. He doesn't like to be tied up – watch out fence you are coming down – he doesn't care for a bit in

the mouth, you will circle constantly while cinching and he acts all the time as if he were starving hungry, which I know for sure he no longer is. Yet, I can call his name when he is standing at the top of the meadow and I hear him neigh and see him cascade down the meadow and up the other side at a speed I didn't think he could achieve. At that moment, my heart is so full, I think it might burst. At that moment, all the disappointments of so many decades ago all fade and dissipate, because they were simply leading up to this.

We saddle up – not without some difficulty – because of our strange little habits and we ride up to the gate. There are 3 dogs and 2 goats in fast pursuit. I knew I should have locked them all up before we left. Trying to get a horse through an open gate and keep out 5 other insistent animals is not to be recommended. In Thelwell's world, they have many sketches about the little girls letting go of their horses and what happens when they make that fatal mistake. The riding instructor is always saying, "Girls, no matter what you do. Do not let go of your horse!" (Always the precursor to the horses headed for the hills, without riders, with the little girls in jodhpurs tearing up the ground behind them!)

Thinking Winston was more of the stationary character, I forgot my 'Thelwell' cartoons, one time, and paid full attention to my goat Charlie who was headed for a big old vine feast all on his ownsome. While I was scooting him back through the gate, the dogs were getting out of the gate; and nothing seemed to be working correctly. I chuckled to myself as I realized I was starring in my own comedy feature. After I had corralled the escape merchants, I quickly realized that I had misplaced my steed. He had moved on down the extremely steep slope and was busy ignoring my beseeching to please come back so we could carry on our ride. I started walking down the slope and then started tripping and running, it was so steep. I was also laughing at myself as I tripped and ran, unable to stop; and he began to run too. And there we were – character actors in our own cartoon. I stopped - remembering the skinny riding instructor in the cartoons. "Do not chase your horse – they will always be able to run faster than you," and leaned casually up against the fence with a fortuitous piece of carrot in the hand. Winston eyed me cautiously and began to salivate over the carrot. I knew I had him.

So now I have my own horse and, though it is not quite the 'Black Beauty' utopia I imagined when I was quite, quite young with my arms wrapped around a wooden rocking horse that I still have to this day, it is still pretty much bliss in the palms of my hands. As we strolled off in the morning mists and I watched the river while he fidgeted about every darn little curiosity in his way, I realized that some passions never really die; you just sit on them for a while. Mostly there is never a good time to pursue any of life's passions, but that when they arrive on your door step, you will know that the time just became the right time and the timing was perfect.

Published June 2011

The box

We spend much of our lives, rushing onto the next thing. When we accomplish something, we are only as good as our next feat. We seldom enjoy the moment or dwell for a nano-second on life's transitory pleasures. Sometimes, at the end of a very difficult real estate transaction, I will pause for a moment, maybe celebrate just a little, remind myself to allow a little teensy, whimsical gift of decadence, because it is, finally, over and I am still alive and then I plunge myself quickly back into the great abyss. That is, seemingly, modern living. It is, perhaps, not until we are in the twilight of our lives that we make the time to reflect on all those special moments we cantered past when we simply didn't have time to pause in life and we take the time to savor them for the first time, one at a time only when, perhaps, time is running out.

It is Christmas morning and my horse is unwell and seems very uncomfortable. He wants to lie down and sleep; he doesn't want to eat or drink. "Get him up!" says my sister-in-law, who is quite the horse lady. "Make him walk, don't let him lie. Sounds like colic to me." Oh no, a colic diagnosis for a horse on Christmas Day – this horse having never had an off day all the years he has lived with me. It seemed like a bad dose too. I walked him in 75-80 degrees for 2 hours and still he wanted to lie down. Any chance to stop walking and he was nodding off. He refused to eat or drink; his bodily systems didn't appear to be working properly either. Panic time on Christmas Day. After the year we had had; why would we presume anything less?

The emergency vet was at our home within 30 minutes, pumping his stomach. "Sand colic," she proclaimed, having seen several recent cases such as his, based on the horses eating off dry and dusty ground and accumulating far too much junk in their systems that they can't pass without assistance. After she cleaned him out with psyllium and mineral oil, he seemed to recover quickly and was soon acting more like the horse I knew and less like a sleepy head ready to keel over, though his stomach was obviously still sore. It was a frightening experience for all of us though and not one I'd care to repeat.

This episode reminded me that the best made plans can go sideways in a second and that we need to always try and find good stuff to hold on to. Christmas Day, we had planned a lovely family day with presents and feasting. The weather was glorious and it should have been a happy, happy day which, for me and Winston, it was most definitely not. Never mind I had a huge vet bill that I had not imagined I would have to pay on Christmas Day, my noble steed was out of pain and still alive. Who cares about the medicine I had to buy or the sleepless nights I endured, checking on him, hoping he was okay, standing up, taking nutrition and water? My baby was out of pain and behaving in his normal way. You cannot dwell on the trivial issues, when the big picture hits you in the head.

And so 'The Box' came to mind. I can't really say it was entirely my own idea, but I am doctoring the concept that passed me by to suit our family. Every time something good happens, you write it down and put it into the box. It could be as small as a new bird landing on the bird feeder, or as large as Winston pulling through from his sand colic. At the end of the year, you pull out the scraps of paper and see how the chips fell in the larger scheme of things and all the reasons you had to be cheerful throughout the roller coaster 365 days you had just tumbled through. I imagined that it would have to make for an interesting exercise. My daughter proclaimed it to be "Dumb", my husband said he'd try and remember to use it. I have already starting using it and we are barely over the cusp of the New Year.

Looking back on the year we had, I'd say it ranked down there with the not-so-good; but I am surely missing a lot of jewels I should wish to remember and cherish. Reaching back, indeed, it was the year my puppy Tucker came to live with us, also the year I went to stay with my baby sister in Turkey. Can't forget that magnificent holiday! It was also the year that my daughter became a Certified Nursing Assistant and the year my husband attained his home inspector license. There, without really casting much of a thought about it, is a cluster of happy, positive things that happened in the year that was; that I could so easily say I was glad to see the back of.

I'm not sure how 'The Box' concept will go for the rest of the family, but I am resolved to give it a go and see how we stand at the end of the year. I document a lot, but not always the good stuff, so this will be a change for me and maybe one that will yield some positive results. With my glass half full, who knows how much better the outlook for the year might be? Happy New Year to all and may your box be full of grateful appreciative thoughts for this one life that we know of, so full of beauty and surprise.

Published December 2013

The Crazy Cat Lady

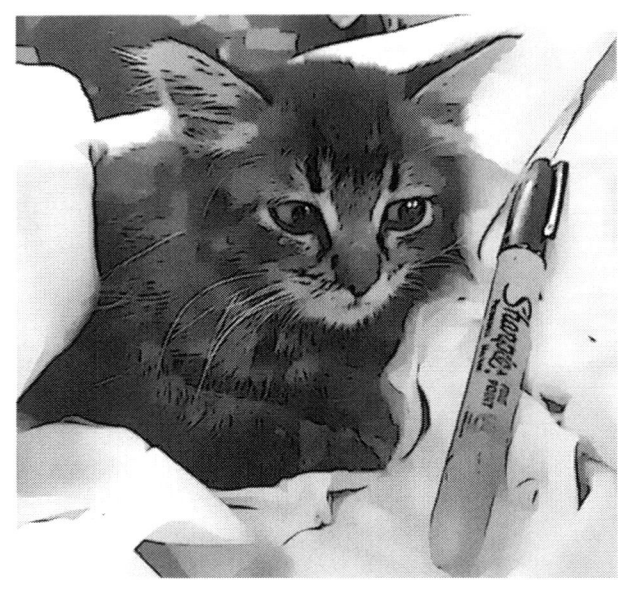

It was not until I was quite old, dating my second and also current husband in fact, that I had to acknowledge that cats were indeed an important part of a home. Since my hubby had about four felines to his name at the time, I had to get over my fear of the feline claw, (which got me in no uncertain terms when I was about two, the memory lingers on), and embrace all that I had been missing in my life; along with the inheritance of two teenage boys, but now, with that, I digress. That is completely another story. Cats and boys were to be part of my life from then on, the package deal and I had better just get along with all of them without exception.

Over the years, and especially since we have had a home in the countryside with multitudes of mice and gophers requiring mo-multitudes of predators to take care of their ever growing population, my love and respect for the cat has grown. Once we had Joey move in with us and live with us for a colorful 11 years of male tabbydom, I became a firm fan. Joe had the biggest personality of just about any pet on the Planet Pet and delighted and frustrated not only his family, but also the many visitors to our home over the years. But you could still never say I was a cat lady. I would be the one corralling the tabby to leave the counter tops, the shower area, the inside of a toilet; just about anywhere the naughty tab wanted to go, while my husband would just laugh and watch the show. I was always the one chasing the tab up and down the corridors, as he fooled me at every corner with his stubborn nature and willful lack of respect for the alpha female in the house.

At the time, our English neighbor at the top of the hill held the title. Any waif and stray that was abandoned in our neighborhood could whiff the scent of 'Cat lady' from anywhere inside the gate of our development and the homeless and needy would always find their way to her door and be taken care of in every which way. And then a sad day came. Our resident cat lady moved and the she was no more in our neighborhood, but there were still many cats roaming around looking for a meal. At last count, our 'Cat Lady' had rescued about 18 cats, most of them still living the life of luxury in her care and, bless her, she did this rescue service for some considerable years; but I had not wanted to take on her role when she left us and never considered the magnitude of such an undertaking. I had enough in my care in the guise of horses, dogs, llamas, goats – oh and my share of cats, I'll have you know. I had more than enough.

But cats have a way of finding another cats, don't they – oh and vacant bowls of cat kibble just hanging out in the driveway, such as they will always find at my place with overflowing bowls of water to boot. Pregnant mamas also know a nice easy birthing room or two when they see it, where some innocent person will take good care of them and their brood, never mind that they don't ever want to be stroked or acknowledged as part of the farm.

Before I knew it, things were completely out of control in Cat Land. Calypso, the feral white and grey tab, had arrived in town – by way of an errant and inconsiderate former neighbor, by all accounts, who just left him behind when they moved. At our place, he found some ladies in need of fertilization, for want of a better term - Mama Scratch and 'Mama' – for want of a better name – both feral, in addition Felie, daughter of Scratch, also feral. It is quite hard to catch a cat if they don't want to be caught, did you know that – and, before we knew it, we had pregnant mamas all over the place. Mama Scratch gave birth to three of her own and sweetly adopted a surrogate that the other Mama had abandoned. Mama gave birth to her own set of three – these are all tabbies mind you, so it gets a bit confusing as to who belongs to who and then Felie gave birth to, we believe three, who currently reside under the back shed. Fortunately, we managed to sweeten, with the lure of wet food, and thereby corral Calypso, also known in our hood as 'Baby Daddy' and managed to prevent him from fathering anymore, prolific though he was. We were lucky to find homes for Scratch's babies, bar the surrogate and we now need to try and corral the remaining who knows how many to get them fixed, find them new homes etc. It is like a soap opera in the feline world and who knows where this will all end? We also have, living in the back of the property – Bona, the black cat, father of Felie – and Sarah the white old lady who has to be all of about 9 now and was the remaining one of two in a 'Buy one, Get one free' special at the rescue shelter years ago. No wonder my cat food bill is crazily high and nothing looks like it is going to change anytime soon.

"These days, we call you the Crazy Cat Lady!" my neighbor told me with a laugh. That is not a title I asked for, wanted to keep, or would have any issue giving away to some deserving person. But I don't see anyone lining up at my place with their arms wide open and their catch cages at the fore. Stray animals always seem to be other people's problem and right now that problem is apparently mine. Not that they are really a 'problem'; that doesn't sound nice, does it, coming from an animal lover. Looking at the tabby kittens frolicking in the sun and having a heck of a time rolling around all happy and healthy; you do have to smile at the part you played in their early development and give a nod to the young lives you perhaps helped along the way to develop into older ones. Maybe I am turning into a bit of a crazy cat lady. I have certainly been called worse. Perhaps I'll even keep that title until a better one comes along.

Lucy Mason Jensen

Published August 2013

The Lousy Pet Sitter

Everyone knows that I am the ultimate animal lover. Just give me a feral cat and a bunch of kittens and I have to feed them, even though more cats to add to, however many I already have, is truly not something I need in my life. There's a lady bug in the pool? No issue, I'll get it out, no matter I am fully clothed. Dogs? Never can have too many. No wonder the munchkins of various ilks show up at my door step in droves and never want to leave. My own eclectic clan of furry wonders take me about an hour plus in the morning to feed, water, groom, sing to and muck out. How do I have time for a regular job? I don't have a regular job per se; I work for myself, so there you have it. No sane company would have me with my animal schedule and priorities!

But, as for having additional time to watch other people's broods, that is not something I have ever really considered. Plus, if you take into account, my own limitations therein.

They say that good fences make good neighbors! Yes, I really do believe that is true. I also subscribe to the good neighborhood concept of helping each other out as needed, when needed, and regardless of any otherwise full schedule you might have. With that said, I did have to chuckle to myself recently at my rather dubious position as neighborhood pet sitter.

My neighbors recently had to leave their critters home alone for an unexpected period of time and needed some help managing. That is when good neighbors, such as yours truly, go into emergency mode. "Don't worry about a thing!" I could hear myself assuring them their critters would be in excellent hands with Super Neighbor over here. "You are talking to the biggest animal lover I know!" I bragged. It was then we discovered that their neighbors – and also ours – were also away and they were supposed to be watching their critters. Aha. Double duty! It sounds like the makings of a bad movie; but it was the week that was in our house.

My first task sounded simple enough. Go and check on the husky pups and give them food and water. Check. Next, go and visit the cats in the garage and do the same. Slight problem there! Mama cat was hiding by the door and took off down the driveway at the first opportunity. "Oh not so fast there, speedy!" I raced after her and scooped her up in emergency pet sitter mode. "Not losing anyone on my watch, missie!" Next it was over to the other neighbors' home with their instruction list and my reading glasses in hand. "Feed the dragon meal worms and defrosted peas. What! A dragon?" Yes, that. Any one who knows me also knows that I am not a huge lover of the reptile. I can tolerate most things – except for snakes – from a distance, but handling or even feeding a scaly one are not challenges that I would ever welcome into my life. And here we have 'meal worms for the dragon' on my own personal platter for the day. Finding the dragon was another issue, since no road map had been issued with the instructions for that either. Once located, no instructions were moreover forthcoming as to how to open said dragon's cage and deliver said mealworms and now well-defrosted peas to rather scary looking dragon, who was, at this point, looking irritatedly up at his feeder. Also needed to deliver fresh water and be in extremely close proximity to said reptile. "Husband!!!!" (He heard me.) Then it was outside to the remainder of the menagerie. "Check on the cats!" the list dictated. "What cats, where?" I did my frantic kitty calls to a resounding silence except for the insistent banter of the chickens looking for something; who knows what. Now how to get into the chicken pen? Peering over the fence like a peeping, hungry fox, I ascertained that the chickens already had food and water; and oh dear, I would have to check for eggs tomorrow once I had figured out how to break into that place. "Husband!!!" (Again, I holler.) Then I had the rather large goats to deal with and the fact that you should never, ever approach full sized goats in flip flops. "Owww, you wretch!" I yelped, or words to that effect as his cloven hoof stepped on my fresh toe nail, (which only recently replaced the one my horse stepped upon and killed.) And then along came the others and they looked as if they could tear up all the other toe nails in one step. Throwing the food at them and quickly fleeing, I then had to turn tail and check that they had water. Food is one thing, but a lack of water? No responsible pet sitter could ever live with themselves if they did not check and double check the neighbor-animals' aqua supply. Back in the pen again with the hefty 12 hooves threatening to tap-dance on a few more of my toes, I skip around the frisky goats to the water trough, grab the hose in threatening mode and complete the water task, then skate out of the barn with no eggs in hand and one sore toe. I check the list. "Give the goats their grain!" Oh no, not back in the pen with those foot stompers! Please say I don't have to do that? But the burden of a responsible pet sitter is a weighty one and we do try and follow instructions even when personal bodily injury might occur. Note to self – when in doubt or in fear of more foot crushing, filter all food through the wire mesh. The animals can receive it just fine that way too.

Husband calls. "The huskies got out!" No, no, no! The last time these energetic pups got out – long story – they ended up in Santa Barbara. "No, this is not allowed to happen on my watch!" I squeal. "Not while I am in charge." I am not, I swear, not going to call those poor neighbor folk up in Stanford and confess, with all else they have going on, that the chief animal lover in the neighborhood has managed to lose their puppies on the first day. "I saw them out, they saw me and promptly took off for the hills!" Husband explained. No, go find them, we have to find them!" I am still squealing.

Two hours later with my voice box sore from calling, 'puppies, puppies' in my inane puppy voice, the little blessings just come running into my garage all thirsty like and telling me they are home. "You little ... $%^&#$%^

... darlings! I am SO glad you are home," (And I never had to make that call, though, like all good pet sitters I did fess up to 'The Incident' the following day.) Husband, meanwhile, spent his evening fixing the lock on the pup gate to ensure that that particular escape would not occur again on our watch.

The life of a pet sitter is not all it is cracked up to be. If I ever again get asked to take care of my neighbors' beloveds, I shall ask for floor plans, steel toed boots and a notarized release of liability. Responsibility such as that needs to come with, bare minimum, a road map and steel caps.

Published June 2013

The month of the cat

So Lily was found in down town Soledad of an evening; seemingly playing with the traffic, for wont of a better description. She was young and hungry and needy, as they all seem to be when they find their way to our home and finally exhale a sigh of relief over a large bowl of kibble. She had the perfectly symmetrical white socks and movie star rose-bud lips of a black & white rock star feline. She loved to be cuddled and held like a baby. And then she was a he. Hate it when that happens. But no worries! The nubs come off and the animal can have whichever name it chooses. Too bad mankind isn't that way. No matter my husband's efforts to make Lily Rose into a Leonard, she will always be Lily to me and an absolute darling in our compote of mixed-breed-rescue-darlings, which seems to increase every time I mention the word 'kibble' and, consequently, go out to buy some more. Husband no longer even bothers to ask if we are keeping them or not. What a question. They cross our paths and they enter our hearts, through whichever window is currently open, and they stay for as long as they wish, or as the Dean of the universe decides. I love that.

"Oh, we can only have the one cat," she says. "Couldn't manage any more." Those restrictive folks always blow me away. What is one more cat, one more dog, that rabbit or turtle or fish, when there are lives to be saved, and these urchins need a home? Extra munchkins are companions for each other. You just do it. That's what you do. I have 5 dogs currently and sometimes that just doesn't seem very many.

So Lily took just a minute to settle him or her self into Solace and be a part of our ever-growing family. She was soon hanging with the big dogs, sniffing at the llamas' hooves and definitely acquainting herself with the large and foreboding horse hooves that trotted all around her. She was fearless and she was happy. To be able to make an animal happy means to me that I have arrived. Period. When you can see it and feel it to the point that it is definitely so; it is a beautiful thing to behold.

A photo arrives in text format from the husband to me. It is of a weensy-tiny tabby thing. "Um, what?" is my casual response, knowing in advance who, in addition, is coming home this evening, that I wasn't expecting on the feed roster. And so it was. A home that husband was inspecting had this tiny bundle lying in the rays of sun in the back yard and waiting to pass onto a kinder world – a world where he could be warm and fed and not alone. The bundle was nearly gone, so depleted of energy and food as he was and, apparently, reconciled to his lot. But husband had water on hand and the cheese sticks that are a staple of his every day lunch and he wasn't ready to give up on a life he just found. He touched the bundle and gave him water and cheese. All of a sudden, the bundle was wildly alive and craving the sustenance he was being given. I'm not a godly soul, but I will embrace a miracle of life when I see one and this was one, for sure. Without a doubt, my husband brought that tiny little kitten back to life that sunny afternoon and then he brought him home; as you do.

As I held his bony little feline body in my arms and begged him to stay around for a while and make me even just a little bit of a believer, I saw the miracle of life come back with a vengeance, as Jesse J - miracle kitten of the week – proceeded to snuggle with me under my shirt, greedily lap up the milk we gave him and chew up the kibble. Though he was just a weeny- tiny, boney thing and looked like a newborn, he actually had many teeth in his tiny mouth and could actually eat regular cat kibble, given just the chance to do so – a fact that shocked me to the very core. This poor baby-kitten-cat had been dying for quite some time out in the elements and all by himself. But no more, I tell you, no more. He is in the arms of Solace now and I am proud to tell you he is doing amazingly well, like the Super Kitten-Cat that he most certainly is. He is sweet and loving and hungry and curious and eager, like all young cats should be. He is another mouth I am proud to feed and I'm hopeful that he will lead a wonderful long life right here with all of us and for always, with whatever we have to share with him.

Never count the heads you have to feed in your household, or wonder how you will ever manage to do it. Somehow, ultimately, you will. Whether you are shadowed beneath the karma of the universe or some other power, you will do it and it will happen. It is the month of the cat here at our home – they keep showing up and we keep making room. We will provide shelter for whoever needs it. Our hearts are full.

Published October 2011

The more I know mankind

The more I get to know some people – their greed and their dark natures - which cross my path daily in my rough and tumble business I call work, the more I love my horse. Though my four legged baby had a tough life, prior to our meeting and falling in love, he remains really straightforward, in that I always know what he wants and what he needs at any given time. I know what he thinks of me and me of him. It's a very pure and simple relationship, just like a mother with her child. When I sing to him at night under the moonlight – why yes, I do, and 'Edelweiss' from the 'Sound of Music' happens to be one of his favorites – there is a calmness that comes over his entire 1100 lb body and an honesty of feeling between us that few human connections could match. His breath is close to mine, we are still and we are one. The more I get to know my horse, the more I wish more people were like him.

A friend of mine was parked at an angle and trying to drop off some bills. I was, equally, parked in a disheveled, probably illegal, way and trying to multi-task, as I picked up the newspaper and talked on the phone at the same time. Her radio was blasting, her engine was running, the kids were fighting in the back; the butt of her vehicle was pointed out into the middle of the road. "How are you?" I yelled above the ruckus, glad to see her. It had been a long time. "Fine, crazy, how are you? You look good!" she yelled back. I wondered to myself if this was the best that our generation could do. A few yells over noise pollution to one another on our way to something else?

"Don't you ever wonder where we are all hurrying to?" I asked her and she proceeded to turn off her engine. All of a sudden things went very quiet and we both pondered this rather large question. "Yes, we are all rushing around to somewhere and getting, basically, nowhere," She noted. There was a pregnant pause between us, a silence that told mountains.

It is when I stop at the end of the day that I, sometimes, realize all the things I have missed in my gallop towards who knows what, in that particular space of light and life between sleep and sleep again. I race home in order not to miss the last sunlight of the day, to visit with my dogs and goats and cats, to seize the chance to ride my horse and feel connected with him, the chance to breathe my last sunset of that special and unique day. If I miss that, which I often do, I feel cheated of my real life away from the hustle and bustle of all that other stuff which is really just a means to procure a pay check and the opportunity to pay a few more household bills, which just procreate daily in any case. At the end of my life, do I want them to say that she worked really hard and missed too many sunsets, or do I want them to say that she adored spending time with all her rescue animals, who stepped inside her heart and became a permanent part of her soul? The answer to that is pretty obvious.

So what do we do, we ponder, as we try and achieve a balance through the craziness? I imagine that we try and set boundaries and rules for our lives and stick to them. If we say we are taking the day off, we set our voicemail accordingly and we take the day away from reality. If it's vacation time, and I sure am looking forward to mine this year, then we take a real time out and stop checking our email every five minutes for all the micro- managing of tasks that we are tempted to do. Your work life does not end because you take the day off. I learned a lot about that when I was ill and could not go to work. We must learn to step outside of our lives and enjoy the heck out of it. Most of my photo collages plastering my walls at home are from trips I have taken outside of my 'regular' life. There are no photos on my walls of my days at the office or the real estate contracts I have written. The images captured are of a vibrant life lived; a life that exists when I have the liberty and wherewithal to go away from normality and have an adventure that lightens my heart.

So here it is late summer and I am already coveting my winter holiday. For a period of time I shall be incognito, traveling, away, out of the country, or whichever term you would like to use to stress the fact that I shall not be returning the call or email that particular day, and tomorrow's not looking that good either. When I go away for my winter trip, I shall be visiting with my Dad, my sisters and my friends. We will be shopping and dining a lot. We shall be laughing and catching up, as if there really is no tomorrow; which, of course, we don't know whether there is or not. I, myself, shall be taking a time out, a time away from all that is normal and I shall probably make a photo collage when I get back to recall all the pictures I want to remember from my time away, along the roads that I just traveled and am now missing.

I shall miss my horse when I am gone. I am already worried as to how he is going to manage without me – and I shall miss some others I leave behind too. I shall also sing some songs to my horse while I am gone, hoping that he catches the tune from some passing star across the ether. In any case, I shall rush back to his side after my few days absent from regular life and I shall catch up with him when I return, plus the odd sunset or two that I shall miss while I am away. When I come back to our shared lives, I shall set a few more boundaries, I am sure, and create a few extra rules for catching sunsets together. The more I get to know humanity, the more I know, when I leave, I shall miss my horse.

Published September 2011

The one-legged bird

The older I get, the more I love it when I can be pleasantly surprised by the human race. In the global view of things, this was not a week for the record books – in fact there was so much sad stuff in the news that I had to turn everything off. It was that awful.

I opened the cage to my parakeets one morning to clean out the water container – as I had done many times before – and my divine Petal – our ice blue and white lady – took off for the skies through the open cage door, pounding her tiny wings towards the Santa Lucia range, as if her entire life depended on it. My jaw dropped. Why didn't I think that that would ever happen? I waited for her to come back. I looked for her in the trees and bushes. I knew her mate Pea would be calling for her. "Birds come back to roost," folks told me, but she didn't. Night fell and Pea was all alone in the cage. In the morning he was still sitting on his perch, head down, not a peep issuing from his downfallen beak. He was in mourning.

The two of them had been rescued together and we adopted them as such. Who knows how long they had been a pair, but I could tell by Pea's demeanor that he was in serious danger of dying of a broken heart – and soon.

My daughter and I took off for the pet shop on the

Peninsula, where she had rescued them as a pair, in search of another Petal to help soothe Pea's wounds. "Do you have any parakeets?" we asked. "Oh no, not at the moment. We have a pair of finches?" said the shop lady. "Wait! We have a one-legged parakeet, she needs a home!"

"We'll take her," I interrupted quickly before anyone else might step in to claim her. Poor baby had been stuck up in a cage on top of a filing cabinet and left to pretty much get on with it, so low was the pet shop's expectation that anyone would want to adopt her. And what a phenomenal little firecracker of a bird she turned out to be. She had no need of that second leg; such was her agility in getting around the cage with her powerful wings and impressive beak. Pea was blown away by his new room mate. Though I had set up the cage with ramps and the like for the disability aspect, Pickle quickly proved to me that she was way ahead in that arena and had no need of special accommodations at all.

With great pride, I posted her photo on FaceBook. "Look at our newest baby, Pickle! She only has one leg. She is a rock star of parakeets!"

"Aw Pickle, look at her …How beautiful …. Thank you guys for rescuing a disabled bird …" The accolades came pouring in through social media. All of this attention for a tiny disabled bird? I chuckled to myself, remembering that the human race, on the whole, was kind and good and compassionate to one another and earth's creatures. All of these busy folks took time out of their busy days to coo over a tiny, disabled bird. Some weeks you need to be reminded of that. This was one of those weeks. It made things in the world just a tiny bit better.

Published September 2013

The peculiar stories of the stolen tomatoes and the clean colon

We stood back in amazement and admired nature's handiwork, contained within our fortress, which was all nicely fenced and double fenced to keep out our pygmy goats, who have no conscience about such things. Our variety garden of tomatoes seemed to be coming along very well, thank you very much, albeit against the odds, and soon we would not need to buy said items from the store. I love this time of year! As the saying goes – there are some things that money cannot buy; true love and home grown tomatoes. It's as simple as that. The little blessings were developing a reddish hue, which made you salivate just looking at them. Their skins were tight and ready for the juice to just pop in the mouth. We were ready. We had rescued them from our goats, this year the snails had been kept at bay, the gophers too; this year, for once, it was going to be a bumper crop. We were going to have so many home grown tomatoes, we would have to also make tomato sauce. It was going to be that kind of year.

"Did you take the red tomatoes off the vine?" my husband made a random and unlikely enquiry of our teenager, who doesn't even like tomatoes. (And I can just imagine the response to that!) He could not think what could have happened. The very red angels we were going to have for dinner, the sweet little rosy treasures, so ready for human consumption, had disappeared into thin air. There was no apparent tussle in the tomato patch, no sign of a rabbit chewing, a gopher gnawing, or the obvious efforts of a cavalier goat cascading with determination over our significant security fence. No, the home grown tomatoes had simply disappeared with not a trace of evidence left behind. It was a complete mystery.

"I am not going mad!" Husband said emphatically. "Honestly, another red tomato has gone!" We both peered with disbelief into our gated fortress of a tomato patch. He was right. There was no sign of any disturbed soil and no telling hoof prints or paw marks, or nibbles to be seen; but our other ripe tomatoes had gone too. It could only be a case of Martians with a partiality to the savory fruit, or a phantom spirit on the wind wanting to have a little fun with their human counterparts. "Tonight you go on stake out," I informed him – and he does love the detective show 'Monk', so I was sure he could assume the character without too much trouble. "We have to save the farm!" And I was pretty serious. I struggle with buying tomatoes from the store, having grown and adored my own season after season. The flavor of store-bought tomatoes is mostly of something that has traveled a long time and been exposed to severe cooling in order not to go rotten. The flavor is not memorable or evocative, just slightly red. There is no amount of money can conjure up the magic flavor of fruits freshly plucked from the vine in your own backyard. That is why I took such affront to burglary such as this.

I read our local paper and saw that suspicious folks had been spotted at 12.31am in blacked out vehicles, perusing our local vineyards. For what? Are these the tomato thieves? Tired of trying to extract copper piping from our innocent farmers or lassoing the cows of our sleeping ranchers, they are reduced to stealing ripe tomatoes from an innocent realtor's tomato patch? I tell you; some folks have no shame. But then the detective in me, as the wife of a Monk fan, alerts me to the fact that our dogs on the porch would not allow such a theft without just a little complaining; so now that theory hits the dirt. If any of you out there are experiencing similar mysteries, let's get together and compare notes. We cannot let this kind of thing get out of hand and mess with the blessing of our existence, not to mention the fruits of our labors and our homegrown tomatoes.

Another strange thing that happened this week was that I had my very first colonoscopy. "Oh no!" I hear you say. "Stop! Too much information!" No, really, I did, and it wasn't that bad. I am here to tell you that the procedure is way better than having colon cancer, and they even give you some magic potion before the process starts that makes sure you have no memory of anything that happened, with any type of scope, in any kind of orifice on your body, in that particular room, that day. After you leave the room, that part of your brain develops amnesia, in a really good way. Kudos to the pharmaceutical companies – or none of us would ever go back for our follow up visits, I'm sure!

I felt so good, the afternoon after the colonoscopy, that I went, not only swimming, but also horse riding. Get it done, I tell you. Colon cancer is a silent killer. It will eat you up, without blinking an eye. In fact, the poster on the wall of my procedure room advised that it is the number two cancer killer in the whole US of A and I don't think many people know that, because there are no pink ribbons floating around promoting prevention and awareness and, in reality, most folks really don't want to talk about anything to do with their bottoms. Anyway, read the poster and absorb the information, I urge you. It is a lot less mysterious than the problem of the stolen tomatoes and other curious tales like it. Colon cancer? Give me a stolen tomato any day.

I am a home grown tomato addict. If you have any information, leading to an arrest, with regards to the mystery of my stolen tomatoes – be sure, I will give you unlimited access to my lovely garden.

Published July 2011

The War Horse

"It became really apparent, really quickly, that this one was a keeper. His soft brown eyes and gentle demeanor led me to believe that he had been this way before. We had met before in another time, another place. The difference was that this time we'd always be together."

The stage was set at the London Theater for another performance of the sold-out 'War Horse.' Critics raved about the incredibly moving presentation of Michael Morpurgo's novel of the same name. There were no live animals on the set of the theater production, illustrating the suffering of the horses from the European battlefields of World War 1; but everyone who attended a performance felt as if the animals had been live on stage, with their hearts and souls proudly displayed on their fur through and through to their whipping tails and stampeding hooves. The horses played the lead roles with the humans only in a supporting role. You found yourself inside the minds of the horses and within their large and bulky bodies. You walked away from the production, feeling as if you had experienced something true about World War 1 and its cavalry on the ground, from the hooves to the bayonets and beyond – the loss and the empathy entombed as one and forever framed as a part of history.

My family took the London theater production of 'War Horse' with them out of the theater district and beyond, deep into their souls and for always; way before we ever encountered our very own.

My horse Winston was just like an unplanned pregnancy. He showed up and the family made accommodations for his existence, as families do. He had been an inconvenience to his former foster family, not mixing well with others and, likely to stress most of the time, while looking as if he would never leave, because no one seemed to want him elsewhere. They had tried to find him a home for a while; but folks were quickly put off by his quirky habits, not to mention his scarred body. He had obviously been a war horse for some time, most likely battling for his existence most of his natural life. Born on a ranch in Mexico, his amenable character and sensitive nature had ensured that some other bully stallion had always been able to push him around, bite him where it hurt and make sure he was forever the last to make it to the feed trough. He had definitely been hungry much of his formative life; no doubt about that. Give that horse a tortilla and he will gladly consume it, hungry or not. To this day, he has never turned down any kind of food, bar broccoli which we didn't push.

Some one had certainly taken a shoe to him with an untrained tool and forced a nail into the sensitive parts around his frog, more than once. They had not watched for the bites on his haunches or the likely cry he made late at night, when the sly stallions and geldings made their position clear and the pecking order became defined at the trough and in the meadow. He had been alone when the young people selected their riding and their working horses, not having the looks nor the physique for the macho type. In fact, he had likely been alone much of his natural born life. But he lived on - a true warrior inside, a war horse - waiting patiently for his chance to victory march on into life and the living.

But character can take you places, or so they say. His character was strong, his soul already defined. He was rescued from the Mean Parts of the world quite by chance and taken to a place where he was ignored much of the time, but hardly ever injured. He was able to rest and feed a bit more than in his previous life, at least. Though he was still the last at the trough, through the muscling and the jolting; the horses were now not so hungry at this place as the last and they always left a bit behind for him to glean. He was grateful for that.

Then he found himself on the move again in another horse auto-mobile and he wondered where on earth he was going to now. Who would want him and for what? Having been there before, he feared for the worst. However, a nice teacher lady took care of him and talked to him when she had time. She told him she would try and find him a good place to live out his days with plenty of peace and food. He hoped she might. That was really all he wanted. She schlepped him around a lot of different places in her large horse trailer; people looked at him with curiosity and spoke in strange tongues, but still he never left the trailer. He was ready to show them how nice he could be, if they would only brush him a little and feed him quite a lot, but he never got the opportunity. "Oh my goodness, he is covered in scars!" he heard some one say, but he didn't know what that really meant. Maybe it meant that he was super-beautiful; show quality in fact. He hoped that was the case.

But on he moved again. "No one wants him," he heard the teacher lady say, which translates into all languages and makes a horse head hang low. He felt a little sad about that. Then he heard that his friends at the foster home, the goats, had gone to a nice place with a big pasture and he hoped that, he, too, could end up at such a place. He told himself he would be especially nice and quiet for the cause. His goats had left his side and he had to be patient in his solitude and hope for a slice of good fortune such as theirs. Then the teacher lady told him some one was taking him as he was; scars and all. They didn't even need to see or visit with him, and, all of a sudden, he felt strong and proud again. Some one wanted him for him and that was such a good feeling. He stood as tall as he could and arched his neck in a way that he knew was attractive and dynamic, like a War Horse should look.

The lady that wrapped her arms around his neck was strange looking. She was grey too and had all kinds of scars on her. She was like a human version of him. She had been nipped a lot and walked a little with her head down. 'Hey', he told himself! 'There's some one out there like me!' He was so excited; it was practically like looking in the mirror. Maybe she would have lots of good things to eat at her place and she'd let him stay a while. He crossed his hooves accordingly in his deepest hope that he would soon find his place and find his peace.

"We'll take him home," he heard the grey, scarred lady say to the nice teacher lady. She looked him directly in the eye and asked him if he would like to go home with her. He tried to ask her if he could eat at least two times a day, frantically moving his lips and his mouth in his own particular way of speaking, but she was already loading him up in the trailer again, and then they were off.

She was as good as her word. There were at least two decent meals a day at this place where his friends, the goats, had also moved to, and there were snacks, too, in addition. No one and nothing would creep up upon him in the dark and bite him to the bone for no good reason. He could hang with his goats or these other friendly dogs that lived in this place, even the odd crazy cat; and it was as if they had all been good mates for years. His trough was his trough and there was never any doubt about that. What a good feeling that was. Fresh water and straw was provided and shelter was right there near the nice people, where the air was cool and the feeling warm.

The War Horse felt the memories of his war days start to fade. He never wanted to forget where he came from or how he got there to that nice place, but sometimes he really did. Sometimes, when he knew he was being especially tricky or he heard the nice scarred lady plead with him about one thing or another; he knew that he should try and stop the image of the bayonets in his mind, or the cry of dying horses in his soul pervade his new life, where he could be different and he could be new himself, as if starting out all over again as a newborn foal. He knew he should attempt to break out of his war horse mode and become a new horse, a horse without scars; but it would only take a curve of the shoulder and a look behind to tell him exactly where he had come from and why he could only trust a little at a time with a small step forwards and often a nudge to the side.

Like a warrior in any battle, some scars can never be completely healed. Some scars make us better and wiser for the days to come.

Winston "Winning Boy" Churchill Sebastian Mason Jensen came to our ranch, exactly when we needed him and he needed us, in the summer of 2011. He will now live out his entire life in peace and luxury, like all our war veterans should. He will never again doubt where his next meal is coming from or who loves him the very most, and who, most certainly, has been waiting for him all of her natural born life.

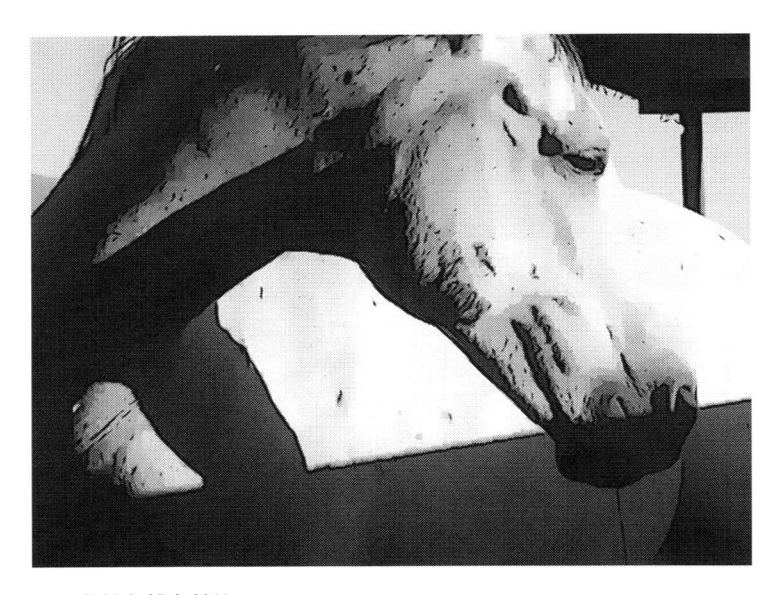

Published July 2011

The Wheelbarrow

"How many today?" "Four. Firm ones." "What's the color like?" "Better. Good even." I haven't been this obsessed about body fluids since my girl was a tiny young thing and I was a first mother, studying the various liquids that came out of her body on any given day with a scientific intensity.

We are talking about the manure from my horse that I study each day and then attempt to maneuver around the property, because, if you let it, the piles can get pretty out of control very quickly. Interestingly enough, my husband is happy to have these *'manural'* conversations with me. Just like a new Mum, I was concerned that my horse Winston was getting too much food – had a cold – had something worse than a cold – had something extremely wrong with his stomach. There must be something going on that made his piles so unseemingly moist; and so the study of his poop intensified in our household. We were all engaged. Fortunately, horse droppings are pretty innocuous, even at their worst on the firm scale; and nothing like the cat things we have to also deal with at our place.

Then along came another challenge and my husband pulled his knee out, trying to dump a full load out of his heavy wood and metal barrow and onto the special manure pile. "How on earth would you do that?" I asked this poor limping dude that I found before me, who was feeling a little sorry for himself with a swollen knee and full barrow – mission not accomplished. He looks down at his flat feet with just a touch of shame and a lot of pain and I realize that woman power would be taking over the barrow duties for the foreseeable future. Not a problem. I am strong, have arms to lift, legs to assist the able back and the strongest will in the world to get out there and clean my darling's stable.

It was at this point, I realized that I had not officially mucked out a stable since I was a young kid myself, helping out with Blackie's stable on my friend's farm; but never mind. Like riding a bike, or changing a diaper, you can get back with it very quickly when the need arises. So we shoveled and we mucked and, all of a sudden, things started to look very prim and proper in that there stable, if that were even possible. The piles were where they should be – in the wheelbarrow – the stable was nicely mucked out, and I was ready to go and haul the manure to its rightful place out yonder. Except that I couldn't. I could not even get the back side of the darn barrow off the ground. I looked around to see if the farmer husband was watching, with his bad leg horizontal – and laughing just a little – as weak old woman folk fails to even lift her barrow, after all her bragging about being able to handle it all just fine and without him.

"That bleep barrow is ridiculously heavy!" I stomp into the realm of the recovering invalid, in full complaining mode. "No one could lift that bleep thing, empty or not. No wonder you pulled your knee out! "I add, for good effect, sidling in semi sympathy into the invalid's realm. And so we had it. An invalid who couldn't dump the load, which had injured him in the first place, and his muscly wife, who couldn't even lift the arms of the barrow to dump the load. (Sounds like something along the lines of a children's rhyme!) A fine pair of farmers we are.

"They make a really nice sturdy, light barrow these days," he offered, helpfully. "That would be perfect for you – and not heavy at all. It has a light body and wide wheels." "Get it," I said quickly, 'And Merry Christmas to me!" Anything that does not mean I have to rely on anyone else is a gift in my opinion and something worthy of a little investment. One of these days I would have my own barrow. I could see it now.

"I'm getting my own wheelbarrow," I tell my overseas friend boastfully. "Excuse me?" she retorts a little, as if she hadn't heard properly. "A wheel barrow, that's what you are talking about? The queen of shoes and handbags and designer this and that is getting her own barrow? What have you become, for heaven sakes, Eliza Doolittle with her own barrow in the flower market?" And there we were and how far we have come. Gone are the days when I think too much about gorgeous Italian leather hand bags and super-dooper expensive designer shoes, until, that is, my glossy girlfriend comes to town. I seldom covet the latest lap top, smart phone or glossy car. I am in tune with my land and my animals these days and this all became clear to me very quickly over the barrow talk. My planets and my priorities have shifted over the course of just a very short period of time. I now love the prospect of my own wheelbarrow on the premises with a wide wheel base and a light lift. I am so darn excited about lifting her up and dumping my own manure without injuring myself, that I can hardly stand myself. I may even name her when she arrives. Never mind that they had sold out of the solid but sturdy number with the wide wheels and we may have to wait for the re-shipment. I'll wait for the Cadillac of wheelbarrows, I'll honestly wait. I can hardly believe it has come to this, but it obviously has.

Sometimes the things you need are so close to the things you actually want, that the difference blurs. May all your barrows be light and easy, may the sun shine through the eyes of your animal. May the days and years be kind to all.

Published November 2011

There is something wrong with my feet

The first Annual Salinas Valley Half Marathon took place last summer, when I was in no position to do a half of anything, let alone a marathon. I do recall looking longingly at the race on the news and voraciously reading the articles in the paper. In short, I was envious of those who had the good health to be able to take part. "I will do that next year," I told myself at the time. It was a goal I would achieve.

Knowing that most things in life are more fun when you share, I tried to gather together a race 'group,' so that we could all keep each other honest and in training for the big day. We were quickly signed up, almost as soon as the sign ups became available – not wishing to have the easy excuse that they were all sold out and, consequently, we'd have to just focus on revving ourselves up for the third Annual. I worked up to my ten-mile feat at the Relay for Life in June and accomplished that pretty fair and square; so didn't think too much about continuing my training for the larger and more difficult trial two months later. Every time I packed my walking shoes and IPOD into my car, planning a brisk lunch time walk, something else in life would get in the way, and I confess that I may have never managed much of a training walk after that big ten-mile accomplishment. Big mistake; huge!

The day before the race, our 'large' group had dwindled down to three participants – and, in fact, they nearly lost me also; since I managed to fall off my chair at work, one day during race week, and hurt my bottom. "Are you sure you are going to be okay to walk?" my friend enquired with some anxiety, making me a tad suspicious that she would be just fine with making my clumsy fall our team's excuse for a no show. But the British are made of stronger metal than that, and, bruised buttocks or not, our Team of Three was going to walk.

Race morning came very quickly and very early indeed. I do not 'do' 6am on a Saturday morning without a really good reason; and thrashing my bod over a 13.1-mile course did not really feel like reason enough, as I looked out over the thick grey summer mists of the valley. The race started at 8am, so there was little time to ponder the day ahead. We joined the masses of serious racers waiting for the buses at Soledad High to take us over to where the race was going to start at the Soledad Mission.

My bus contained a lot of serial marathon participants. "Oh, ya, did you do Boston? Weather was a bit tricky!" A hoot of laughter came up from the back row. "How about Chicago? Insane!" some one else wooted. The smell of 'Ben Gay' and sports creams filled the air. Lithe legs and thighs made not even a ripple on the bus seats, I noticed. Trim, muscled arms poured out of miniscule little running vests. These folks were in it to win it. How were we all going to start this marathon adventure and not fall over each other? I could only imagine it was going to be a logistical nightmare. Luckily for all of us, the organizing folks had done this before and had the Fast and the Serious lined up in the front row and various stages of Fast and Serious after that, until you got to the Slow and the Losers at the very back. We took our rightful places at the very back of what seemed like a huge mass of people and got ready to go. "Hey, wait a minute!" I exclaim. "We must be going the wrong way – this is in the Greenfield direction!" And sure enough we were going backwards on our marathon before we were going forwards. We soon got a good pace going in the cool misty airs, however, and the field seemed to settle nicely into its pace. A rather disabled fellow with a gimpy leg was struggling ahead of us. "Oh poor guy," we whispered. "How on earth is he going to finish?" We kept our eye on him and overtook him quite severely at one point on a downhill slope, just to show that we could, but then he left us in the dust for good. A perfect example of never judging a book by its cover, as my Granny used to say.

Somewhere just after mile marker number nine and the six feet in our team started to complain. Whether it was the climbing hills or the tough gravel under foot, I'm not sure; but we all started to have owies of one kind or another almost simultaneously. "My toes hurt!" Letty exclaimed. "This is freaking tougher than I thought it was going to be," stressed Leanne. And the balls of my own tough feet were also beginning to complain. Luckily I had thought to pack my trusty canister of Vaseline – thank you, marathon runner sister Mary - and a clean pair of socks in my sporty fanny pack, so we all took a mini pit stop, where we also shared band aids with a fellow Soledadian from our school district who was sporting a bad blister; and strolled off again, our hands up in the air, as if in celebration, when in fact, our fingers were simply swollen like sausages from too much hanging down below the heart.

The language deteriorated sharply around mile 11 and I knew I was in trouble when I kept trying to walk on the outsides of my feet, because the rest of them weren't feeling so good. "Ok focus on the parts of your body which do not hurt!" I encouraged my team, in cheerleader-like fashion. There was a silence. "My nose feels pretty good," I noted cheerfully and heard some blank-blank expletives in return. The strawberries at one station felt like a shot in the arm and the kindly glasses of Gatorade certainly helped us to limp in through the finish line, though the chocolate energy gloop did not provide the same life-enhancing effect that real chocolate might have.

We were not exactly treated like award winning finishers, when we lumbered through the finish line at Pessagno Winery; but we finished and that was the important thing in our book. Plus, we didn't even finish last. All the award winners had already got their medals and trophies when we showed up – we even saw some Fast and Serious folks walking with their medals backwards along the course, as if they hadn't had enough already. But the Three Team had had more than enough and all agreed that a half was plenty for everybody.

A word of warning for any rookie half-marathoners: never take your shoes off at the end of the race and enjoy the cool grass between your toes. I promise you, you'll regret it.

Published August 2011

When the animals speak

All my animals are rescue animals; other people's throwaways if you like, but they are truly my gifts. Proper animal lovers, real human beings - in my opinion - could never discard an animal. It makes me so furious when I witness such a callous disregard for life. There are too many animals out there needing a loving home; you can look to the shelters for your companions, or you can let life bring to you what you deserve. It was always that way with our motley crew of strays.

One way or another, over the course of time, they walked into our lives, found their piece of paradise and stayed on to become members of the family. Never mind I had always dreamed of having another Lab in my life. I'll always be happy with what shows up. Baxter was found at the shelter, Sophie was dumped on the streets of Soledad, Joey found us at the shelter, as did Chloe and Sarah. Dug walked into our garage from who knows where and so it goes on; so much so that I mostly forget just how many animals I actually have, until I look at my animal feed bills for the month and mildly notice that they cost more to feed than teenagers.

There is something so special about abandoned animals that touches your soul and makes every day a better one. They intrinsically know how lucky they are, that they found you and your home, and, in their adoration, they never stop reminding you of that. They crawl up inside your heart and they stay there. Their love is an eternal fountain and their loyalty to you becomes so quickly engrained in their being, that you, in your turn, crave it as part of your daily bread. Theirs is a special talent, as if they know that their existence under your roof rescued them from a dubious existence elsewhere – or even death - and guaranteed that their life, from that moment on, would be full of kibble,

Friskies, love and joy. Check out an animal's response to a person and mostly you can tell if the person is worth knowing or not. It's an interesting test.

My first rescue animal, Baxter was rescued from the freeway in Gonzales at 3 months old. He has always had the sweetest soul. Simply put, he adores us – all of us – and also welcomes all our various waifs and strays to his domain. He is the alpha male, but without a shred of dictatorship. He loves all living things equally and puts up with everything from a blind cat that needs to snuggle to the wet, pond-smelling kisses of the new pup. He also has unusual skills. When my daughter would catch the school bus home, some how he knew exactly when the bus would be coming along Metz Road. At just before 4pm, weekdays only, Baxter could be seen sitting at the point in our yard and waiting for the yellow bus to bring her home to him. Don't ask why; he just knew.

When I was going through chemo, my dogs would lie in a circle around me on our deck and they would stay right there for hours on end, knowing that I needed watching over and that that was their designated job for the day. I would look up from my drug-induced haze and instantly feel their warm eyes upon me, looking for instruction, yet all the time hosting protection for their mistress. Mostly I wasn't capable of any instruction, but I could sleep peacefully on, knowing they would never let anyone near who wasn't supposed to be near.

Our cat speaks in his own way. He is a male tabby with a big attitude and he always tells us, in his own inimitable style, when we are not paying enough attention to him. As a mature cat, he knows exactly how to get our attention, even though he does know better than to exercise the bad habits he has gathered over his lifetime. He just can't help himself. He will get on counter tops, perch himself on the dining table. He goes anywhere he knows he is not supposed to be, when we have not quite fulfilled the task of making him feel completely full and comfortable, which is our life's work, as far as he is concerned. He has asserted himself so much in our household, that the dogs step aside when he walks in the room and we, the humans, hurriedly pop the cap on his wet food, in order not to deal with his wrath and spite and his insistency to be immediately served by us, his humans. He is a 6lb dictator and we'd be bored without him.

Our Princess Pom/Chihuahua mix Sophie is the smartest cookie of them all. She was thrown out of a car in Soledad one Halloween night, after her former owners had bred her to her max and were done with her. She was starving, flea-bitten and afraid, when we witnessed the foul deed being done and picked her up from the dark street. I've never been a fan of that type of dog, but she found us and quickly fell in love. She has enormous attitude too and tells any big dog around her that she is the boss of them, no questions asked. She also has huge survival instincts and can be seen burying small bones for a later snack, or tormenting the other animals with a cosseted taste treat that she has been guarding all day long. We joke that we could drop her off any place in the world and she would survive, witchy little thing that she is. She'd probably also hitch a ride, while she was at it, and be back home in time for supper.

Our birds speak to us, just as our dogs and cats do. They settle around our house and have their babies. They tell us, in no uncertain terms, when we are out of seed and will buzz the tops of our heads, if we just happen to casually walk by and do not quickly refill the feeders. They speak loudly, sing well, eat bugs, flaunt their babies and bring their friends over to visit. In our turn, we create a habitat where they are safe and have everything they need to survive and to thrive. We build ponds for them and, every day, they splash and drink with glee. We keep plenty of foliage around, where they make their nests year after year. We make sure they are well fed during the winter and they even stay on over the summer, when they can bask with us in our home we call Solace and chitter-chatter their days away, in a place where they are safe and they are welcome. And what better life is there?

Taking care of abandoned beasts and even wild birds fills my heart so full of love that I find myself looking even further afield for more animals in need, though, in truth, most of mine find me. I've always wanted my own horse, one that no one can take away from me. Maybe I could rescue one of those and love it to pieces, make up for its previous life of semi neglect. We have pigs now, but they will be leaving us fairly soon. Perhaps an abandoned goat would like us and we would like it. More dogs? For sure, I don't need them, but probably they will show up needing me. You never know when another panting tongue is going to arrive and need a drink at your place. For, what I have discovered about rescuing animals is that when you think you've rescued them and given them the home they need, what happens is they end up rescuing you right back. Not only do they save you from the clouds of a darker side of life, but they make a permanent home inside your heart.

Published April 2011

With every season

My mother used to say that autumn was her favorite time. She would recall the lovely changing colors, the wonderful feeling of carrying and delivering babies that time of the year – which she did twice, to my certain knowledge. She also despised winter; so autumn was a tricky transitional period for her, never really knowing which way it was going to go; either forward to winter and despair, or back to summer and delight. That is one of the great unknowns; when autumn is going to accelerate onwards to winter, or take a swift reverse gear and become summer once again, especially in England.

I myself recall the Indian summers, when I was away at school in Saffron Walden, and we would be wearing our mandatory, thick, winter-green uniform and sweating under a September blaze; or trying to play hockey in full gear with the sweat dripping and our hockey coach yelling at us to run just that little bit faster down the bone dry hockey field. I do remember those days when I questioned the seasons and our expectations of them. But mostly I loved the autumn with her long afternoon shadows and crisp early morning promise of the long winter sleep ahead. We were, mostly, still eating ice cream and playing tennis, when we weren't supposed to be – also crunching wonderful fall leaves under foot and living eye to eye with the wiles of Mother Nature.

Now, in this part of the world, we don't see much by way of fall colors or the changing of the seasons. If I didn't have the grapes to watch, I'd be lulled into thinking that just about every season was a summer one. Though my dog Baxter and I loathe the bird cannons at this time of year, (we are both deathly afraid of the bangs), those noisy instruments, which, pretty unsuccessfully, try and ward the marauding flocks of birds away from the ripening vines, they do herald a turn in our seasons. They signal the time when we will soon be seeing huge trailers being dragged alongside the vineyards ready for their loads of fruit and when we will be kept awake at night with the picking machines doing their seasonal job. They remind us that Halloween will soon be here, followed shortly by Thanksgiving and then Christmas and the end of another year.

How can we already be looking at the last quarter of this year? Our ripe tomatoes and ripening apples should give me the 'hello' that I am looking for, but I still cannot believe the swift cantering of time. It has been almost a year since my last chemo. (I see my daughter's eyes roll. "Oh no, not more talk of breast cancer!") No, my lovely, no talk of cancer, only of recovery and looking forward! My lovely nurse Rhonda told me that it would take at least a year until I recovered from the effects of the chemotherapy and she was right. I could not believe, at the time, that it would take that long, but, honestly, it did. People ask me how I'm doing and I reply that, mostly, I don't have time to think about it, which is probably the best recipe for recovery in anyone's book. If I were to sit in my chair and watch my tomatoes redden, I would almost certainly have sent myself mad with all the dreadful things I could imagine that might be going on in my body. But no; as soon as I was able, I was up and about, back to work, driving, traveling, doing, seeing and, simply, being. I have already accomplished two items on my bucket list, I most likely would be still compiling, if things had been otherwise. And now, in the third quarter of this year, I am here to say that our fall this year is an extraordinarily beautiful season. It is unpredictable, just like life itself. It can still have its summer fog and its winter cooling. It can blaze like high summer or storm like January. We just never know what we are going to get. But with that unpredictability comes a certain gratitude for the gifts of each day and the spread we get to enjoy, no matter the season. When you have felt clouds inside your heart, you are happy for any season. They herald a new day; one where you are still alive.

And I won't mind when we pass into the winter season with her swift blanket of darkness and cooling airs, along with her kind buckets of rain for the parched ground. We will welcome that time just as we welcomed this; knowing that the only guarantee in life is change itself and that, always, change it will.

Before we know it, the twinkle-twinkle will be on the homes and the shops will be full of glitter. Then we will be looking forward again, around the corner of that particular season, to another year full to the brim of opportunity, adventure and surprise. With every season there is a pleasurable anticipation attached to it. I know that now. It is very simple. It means that I am still here.

Published September 2011

THE ANIMALS TEACH US:
Humor, Joy, Trust, Love

These tales were published in South County Newspapers 2014-2016

53 and fabulous

During a recent visit overseas, my old friend and I were sitting across from each other on the sofa, chatting away as we do. "You are a bit blurry," she tells me. "You are a bit blurry too," I say. We hadn't even had a sip of Bailey's between us. I tried on her glasses and could not believe how different the world looked now that I could see. I literally gasped with wonder at the symmetry of her face, the green clarity of her eyes, the sharp outline of the cat upon her lap. I needed some of that; I needed to be able to see again. I had been too long out there in the dark.

It's been a long journey to relative myopia, where I'm currently standing, to where I was before. Right around 45, I began a relationship with 'The Readers', beginning at the dainty 1.0 level of magnification which seemed very civilized almost at the time – borderline intellectual if you like. Now I am well over the 3.25 mark and also squinting at traffic signs, or the television, or my friend's face; it became beyond time for a change. My friend's glasses showed me the way and then there was no stopping me.

Back home and it was time to go and see a real optician. I had been to see a pretend optician a few years ago and they had scared me into the world of the peepers forever more. They had prescribed a pair of spex that literally made me feel sea sick - a very terribly awful thing to suffer when you were supposed to be improving your sight, nothing more. I wore them once, tried to get some help, failed and buried them forever. An expensive mistake.

Boldly going where I had never been before, I casually strolled into the eye glass emporium in the Mall. Surrounded by bright lights and designer frames, I felt as if this was a place that could bring vision back into my life. They seemed as if they knew what they were doing and had been doing this for a while. Soon I might be able to see again; I might have some definition to my every waking minute. The optician lady ran all kinds of tests on me. "How is your night vision for driving?" she asked me. What a loaded question. I no longer see at all to drive at night. I don't see that well to drive period! My palms started to sweat just a little. "I really do need glasses, don't I?" I whispered, feeling a little emotional. "Yes, you do. Lots of people do." The optician lady discussed my options and decided that progressive lenses would be best for me. I selected my cute Ray Ban and Ralph frames and imagined how life would soon look with my new face wear.

Bother, now my feet are really starting to hurt. For sure I have bunions and who knows what else. The left and right of my foot are splaying out and resembling a rather mal-formed brick. None of my winter boots are feeling good. Oh and, in addition, the sciatic is super twingey in my left leg. What else? I can't afford all of these medical bills – I'm going to have to stagger my doc visits. Eyes, feet, leg – oh and the ear doctor needs a visit too.

"What should the title of my story be this week?" I ask my trusty buddies, all of us 53 and in varying stages of half-century body deterioration. "Band Aids and Bunions?" or "Fabulous at 53"? The text came winging swiftly back across the ether and through multiple time zones. "Ladies! We are fifty-three and fabulous. No talk, please, of disintegrating bunions. Let us bound joyously – albeit with three pairs of glasses around our necks – through the decade. Onwards!" I can always count on them for laughter, as I grab my extra pair of spex and try to read the swiftly returned text and return it.

Sometimes I do feel fully fabulous at 53 and sometimes I just feel 53, however that is supposed to feel. I'll let you know, for sure, once all of my body parts have had an overhaul and I get to rejoin the human race, laughing as I go. After all, what is the alternative?

Published October 2016

A marvelous feral called Mama

Out of the corner of my eye, something skitter-scattered along the shelf by my desk. I almost screamed. Every now and then, I'd catch sight of a tail turning a corner. Like it or not, old buildings have mice.

A pretty calico cat began frequenting our back cage area. She would see me and hiss-snarl. But I can't see an animal go hungry, so I brought kibble to work and made a daily habit of putting down water and feeding her. If I tried to get too close, she'd hiss-snarl, as if ready to attack. "Bite the hand that feeds you? Yeah, right!" I'd whisper. Then, a few days down the road, she'd see me and lick her lips. That was the beginning of our love affair.

Soon I realized that she was fat with kitten and I fed her up a bit more. I discovered that she loves wet food, milk and cheese in no particular order. She gave birth in the back of the cage to 3 healthy kittens. And now they were a feline family of 4. Once the kittens were weaned, it was time to bring in the cat-lady to trap, fix and release – at least our Mama. One black kitty stayed home with the cat-lady, the ginger came home to Solace with me - Kitty Kate - and the other black was just in the right place at the right time to secure a forever home. We felt good about all of it. And then it was just Mama and me again.

We'd call for her every night when it was feeding time and see her slinking across the parking lot licking her lips. My colleague bought her a shelter with a bed and I put a blanket over it to keep out the wind. I caught her sleeping in it one day. Then came the huge change, the 360 in our relationship, the marvelous thing. I went out to feed her and she wrapped her body around my legs. She let me touch her tail and then turned her back on me to feed in peace. I could touch her tail and her back while she fed – we had crossed enormous rivers from wild cat to semi-domestic love-bug, enjoying her first trusting contact ever with a human being. I felt so proud and happy, a tear slipped down my cheek. Some people think they have succeeded if they make pots of money at work. I feel successful when a wild street cat trusts me enough to wrap herself around my legs and turn her back to me when she eats.

Mama is one of the mascots of South County Animal Rescue – or appropriately the acronym 'SCAR' She gives us hope that many, many more so-called unadoptable animals can be safely rescued and placed in forever homes.

Published February 2016

Be still my beating heart

I rescue animals; that's what I do. They show up, I take care of them, I persuade my husband we are keeping them and we give them a home. That's what, in short, we do here at our home up in the hills we call 'Solace'. From multiple dogs, to generations of cats to other people's horses and even horses that people said possibly couldn't be saved; many have found a safe and happy home inside our fence line and I want it to always be that way. Again, that is what we do. It is my life's work, if you like; without sounding self-inflated or pompous in any way. Some folks rescue children, others donate time and life to a religious institution, some just wallow in themselves their whole entire life long. I give what I have inside myself to the animal kingdom. The animals talk to me, they really do, and I feel moved to talk back. If I were rich, or even moderately comfortable, (scratch rich), I would build a whole sanctuary for animals in my back yard and never have to question me, myself, I or even the husband on whether we had the means to rescue another soul that needed a safe place to rest his innocent head and hope for a meal. The souls we have rescued over the past 12 plus years of living here now most likely can't remember another place they lived before they ended up here at their forever home. In the case of our dogs Roscoe, Baxter, Sophie and Dug, plus many of our cats, I'm sure, and most definitely my horse Winston, the fact that the memory fades in time can only be counted as a blessing. I plan to be their home and their sanctuary forever. We will be all they remember and thank goodness for that.

But I do have a problem when I fall short in my calling. I cannot handle failing at the gate, not having or doing enough to make the difference, step in, be the catalyst for success and savior. Abbey Rhode is our elderly lady, our mare extraordinaire. We took her in when a friend was losing his home. He had had her in his life for a very long time and wanted a safe place for her to fall, since he would no longer be able to take care of her. He knew she would have it with us. When she came to live with us, she was still a spry 25 year old with lots of piss and vinegar – as Granny would say – meaning pep and get up and go, and a raging sense of humor to match. She loved to run up hills, especially if she were racing Winston, my horse, to be the first to arrive at the gate. She lived to be first, to be the alpha female and the one with brains enough to win every time. We laughed at her antics to thwart the gelding at every post and succeed almost always. If he caught her 'visiting' his stable, we knew there would be trouble in paradise; because no one gets to visit his lordship's stable without an invitation; but visit she would and there would be heck to pay when she got there. She did it all the same, because she wanted to and because getting Winston all riled up was a valuable part of her day. She would clip- clop down the hill swinging her pretty tail and watching for him, as he sidled up beside her, ears back and looking as if he might nip her pretty rear. Then she would chortle in her throat, throw back her head, sing out a little pitiful whinny and throw her back hooves up into the air, playfully mind, with no bad intent intended. They would play their little game and do their rounds and then later I would catch them napping close by each other at the bottom of the meadow. Just like siblings, I would say to myself. Fighting and loving all the way to nap time.

And then, one day, she started tripping. She had a hard time getting down the hill to the meadow and, sometimes, even as far as the gate to the meadow. She found it tricky to lift her hooves to be cleaned and she wasn't eating like she needed to. Her ribs became more pronounced and again I was losing the weight battle I had been engaged in with her since she came to stay. From the alfalfa to the oat hay, you then go to the rich senior feed, the supplements, oats, apples, carrots and molasses. I found myself trekking out at night time to give her, what us Brits call, some 'hot mash' – a compilation of heated oats, sugar, molasses and whatever else an ailing horse might fancy. My girl doesn't care for apples, she prefers carrots; so her 'cake' is iced with carrots every night. I stand by in the freezing dark, stroking her skinny neck and begging her to eat the hot food and stay with us a while longer. It's a pathetic sight really, me begging and her choosing not to eat. The power game and the agony are immense. I want her to gain strength and stay; she has the ability to decide, thank you, I choose not.

I find myself researching end of life options for equines, I put myself in that place, that day, when I need to hug her skinny neck for the last time and let her go to a place, hopefully, where she can, once again, run up the hill at speed and torment the gelding, but in a younger body with no pain. "You are going to need to tell me when it's time," I whispered to her in the dark the other night, when she was being particularly picky about her food and I was allowing myself to get more and more upset about it. "I am not going to be able to make that decision on my own", I found myself telling her, as if she could understand me and, who knows, maybe she can. And I do hope she will do that and not make me have to play God; but more I hope she will rally and starting eating better, moving better and making us all believers again in the power of the will over the fleeting abilities of the body. I know she loves her life here, I know she still has more to give us and we her. I will her to will this too.

Be still my beating heart; this part of the journey is the one I am least capable of completing without enormous assistance. I find myself wishing that I could pass before my animals in order not to suffer such intense and agonizing pain; but then that would not give me much longer on the planet, I'm not done with my work here and we are never satisfied anyway, are we humans. I find myself musing on the words of my lovely granny Myrtle, "It is better to have loved and lost, than never to have loved at all." And she was right, of course, and we all do all of the time. We love, we love entirely and completely. And then we lose and the pain is excruciating. But, from where I'm standing, the heart aches even at the thought of it and I'm not ready to go there, not even remotely.

I'm off to the stable in the dark and the cold now, to see if I can get her to eat a little more and be with us just a short time longer. It's a race against a clock and a will that I cannot win, but I will keep on trying.

Buttering toast for the Chihuahua

It is breakfast time at Solace. "Honey, we bought a zoo!" No, wait. "Honey, what we have put together here in the place we call home is a zoo!" All these different animals with all their varying needs and wants. We have front yard cats and back yard cats in the horse box. About 20 odd feral cats wander these parts, some more tame than others. Due to the fact that some animal shelters will immediately kill feral cats and that is not the way we live, we choose to catch, fix and release our ferals – hence the rather large number who reside here at Solace. (For the record: many feral cats will ultimately give into your need for a cuddle and actually enjoy the heck out of it, if you persist. Also, we no longer have any problems with vermin around here, which counts for a lot. What goes around comes around.)

Moving away from the cats to what we call our 'terrorists' or pygmy goats; Elvis and Charlie will get veggie and fruit cuttings of a morning, also alfalfa hay and some toast – preferably well done, if you please, so they can crunch-crunch to their hearts' content. They also like chips and crunchy cereal. There are large dogs, who get a whole cookie, and smaller, plumper ones who only get a half. Our little princess Chihuahua, at the ripe old age of about 9-12 – no one really knows to be honest - has few teeth anymore and can't manage much in the way of cookies, but she will never say no to a slice of toast or bread that she can suck on – not too crunchy if you please – and she really loves it if you'd butter it for her, the more butter the better. Then she will proceed to lick all the butter off and spend the rest of the day guarding the remnants of the toast and growling at any of the other dogs trying to do a detour anywhere close to her and attempting to steal her bounty. It's her little power trip. It's all she has, small as she is. She has always done it and always will. Heaven help any animal, large or small, bold enough to try and pull one over on that little Madame. She has a snarl much bigger than her actual size and an attitude that is way out of proportion. My other dogs are big, but they know better. They respect her almost as much as they do the cats. Wish I had that kind of time on my hands to guard my one piece of toast all day and growl at everyone around me!

And all this early-morning detail is way before I have even got started with the horses – the most spoiled equines in the universe, if you don't already know that. My horse and his requirements are eternal. His needs, first thing of a morning, are a small snack when he first sees you and nickers his way swiftly into your heart at the start of your day. Carrots and apples are acceptable – preferably sliced. Then, from the starter snack, you must move swiftly into the heart of his appetite: his hay. He is okay with orchard hay or oat, but, given a choice in the matter, he really loves alfalfa and quite a lot of it, thank you very much. And don't even think you can take some time out petting the dog or pondering the feeding of the llamas or goats in advance of his lordship's meal. That will not work out well for you. He is King of his hill and must be first to be fed, in order for the rest of the morning's schedule to flow relatively smoothly. My horse, Winston, will reach out desperately for his first bite of a morning, stretching his neck, with starving vigor, for that first tear of the green stuff and then chomp, with his head happily nodding, as if to say, "Thank goodness for that. Nutritional redemption at last! I honestly thought I was going to die of starvation." Mind you, my horse always thinks he is going to die of starvation – that is what happens when you rescue an abused animal. He is just a little high strung when it comes to issues of the belly. The residue of abuse lingers on, way after the actual symptoms have been firmly put to bed. Despite my regular spoiling of his royal being and supplying all his needs and more, he still stresses about his supply of food and where the next meal is coming from. Probably always will.

So, the horse gets his morning meal and then the water troughs can be filled, goats or 'terrorists' also fed and llamas fed in addition. Mucking out can then be accomplished and the flow of the morning can be seen to move in the right direction.

"It all starts with the horse," I explained to my ranch hands, who will be manning the considerable fort while I am gone for a few days and have been in-training recently for this dubious honor. "Always start with the horse and you can't go wrong." "Wait," they say. "Wait. You deal with the dogs first and then you deal with the horse?" Well, yes and no. You are prepping for your dealings with the horse well before you are even thinking about dealing with the dogs. And then the flow starts – thinking about the horse/cats/dogs/horse/goats/llamas/horse/horse. This was a very hard schedule to explain, I discovered. I just do it; I don't explain it!

I had to stand back from my own crazy ranch schedule recently, as I was attempting to train my neighbors. Our routine was nuts, I had to admit to even myself. Who chops apples and carrots for the horse in the morning and then gives him vanilla crème cookies in the evening, just because he loves them so? Who asks for bones at the butchers for the dogs and then bakes them in some yummy sauce for them? Who makes toast to the specifications of their goats, because they know the goats like their toast a little dark? And really, honestly, really, who butters the daily softly-toasted toast of their ageing rescue Chihuahua, because they know that is exactly the way she likes it? Yes, guilty on all counts, your honor. And I wouldn't have it any other way.

It can just be a little difficult, I've discovered, to translate all these strange and unusual habits to your ranch hands-in-training, so that they can run your place as seamlessly as possible while you are away. At the end of it all, I'll tell them again, "The main thing about a ranch is water and gates. Everything else can be forgiven, if you forget." Though my ranch hands are of extremely superior caliber, I shall be reminding them of those two things only as the key to keeping everyone alive in my absence.

Everything else is just gravy.

Now if I could keep my cookie monster husband out of my horse's vanilla crème cookies, we'd be in really good shape! I busted him the other day, when the store was out of vanilla and I had to buy the lemon ones. He slipped up and confessed that the lemon ones were not as good. The husband chowing down on the horse's cookies? Some things you just cannot make up.

Published February 2014

Carpets & Cowgirls

In the modern world, it is commonplace that the man and the woman share the workload, whether in or outside the home, with children or without, on the farm or away. When I was sick and unable to work, my husband was working for all of us; that was how it was going to happen for our family during those long, tough months. And then, most recently, when it was his turn to go under the knife, I dutifully reciprocated and stepped up my game as the all-doing in the house. These days, the sexes maneuver their lives on a much more even playing field, I've noticed, than in the days of yore. We all do what we can, when we can, within our family and on behalf of our unit, for it to function and work its way through that tricky time when the plates have shifted and the players are not in their comfort zones; but everything still needs to continue on and get done. So, pretty or not, we make it happen. Most houses these days require a two-partner working engagement on every level; but, I'm realizing, we are just not all practiced on all levels to our highest potential.

Recently, with my husband in recovery from surgery, I've noticed just how much he does around here. Pick up hay, straw and animal feed and unload into an acceptable distribution bay at the house? That would be his job.

But, not at the moment! Mow the front and back lawns, weed and beautify? Again: his arena of expertise. It's not happening right now. Cook meal after meal that will tantalize the taste buds and satisfy the growling stomach to the family's satisfaction? Him, again! Man must eat in order to exist. Thus, it can be, when familial plates shift, as they are wont to do; that the other side of the partnership, the person who does not normally do these things, can somewhat panic, when they realize for a certain chunk of time, it's on them and they had better make it happen for all – quickly and efficiently - as if they'd done it all their lives.

I own an official culinary repertoire of about 3 dishes that are considered acceptable in my house: spaghetti, lasagna and roast chicken and I'm not bragging at all. That would be about it. I am also occasionally allowed to do a fry up for brunch with eggs and bacon, but I usually burn at least the toast and am immediately fired, so I am not going to count that. Thank goodness for the three dishes; that is all I can say, with regards to our most recent expedition with me as chief chef, oh and the fact that the patient didn't have much of an appetite in any case. (Oh my goodness, I must work on my culinary repertoire; it is really lacking!) But we got through it, thankfully, with very little disruption to our gastrointestinal tracts or our sense of humors, I'm glad to be able to say.

Then the patient was feeling a little better, well enough to be a danger to himself, seemingly. As a man starting to feel a little better, he eye-spies a heavy piece of equipment that is out of place in his front yard and, like a healthy man, muscles in on said piece, maneuvering it away from where it was to where he thought it should be. "Noooooooooooooooooo!" his wife could be heard screaming, as she practically experienced his newly meshed area split with the strain of it all. "YOU ARE NOT ALLOWED TO BE DOING THAT! I HAVE TO DO ALL THE HEAVY LIFTING FOR THE INDEFINITE FUTURE AND DO I MAKE MYSELF CLEAR??" As 'The Wife of The Patient,' I went off the deep end, as they say, and put said, super-remorseful patient back in front of the television and in his chair, where he quietly was before said incident. And so it was down to bossy me again. Can I lift a 50lb bag of dog food? Why no, I cannot. Can I lift a 40lb bag? I am quite proud to say that, yes, why yes, I can actually do that with no apparent, lasting damage done to my ageing spine. And so it was that things started to change in our arena. I would be doing some heavy lifting, within a certain and very limited range, and whatever was out of the range would have to wait for another day, maybe never to happen again. I could cook a bit, if necessary, and people would eat it if they were hungry and not, actually, die if they did. Things moved along, trickily, but surely, those first few days of recovery in our home, where our plates had shifted and where I quietly missed our old life and resolved to try and bring it back to life again.

Deeper into the recovery, the woman is at work and the man is at home cleaning house. "I'm going to clean the carpets!" he announced. They are covered in hay!" "What?"

his cowgirl-bride responded, with a sudden afterthought of "why yes, oh yes, of course, all my clothes are covered in hay! Hay rules! And that would lead any sane person to assume that, yes, my house must be covered in hay! I'm a cowgirl, remember?" And with that, he remembered. Of course, he did! She might be trying to cook the odd dish, now he was in recovery and all. She might be pretending she was Suzi-Homemaker, Nancy-Nurse or some such 'Pretty Pretties' not often seen on the ranch with dirt under their nails; but his partner was truthfully more of an 'Annie-go-get-your-shovel' type or a Calamity Jane enactment, more at home with a pitchfork in her hand and hay all over her clothes, than at home in the kitchen trying to figure out some kind of edible thing for dinner. No wonder she wouldn't win any awards on the homestead! His broad, she was much better outdoors or at work; he knew that and he still loved her for it! He could clean the carpets and she could clean the stable; and, at the end of it all, the ranch would be a better place in the larger spectrum of things. Together, in both of their recoveries, they could get it all done from the house stuff to the stables and back again. Cowgirl and a carpet cleaning crew— a match certainly made in heaven.

This story is dedicated to "The Husband" and 18 solid years of being not only his cowgirl, but also his lousy wife.

Published April 2014

Dogs on a Diet & a trip to the ER

"He's 8lbs overweight," she tells me. I knew it was coming; it had to come from her for me to know it was true, but I shuddered all the same, as the truth echoed through the chambers of my heart and back up to my brain, where it was slowly chewed and processed. He loved his chow; this would not go down well. In his world, this was going to be tantamount to abuse, at the very least - or torture.

"I will try and run with him on a regular basis," I tell my daughter. "That will probably help a lot."

"Not enough," she tells me dubiously. "8lbs is a lot of weight." And there we had it – radical measures were in order in the Jensen household, as can be the case when we have all blown our wad – and, this time, not just the humans apparently. Our dogs would all be going on a plan. Think one, think all in our house, or it never works. Just look at my husband and I and any plans we might have to separately lose some extra flesh. Just doesn't happen. Little skinny, neurotic Sophie would be the only one to escape the wrath of the diet doctor. She was just a few pounds total in weight anyway and couldn't afford to lose any more. Her morning's bread and butter were safe.

The first morning of the plan and there they all were,

five smiling faces all lined up in their happy places and waiting for their morning cookie. When the half-a-cookie treat, with bonus half a carrot appeared, there was some disgruntled mumbles among the troops, as they tried their best to steal the other's half cookie or trade with the carrot. "No, no! None of that!" I insist. "Carrots are good for you. We love carrots!" And normally they do, when I am trying to give carrots to the horses, llamas or goats. But, Mum, in place of the morning cookie? Now, that was another thing entirely.

"After 3 weeks, a new plan becomes *the* plan you know and can stick to," I read and wondered if that was the same for dogs as for humans, because the half a cookie thing didn't seem to be gathering any fans day 2, 3 or 4 into our new world, where we would all be about 8lbs lighter, ideally, come our next weigh in.

It was the early morning of the blood moon. "Wake up!" he says. "It's 5am and the moon is up," and sure enough she was and weirdly transfixing in her yolk yellow shroud and reddish glow. Transfixing and a bit spooky, if I can be honest. "I love you," he said, (not something he often says.) Followed by - "I'm going to pass away today."

"Well, if you do, I shall be royally upset!" I retorted, "So please try not to!" I went back to sleep and he did not.

When I finally got up to make my coffee, he was sitting in his chair and he didn't look very well. "I'm tired," he said. "I feel a bit dizzy too." Oh great, he has a bug, I thought and went about my business. He did look a little sickish and grey about the face. "I can take you in to see the doc?" I offered, helpfully, clock-watching as type-A people are wont to do, with just a modicum of anxiety, since I had an open house scheduled at 1pm. "No, I'll be fine. I'm just going to rest," he said, but he did take his own blood pressure - something that should have clued me into his general feeling of unwell.

On my way to work, something told me that all was not well in the kingdom of Jensen and I had better call in the big guns. The Daughter. "When are you coming home?" I texted her". "When do you want me home?" she replied. "Now." I said. And there we had it. I never say "NOW" these days. She knew something was up.

A bit later on:- "I'm taking him in to the doctor," she said breezily. "His pulse is crazy." (Hadn't even thought to check the pulse!) Thank goodness we now have some one with some medical savvy in the house. A little while later and my anxiety levels are rising. "He's being taken by ambulance to Salinas Valley," she tells me. "You're kidding me," I respond quickly, still texting. "Yes," she texts back and then I have to call her. "You're joking?" I quiver, hopefully. "Nope." She's as cool as a cucumber. She is not joking.

The day fell apart. We were supposed to be going out for a nice dinner that evening. Nothing mattered anymore. She and I arrived at the ER to find him all hooked up and looking a little bashful. "Sorry," he said, as if there were anything he could have done about any of it. We waited and watched, as you do in the ER, listening to the unfamiliar sounds and watching all the machines with their language that didn't make any sense. The doctor presented the options to us; the best one being that he stop my husband's heart and then re-start it to try and regulate the heart beat. That didn't sound good, but he assured us he does it all the time with enormous success. The husband wanted that option.

There is nothing quite so scary as watching a loved one have the lights taken out of them and then have their chest charged with electricity to such an extreme that they levitate and not in a gradual way either – it was an aggressive jolt up into the air. My daughter and I sat by his bedside and watched this happen with a gasp.

I was eerily reminded of his words from the morning, "I'm going to pass away today," because that is exactly what happened. I'm also supremely happy to be able to tell you that he didn't stay passed away; he came back to us, thank god - with a super sore chest, but a regular heart beat.

As for the diet crew back on the ranch, there were a few days there, when the rations were probably a little slim - definitely a little late - and perhaps they lost a few pounds over the course of those stressful days when they got fed later and more infrequently than I like to do ordinarily. However, I do know this. They have also grown to be a little more accepting of the carrot treat over the past few days, so much so that they will actually take one of the orange numbers from me and give it a go, before giving it up to a brother. I don't know that it will take them 3 weeks to get used to the new plan, but I'm sure they will get with their new program way before the old man gets with his.

You can't teach an old dog new tricks? I'm really thinking you can.

Published 2014

Either Madness or Grief

"So," she said." My report card wasn't quite as good as it may have seemed." I paused and swallowed long and hard. One of those moments frozen in time, when the screen did actually freeze, Sometimes it is good that the other person cannot see your reaction on FaceTime. "It wasn't actually that great," She confessed finally; the Queen of understatement.

My baby sis had let the entire family go through the Christmas season imagining that things were okay in her world, that the cancer was being kept at bay, that we could all relax just a little and let modern medicine do its magic, as it seemed to be doing like an absolute miracle. She had kept it from us so that we could all have a nice Christmas. And then, post-Christmas, the truth was revealed in all of its cold and cruel reality; just as it needed to be.

"There are spots here and there, including the brain. I have fractures in the pelvis, hip and spine. The osteoporosis is really eating me up …" Her words went on. Everything else became a blur after that and I began to immediately grieve for the magic I had expected, the sheer miracle I believed she deserved and that would happen for her and for all of us. Our dreams for a miracle became soaked and soggy in our tears.

Every moment of every waking day after that became mixed with this news, meshed and tainted in a dark way with the fondue of our family's reality. Baby girl was really dying now and she was telling us there was not going to be a way to stop it. "Don't change your plans," she tells me in her cheery way. "I'm not going anywhere in a hurry!" Our plan had been to go and see her in June when the weather was better in Turkey and we could all enjoy it together. Now it seemed like such a long time away.

It is worlds away from where I'm currently standing and where all those cancer cells are growing and that osteoporosis is eating up all the fading bone mass, as we speak. She is there and I am all the way over here. It is hard not to just jump on a jet plane and stay glued to her until infinity, or whenever we are forced to part company. She is my baby sister and it is my job to take care of her and protect her. As I flounder my way through these days and my inability to do anything really constructive but focus on the aches inside me and my fury at the world, she tells me she is off to Venice with the love of her life to celebrate her 46th birthday; and how beautiful is that.

She has explained to everyone the situation, she has set to the side anyone's hopes and dreams for a miracle cure. Yet she is still living her life on her own terms, with each day an absolute blessing, full of love and laughter and appreciation that she is still here. I tell myself you have to take the pleasure with the pain.

Rosie Emma Alexandra Mason Arican is my baby sister.

Published January 2016

Finding Fur-Ever Friends

"They have been hanging out in the Mission District for over a week," she said. "No one can even come close to them. They are just there, waiting, we guess, for their owners to come back and get them." My friend managed to pick them up and give them her hamburger. They were super hungry…

"Can you take them in?" she asked me. "I took in the last one." And there we had it. This was the two and fro of a quasi-rescue outfit that had been evolving over a period of time, without us even realizing that anything was growing before our very eyes.

Jack and Jill – two dachshund/chi mix – maybe a mother-son duo – were a little the worse for wear when they came home with me to Solace, my home. Jack had burn-singed ears, Jill had a slash on her back that was slowly healing. They both had a cherry eye condition and a fear of humans. Breezy, a pit-mix who had been initially found on my land and then taken into her home a while back, was the one before and she was being housed with my friend. We had a rescue outfit for a while that we didn't even know about.

We built a pen for Jack and Jill, where they would be safe and fed and warm, with a nice, good-sized area to run round in also. Sadly, they were not able to mix in with my other five pups for various reasons – they also could not be in the ranch situation with a horse and llamas and goats. We still learned to quickly love them. And that is what you do when you are an animal lover. You find a way to make a sanctuary for a soul in need. The feral cats that showed up at home and at work. We trapped and fixed and released them back to their environment, as civilized people do in a civilized world. You do not euthanize -without a hope in the world. You do everything you can do to save a life; every life has a right. And, with that, evolved – slowly – the South County Animal Rescue with its "Fur-Ever Friends" tag line.

Andria and I - along with our whole board – have fostered and rescued needy animals over time - and we had found huge holes in the organized rescue situations established to help, mostly due to over-extension of their services and their physical distance from us. Too many animals, too few organizations available to help. Though some County organizations were willing and able to help our remote communities, they were so inundated with their own challenges that it took too much time for them to be able to step up and help with this type of time immediacy. We needed to fill in the gap. It was staring us in the face. And so, gradually, we were born. Ready or not, the social media of today allows for a swift and powerful outreach to your target audience.

Initially, we are looking for sponsorships to help build the organization. We are looking for partners. We are looking for "Animal Champions" to help provide safe houses for our rescues, as well as foster homes and supplies. Start up costs are significant. Our goal is, ultimately, to have a local facility; but, to start, it is just two founders, a small board of Directors and a little community interest that we hope to grow. We will be applying for grants and hoping for the very best.

If you have it in your heart to help us – however small your abilities – we would like to hear from you. The animals need you.

Published January 2016

Finding Love in the Mud

"El Nino is coming," The Experts assured us through the never-endingly arid, corn-colored months - like a promise we could almost reach out and touch. As we sunk, deeply depressed, through endless water-rationing, drowning in the sadness of the dry bed lakes; they promised us that a pineapple-express like system would soon be greeting us and loving the heck out of us with its buckets of wet stuff; almost, seemingly, solving our water problems. They reached El Nino out to us like a carrot on a stick to give us hope that all was not lost – our farmers would be able to farm again, our people would be able to work, our hills would be green once more.

We didn't believe them really – let's face it, they are quite often wrong. We figured the highs would push the lows away and up to soggy old Washington State where they usually land and as usually happens. We couldn't imagine what might be the next thing to come along to help solve our dry, old water problems; but we didn't think the meteorologist's dreams would come true and fill our pails with water, like manna from heaven. Maybe The Experts would find the way to ultimately desalinate the ocean in an affordable way and the stress would ease that way. We certainly didn't expect El Nino to come blasting through; not really.

January hit and along came the buckets cascading from the sky like a late Christmas present. The hills went quickly from green-hued to lush. Water flowed across roads, the alley from my horse's stable became a mud bath I wasn't accustomed to. I loved it the first few days. I closed my eyes to the heavens and said, "thank you and yes please, please send more ..." (I now think I was just a little kidding. What I meant was, send a little rain every night and then some sun during the day, please. I think.)

Our ranch is now a huge mess and likely to remain so. The straw I placed over the mud just serves to make the alley into a skating rink. My clothes, boots, jackets are all covered in mud, my dogs need their paws dried at every doorway. This wet-winter lark is a whole different ball game that we had forgotten about during those difficult dry years, those winter months of stressing because the rain wasn't coming, the lakes weren't filling and the ground wasn't soaking.

It is a natural syndrome that is so important for our State as one of the growing capitals of the world that we must not complain, I tell myself, now it is here. We must enjoy working in the rain, driving in the rain, learning to love the interiors of our houses and not our horse's backs. We must worship the rain and ask her to keep coming. I was telling myself this the other evening as I was endeavoring to show a home and the wet stuff poured down the back of my jacket. "Get yourself an umbrella!" I heard someone say and I almost laughed. "Umbrellas are for the Brits, who count on this stuff all the time. Here in Cali, we get just buckets of the stuff one year and nothing the next. Who needs an umbrella for that kind of unreliability?"

In the meantime, I must learn to find the love in all this mess and hope upon hope it's enough to, ultimately, give us a really glorious summer that we will all be able to enjoy without even a whisper of the word *drought*, let alone the words *water rationing*. We are always subject to change. That much I do know.

Published January 2016

For the love of a stubborn man

So it came to pass that stubborn man looked upon stubborn woman one fair morn and he doth sayeth, "So wife of mine, if you were to imagine that stubborn man were in extremeth of pain one day and then also the following day, say in one certain area, per chance, over and over again, what would then one stubborn woman say to one very stubborn man?" It was a modern day plea for help at its very finest. With this somewhat pitiful speech, it came to me that this stubborn man was asking – excuse me, begging – the woman in his life to force his very stubborn self to go to the doctor and be quick about it. If I hadn't been so super concerned at the time, I might have done a victory dance and then quickly encouraged him to do some more theatrics, because he was that good.

And so it came to pass that stubborn man made his own doctor's appointment and also attended it. Just as we thought – this was an extreme measure that said stubborn man was operating under and the ensuing result was not that great. "Surgery!" the great doctor announced in great Mighty Doctor format i.e. "I will send out a referral to an operational doctor and they will then call you to get going on said very important operation that you actually need super soon". Heck. And then the rest of the world falls down just about to your ankles, because this is not a good thing for anyone, least of all stubborn man and super-stubborn woman who are rather busy and who do not have time for such inconveniences in life such as surgery. But that is life, isn't it. 5 steps forward and 10 back.

But super-stubborn woman's first reaction was actually huge relief that said affliction was, at least, not something super-spooky, as had been her first impulse. Then she went through the whole gamut of worry, concern and stress before she came back around to practical thinking and the urge to get through this thing and back to some semblance of normality. Then she goes back to disbelief and then back around the corner to super-relief and left around the block to the other place. It is really very shocking when these types of things happen to your family — and also, when you had least expected it.

This was also the week that I got hit by the cold of the century — in my humble opinion — a cold of such magnitude that it sent me to bed two afternoons in a row and had me reaching for various different types of medicine over the course of day and night to ease said affliction. Sore throat, coughing, congestion and extreme levels of mucus plagued me for some days over the duration of this very strange week. This coincided also with a rather good amount of rainfall that we had been dreaming about for some considerable period of time; and so it came to pass that the plates, they were a-shifting in the Jensen household. Stubborn man has to cancel several jobs he had lined up because of his inability to really do much of anything until the surgeon took care of his problem. Stubborn wife, in her own way, decided that she would have to take on as much work as she possibly could during this fallow period in husband's working life. "I hope you don't divorce me because I am so useless," stubborn man could be heard saying to stubborn woman in the early stages of his diagnosis. "Oh no, stubborn man," She could be heard telling him in no uncertain terms. "til death us do part, buddy boy!" she warned him. "But you can expect to find my foot firmly planted up your hind quarters, making sure that you follow all of the doctor's orders post surgery – oh and my personal ones – while you get yourself back to health!" Thank goodness we have a nurse in the house to change his dressings and watch over his wound. Our son will be coming to monitor his movements and cook our dinners. For my part, I shall be doing my best to keep some money coming in and the wolves from the door, as Granny would say. I shall also be a Grand Champion Cheerleader during this time – just in case we need one.

And so this is indicative of a good marriage, I'm thinking. A solid union shows its best colors in sickness and in health. It is forever and for always, as far as I'm concerned, with all the bumps in the road along the way that life deals us. We do the very best with what we have to work with and we act as brave as required with the head held high.

Too bad husband had to cancel some really good jobs after his diagnosis and husband will have to take a really good look at his life and his livelihood from here on. He will ultimately be fine, as will we. We will all weather this together, as a family should, and we will come out the other side as equally stubborn and solid as when we went in, just as a man and wife should, with their adoring family all around them, helping them to pick up the pieces of the days left fallow.

Published February 2014

Good work is not easy

They say that anything worth doing isn't easy. They are not kidding. When we started the local animal rescue back in the beginning of 2016, I don't know what we expected. We knew there was a lot of work ahead of us, but the work was important as was the need on our streets, the endless streams of homeless animals wandering starving and needy in our communities, the horrifically blasé attitude towards an animal life and our quest to save them from the alternative of what might await them if we didn't step in. Luckily there were several other folks out there of the same mindset. And so, our group was born.

Fortunately, one of our group had a home she was willing to use as a safe house for the needy babies that seemed to instantly arrive at our doorsteps. We expanded our foster home base to accommodate the need and many of us took in additional mouths to feed that we hadn't counted on. This was all out of our own pockets; packed up with a lot of love and good will. It amazes me how many stray dogs there are wandering on the streets in our small towns. Do people just open their doors and say "Go"? If they realize that a dog is as much work as a child, do they just drive them somewhere and throw them out on the street? In my experience, I would say yes, they do both of those things. This is totally unacceptable. An animal is forever; like a child. One of our goals is to educate our populace of those very same things.

And so our work began. A group of energetic animal lovers, who were already rescuing animals, with big hearts and small bank accounts – never a good combination. Silky – a slim, beautiful girl – had eaten some plastic and needed emergency surgery. We opted to try and save her to the tune of about $2000. We won, as did she. She has already been adopted by a lovely forever family and is doing well. Romeo was surrendered by a family who could not take care of him. We took him in as a surrender and he became a forever friend of a delightful young man in Salinas and his Mom who said she didn't need another dog … We love success stories like that. His Mom tells us that Romeo sits outside her son's room waiting for him to come out; he is so adoring. Amber, a sweet cocker spaniel, was surrendered when her family was divorcing. We homed her to a beautiful situation. James, a gorgeous lad, was dumped on Metz Road with an enormous fear of humans. We furever homed him too. We do not arbitrarily home dogs. We do adoption contracts with the family, we check the home is a safe place for our fur baby. Our babies must have their shots and be spayed or neutered. We proceed with caution and then we feel proud. We have done a lot of good work in just a short while. Several generous folks have helped us along our way. Our first fundraiser brought the animal lovers out in droves and, through their generosity, funded Silky's surgery in almost its entirety.

Good work is never easy and it certainly is not free. But it is what makes life a very rich place to live in and it gives you a peace and a satisfaction you can never get from just a pay check.

Published May 2016

Lizard on a hot tin roof

I feel as stretched as a lizard pinned down on a hot tin roof right about now; and if that doesn't make any sense then neither does my life. Sometimes you feel so immensely overwhelmed with life that you want to run and hide in a dark room with your hands over your ears to keep out the noise. That does not work well when you have a house full of relatives, a family that expects your attendance at regular events such as meals and laundry, and a job that keeps on sucking your blood most parts of most days.

Watching the lizard cavort across the logs, fall brutally between two sticks and then get itself just a little stuck between two timbers, when it tried to rescue itself, mirrored how I'm feeling these days. I keep trying to get ahead, I keep trying to climb the Mount Everest of my own existence, but the harder I try, the quicker I fall back down again and get squashed and bruised between at least two of the sticks, which are somehow set up to trip me.

It's the modern way; so they say. We try and we juggle and we sometimes fail miserably, we do. So what can we do? We cannot cease to exist. We cannot really hide in a dark room for very long; regardless of the known benefits for the universe to stay firmly away from pre-menopausal women, (sometimes we *need* to be locked in dark rooms.)

We have to believe that the morrow will be somewhat improved; that there will not be two escrows that fall out with the drama of crashing shooting stars every single day. We have to soldier on and weather the storm. We must see the bright side of each day; not knowing how many of those things we have left to squander. Here is my latest, brightest compilation on that particular melting pot of ideas:-

Hug and stroke dogs at least four times a day; more if you have the time. They make you feel like you rock, you totally rock; and when they are making you feel that way, they feel that way too. Nothing has that same ability. Cats are good too, except that most of them will get quickly bored of all the attention.

Eat chocolate. It is the simplest most divine pleasure; as close to god, just about, as you can arrive, in one second. You don't have to eat a lot; just a snickle on the end of the tongue and see how long it can last.

Drink wine. It is another of the most divine pleasures in life. It has to have been created in heaven – wherever that is – by some really old souls who knew what the rest of us needed. Don't waste your time on cheap wine; life is so definitely too short.

Exercise. It is such a gift. You don't have to be a major athlete to do it, just get a pair of well-fitting sneakers on your tootsies and go out and do something. Even if it's only fake karate or pseudo ballroom-dancing in your living room while you watch 'Ellen', it's so very important for your body's blood flow and your sense of well-being.

It can also keep you away from needing the dark room as much as you possibly do.

Don't over-book. Life is one day after another. There will be 365 days to the year and you do not need to fill each one chock-a-block with something to do. Cherish the days of nothing and take your gift to heart; you may not have another one for a week or so. Do the same thing for your children. Every minute of their existence does not have to be filled with something scintillating which makes them a sure bet for Harvard or Stanford. Really, truly. Sometimes it's okay to let them play XBOX or chat to their friends on 'Facebook'. Remember what you forbid them to do, they will just do at some one else's house.

Give yourself a daily time out. That requires a few minutes of nothing each day when you sit and look at the birds, the sky, the mountain; whatever toots your horn, and you do not check email or talk on the phone, and you definitely don't speak to other people. You cleanse your psyche; a colonic for the soul. Some other people might also call it praying.

Try to laugh more than you do. Whether it's watching a season re-run of 'The Office', or just chatting with your young one – they've always got something funny to say. Stretch the laughter lines of your face; and put one more character line around the eyes, why doncha? I'm a firm believer in the powerful release of laughter; cough up the tension, get it out. Follow the example of the children; they can teach the adults a thing or two about laughing. They do it much more than we do.

Find a fabulous book you can't put down and feed your brain some mind candy. It's a vacation for the mind truly to go somewhere you were definitely not planning to go that day. If you can't afford a book, the library is full of wonderful choices; all free.

Plan something fun for somewhere down the road; but not so down the road that you feel doubtful you will ever make it. If you can't plan a vacation, plan a mini visit somewhere; even a day out somewhere fabulous, or preferably a night too can give you the makeover you need and help you with that stretched out feeling. The world will not close down if you take a day off; you will not be fired from your job, or have clients banging down your door to cancel contracts. No; it is for the betterment of all and we have to allow ourselves to be a little more healthy-minded than perhaps we have become in this rigorous planet of land mines across which we tread.

If you too are feeling like a lizard on a hot tin roof; you've fallen off the burning roof into the wood pile and feel like you can't get out, then know this; you are not alone. There are too many of us feeling this way and it needs to stop. If you can't get hold of me one day, don't worry; I'm either in a dark room with my hands over my ears or I'm taking the day off. Don't laugh; it might happen!

Published December 2014

Making a difference

She was dumped – a common occurrence in these parts. You don't want something? A wife, a kid, a dog? Just dump it; it's the modern way. There can be no accountability, if you just open the door and let it go and become some one's else's problem; or behave so badly the State has to step in and take over, where children are concerned. My cousin wanted me to take on her teenage son. I was horrified when I realized what she was asking me. "I don't do kids," I was forced to say. "I can do animals all day long; but I can't do children." I felt horrible having to turn her down. Having raised three of the two-legged species already – sometimes better than others – I feel qualified to say that I graduated from that particular course of life with maybe a B- and I likely won't be going back to school to study it again anytime soon.

Fortunately, we are all made of different mettle and my friend collects children like I collect animals – to my mind, a much more challenging endeavor. Years ago, she qualified as a foster Mom and then adopted one of the children she was fostering. Then she foster-failed another child, (i.e. adopted her!) Once she found out that all five of the other siblings – if I remember it correctly – were in the system, she foster-failed all of them too. And now they are one huge happy family and the children get to be together forever and they even get to see their mother who couldn't care for them, but wasn't cut out of their lives completely. That type of selfless behavior is worthy of very special recognition, in my estimation. Incredible rare generosity of spirit of Disney proportions, worthy of a year's free groceries or a visit from Ellen at the very least. People like that are extremely rare; I hope those foster fails – those lucky, lucky children - appreciate that down the road.

And then there's us with our small animal rescue and we try to make small differences where we can. "Do you still sell real estate?" she asked me. (How on earth does she think I pay for all this kibble?) Then I realized that I have aligned myself so heavily with the rescue of the animal world these past 8 months that I may have forgotten a little where my bread and butter comes from. Yes, of course, I still work in real estate! Do I look like someone who is eligible for retirement, or even who just won the lottery and can now build her own shelter?

Driving abandoned cattle dog Thelma to her, hopefully, forever home recently – her nervous panting and licking and agitated demeanor made me step inside her paws for a few minutes and imagine all the thoughts careering through her head. "Where am I going? Why am I going? I don't want to go …" She was looking around and processing her environment, then coming in for a head stroke before panting and looking around again. I made the mistake of turning and looking at her before I drove away from her new parent's home – that poor abandoned girl whose former owners didn't care whether she lived or died. I shed a rare tear for all the babies we couldn't save. Then I kicked myself in the rear end and went off to work some real estate. Later on, her new Mama sent me a photo of Thelma sleeping peacefully in the sun in their back yard. "I think she likes us," she said and I felt as if I had done a good day's work.

If everyone who could made a little difference where they can – whether in the fostering of children or the rescue of animals – and all the other places of need in between – from the line of a great song - *what a wonderful world this would be.*

Published August 2016

My forever girl

I've always been partial to border collies; ever since I fostered Allie, a large muscle-bound Collie-Lab, who stole my heart a few years ago. Technically, she belonged to my daughter's boyfriend and, somehow, when the relationship went south, I got custody of the dog. And then he wanted her back and I didn't have her anymore. There was a huge hole in my heart and it took me a very long time not to miss her. Over time, my other 5 canines eased the pain, leaving me calm in the knowledge that I would, one day, have my own crazy-collie-girl. For those of you not in the know, the breed is quite something. Demanding, ornery, conceited, herding, energetic and deeply loving and loyal. If they don't get enough exercise or 'work' in their day, they can be extremely naughty; which is why a large land mass is recommended for them to burn off their energy. I just love them.

I was getting ready to go and see my sister in Turkey. I eye-spied a gorgeous border collie on FaceBook, such a great modern forum for lost-found dogs I've noticed – indeed, the viral bulletin board for canines. 'FOUND ON CASTROVILLE BLVD, BORDER COLLIE!' She had a deeply sweet-shy face and the conventional black and white coloring I love so much. I tentatively messaged back, enquiring if they had found the owner yet. "No, and we can't keep her," the lady responded. "We already have 3." I explained to her that I was the President of South County Animal Rescue and that we could maybe help. I would be leaving the country for a week, but then I would be ready and able to assist.

I'm packing my case to leave and receive a message,

"We know you are leaving, but we really need to home the dog. My husband is getting too attached." My heart leapt. No one had claimed this beautiful girl and here was my opportunity to claim my very own border collie. The one small problem being that I was packing up to leave the country in the next few hours.

Fortunately, I am married to a saint; a fact I may have mentioned before. "Honey, we need to leave a little early for the air bus," I tell the saintly husband. "How so?" "We need to go via Castroville Boulevard and pick up a foster," I half-lied. "If we don't get her, they are going to have to take her to the SPCA." "Foster, hmmm." He was onto me. He knows me so well.

We pick up this dear sweet girl, hugely underweight with a large, healing gash under her leg. They told us they found her on a highway median and couldn't just leave her there. Who knows what her story is. We took custody of her and I felt just a tad guilty, leaving her with daughter and husband while I jetted off to see sis.

"Thanks man," husband tells me later. "She puked all over my truck." As I mentioned before, he is saintly. But, by the time I arrived home, she was settling down nicely at Solace. "I don't think I'm just fostering her," I whispered to my daughter. "No, we know, Mom," my daughter smiled back. And there the universe righted itself just a little and Jaxx Jensen came to rest and play at her fur-ever home in the hills South of Soledad - our home we call Solace - where she would no longer know hunger, suffering or neglect. My heart is full.

Lucy Mason Jensen

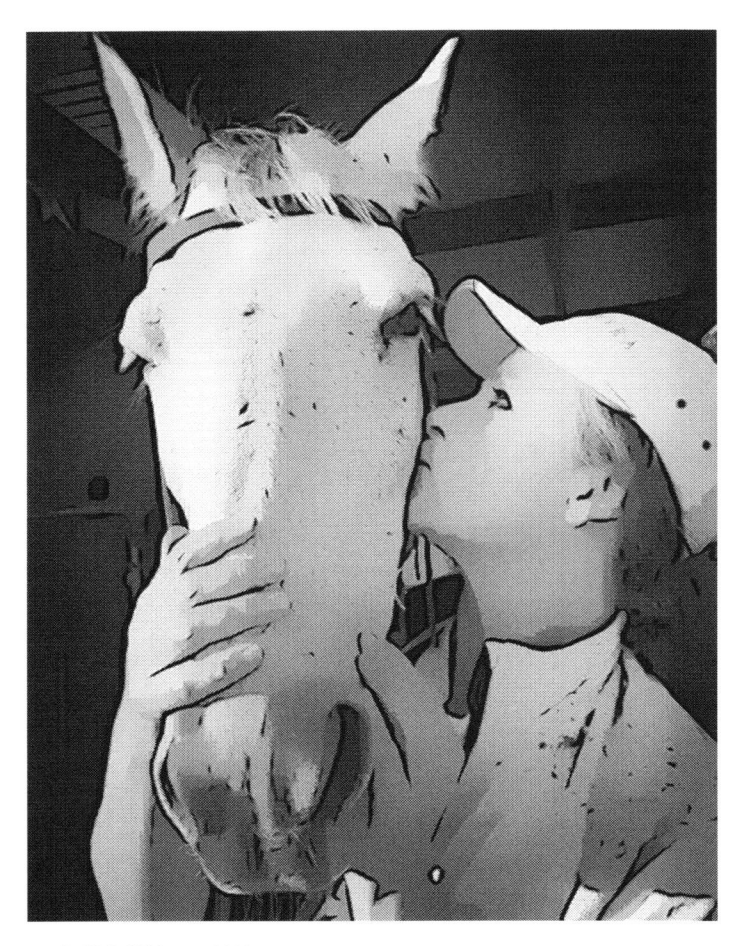

Published February 2016

Puppies and Plane Rides

"I'm just so sad I don't know what to do with myself. I walk in a room, walk out again. I don't remember why I'm going places and for what. I can't sleep, can't work. I'm a mess." Thrown to my knees by my sister's most recent diagnosis, there were several days when I could, honestly, barely function. Luckily I have old friends to hear me out and try to guide me back to everyday life.

"Do you want me to come over?" She asked "Well, of course I do. When are you coming?" Came my swift response.

And so the dialogue goes with an old friend when they know you are hurting and want to try and soften your pains. "Plus we are going to have puppies." I came in for the kill.

"Puppies? Puppies, what? I'll figure it out." I knew I had her with the 'P' word. I knew she would come. And that's how it goes with old friends of near 40 years. Never mind that we live on different continents and time zones; when one needs the other, we are just a simple plane ride away. And so the plan was born. She would be coming over to distract me from my personal agonies and I would be supplying her with some serious puppy time. That's what friends are for; everyone needs agony aunts in exchange for puppy time. So she flew from England to America, as you do when your old friend needs for you to do that. She also came bearing a lot of gifts – including chocolates, bath essence, champagne and homemade chocolate cakes and flap jacks – lots of my favorite things. "Rain drops on roses and whiskers on kittens ... these are a few of my favorite things ... when the door slams, when the bees sting, when you're feeling bad ... these are a few..." And it all helps; you know. Distraction is key, when you can't get your head around some of life's tough hand-outs. Distraction and gifts and chocolates and champagne. It all helps to ease the pain and move the mind over from gripping, endless sorrow to hedonistic pleasure. I write a note to self that I will try to pay that forward in the future, as required.

Her visit was a breath of fresh air. She organized me, she cleaned my home. She swept and clipped and washed. She laid out the chocs and the champers for me and she played with the puppies. She showed me the things that were within my control and those that were definitely not.

"We are going to be having another litter," I broach tentatively. My foster dog Molly is also rich with pup and due any day. "It would be great if you could stay on and help with this lot too." But I actually didn't say the last sentence – that would be unfair to her life in St Elsewhere and her own husband and puppy waiting at home for her to go back home and organize their lives and bring a little chocolate into the house for them too. So I stayed quiet on that front and remained hugely grateful for the days she did spend with us and the lasting effect she had on my psyche. Bless you, dear friend, for giving hugely of yourself and all you brought to Solace – and I'm not even talking about the chocolate and the champagne. See you in a month, girlfriend, when I come over to stay at your house and the fun kicks up a notch all over again.

Published April 2016

Queen Victoria and the Diet Princesses

Oh my golly gosh; the more vacations I take, the more I am convinced that 50 is the perfect age for retirement and I just need to be able to do more of that and take more of those. Can you tell I just returned from a blissful vacation? From the clear blue, bath-warm beauties of the Mediterranean to the stormy billows of the North Sea, I was there and I was present and I was oh so happy for all of my nearly 3 weeks away from my normal life in my normal world, which is here and at work.

My baby sis is doing so well, all things considered, and thanks so much to all of you who ask after her and continue to do so. You have no idea how much that means to me. It's as if she has a cheering squad that she has no clue about, dancing their little hearts out in her name, helping her to cross yet another finish line she had no idea she could make. We spent precious days with her at her home in Turkey this time around, in celebration of my father's 86th birthday. We laughed – a lot – actually had tears streaming on more than one occasion. We ate together, swam together, walked together, did all kinds of normal things together that ordinary families should be able to do and it was made all the more precious by our actual knowledge that the doctors would call her "terminal" and we just call her "Rosie", because that is who she is and always who we are when we are around her. Yes, it was that kind of trip. My middle sister and I escorted our father over to see our baby sis in Turkey for his birthday treat and how perfect is that. Even when he did not really feel like celebrating one night, we helped him out and ate our dinner under the stars without him. We saluted the full moon and the pathway of the moon across the sea. We made sure he was all well accounted for on his birth week and more. We held tight to all the moments we had together and we hoped for more. That is what you do when some one titles some one in your clan as being 'terminal'. You live today as if it were your last and then you kiss the ground when another day is granted you. And another after that. Our family knows all about living like that.

And so it was that I felt strangely okay about leaving my baby sis in Turkey this time around. Firstly she was off on a trip to Spain with her girlfriends and she was feeling more than just okay about that. Then, it was that we were going to see her again really soon, just a few months down the road and we already had our travel tickets. That does help, I've found, when it comes to saying good bye. It gives you a warm security blanket that you had no idea was so very important. You really do need another date in the diary, or it all feels too final.

So we parted with hugs and smiles and "see you soons" and it was off to the East Coast of England for a reunion with the girls. We have been friends since we were 15, so we are always glad for a chance to catch up and revisit on our 15 year old selves that we still feel are pretty much in existence. We laughed a lot together, oh my goodness, did we! We lay on the beach and drank champagne, we visited fond spots, we shopped and ate together and the hours they passed much too quickly, as such times are always wont to do. We talked about our 'meno bellies' (menopause equals too much fat around the chest and belly areas) and we promised one another that we would have just a bit more boney dominance the next time we saw each other face to face in October, when we would have the chance to kick up our heels again, together, all being well. We would be more in line with the 'babe' look than the grandma look, when we met again, we decided, and that would work well for the all of us. We signed up for the 'Fitness Pal' app in our smart phones, where we could share our success stories and encourage each other along the way. My friend's critique went something like this - "Kate needs more encouragement. Please make sure you do that." And we all got a good laugh at that. "Carey has not consumed enough calories. It is likely that her body will be storing fat, because of near starvation." Roared with laughter over that one! Sharing with old friends is so much fun. Whether or not we actually look any different when we see each other in the flesh once again in the fall, at least we had some fun along the way while we were apart, and sometimes, at each other's expense!

And so it was that I needed to make the trip back across the pond to the West Coast, where I had some newcomers in place and waiting for me in Solace. They had moved in while I was away, as can happen in our near animal sanctuary we have built here. Three ladies of a certain age – we will call them Queen Victoria, Anne Boleyn and Princess Charlotte – had moved into our Secret Garden and were making themselves pretty darn comfortable, thank you very much. Not to negate the rather pushy curiosity of our young tabby cat who kept visiting them and wondering at the flap-flap of their wings, they were living in rather peaceful serenity in the gardens surrounded by only lovely red wood trees, limes and water and sharing the space with only a very private and respectful turtle.

I was delighted. Fresh eggs at last. The first few days I enticed them with my yummy collections of snails and the like, in addition to their daily scratch and laying pellets. They seemed to like me, they really did. The large eggs they produced in the flower pots gave me a great respect for such an enormous feat of nature. How does such a small thing produce such an impressive thing? Then, one day, Queen Vic seemed a bit off. She sat quietly under the shade of the wagon wheel and didn't jump up when I brought in the snails or cluck impatiently like her sisters, when she saw the arrival of the morning bread and butter. I went over and stroked her. I had never stroked a chicken before and she seemed to like that too. As a former battery hen, I doubt anyone had ever stroked her feathers in her whole life. "Come on girlfriend," I told her. "You have to rally for the sisters, you have to rally for me. You just got here and we have lots of fun to have together!" I put her own little dish of water before her and a large juicy snail.

She looked at me strangely as if to say, "You are a very funny chicken." Later that day, she had moved from her former spot, but she still wasn't clucking around. She was still quiet. I knew her time was close, so I petted her some more and thanked her for the eggs. She was gone the next time I visited her and I felt very sad, as I always do when one of the family goes away and there's not a darn thing I can do about it.

Queen Victoria was buried near Carey, the cat, in our front garden. The circle of life goes on. The next time I visited the girls, they were clucking around the pond area as if nothing had happened. You do wonder if they realized that their flock had been depleted by one third. They carried on, as we all do. We carry on, until we can carry on no more.

And as for the Diet Princesses, they are carrying on too. Some days are better than others. Some days the confessions go something like, "Drank a vodka and coke. Then another one. Then I ate a box of chocolates." Some days, the diet halos are stacked up on top of the diet halos and they read something like, "I ate nothing today except for a small tomato. I gained a pound." Then we have to laugh and we have to laugh some more. Without laughter, where would we all be? Can't wait until the Diet Princess convention in the fall.

Published May 2015

Sweeping the stable

I can still hear it now. "Lucy is not domestic. At all!" It was my mother's voice. I think the noise started at around the time we had 'Domestic Science' as a subject at school, where we were supposed to learn how to cook, sew and clean. Perhaps this was not one of my better subjects; I don't really remember, except that I did not care for it very much. Whatever, this was a prophesy that, over time, became true.

In time, my younger sisters became really good cooks – I did not. Others learned how to patch a hole, or unplug the vacuum. I did not. More to the point, I could not have cared less. Whether I can actually cook a decent dish or two from my limited repertoire, when pushed, is a secret that I might care to share or not, at this late stage in the proceedings. Fortunately I married an extremely good cook and our son is a professional chef; so who really needs to add to that competitive pile? Note: I do like to eat. I just hate domestic competition. So, can I cook if I want to? I'm not telling. It was always so much easier to just not go there and I'd like to stay with that while I can.

One of our family's great jokes was when I became the 'Executive Housekeeper' of a large 300-bed convention hotel in Baton Rouge, Louisiana. "Lucy is not domestic! How could she be in charge of a cleaning crew, a laundry and all those bedrooms?" But I was and I did a reasonable job, I think, for some one whose reputation had always been the complete opposite of a domestic diva. My hotel crew liked me at least and I considered that the most important thing of all.

Years away from all of that and I still really couldn't care less about the cleanliness of my house. Every once in a while, I will look at my nightstand and see the layer of dust that needs my attention, or suddenly become aware of kitchen counters that could super-use some elbow grease and bleach. I will then, reluctantly, put on my rubber gloves and go to work. Does it bother me if I don't? Not a bit. If some one is coming to stay, then I can get a little excited about dust on the base boards and grimy windows, but that doesn't really happen that often. Certainly not often enough to alter my reputation!

But now talk to me about my stable and then tell me I am a complete nut! I love a clean stable – I really, really do. Every morning I can be seen out there sweeping my stable mats and scraping out dirty straw and bringing in clean straw and shavings. That gives me the most immense sense of satisfaction there is, alongside the fresh air, the music from the record player and the bright, bird-filled skies. Coupled with clean, full water troughs and a horse that lets me love on him just a little and I am a happy woman.

Recently, I found myself sweeping all the way down the horse's alley away from the stable. It just looked so perfect like that with lots of even sweep marks. All the goat pellets were swept away and there was a clean and fresh alley way for my horse to stroll along and do his business upon, as he came and went to and from the meadow.

"Really?" husband questioned. "Really? Now you are sweeping the alley too?" And yes I was and it felt really, really good. So good I had to laugh at myself. Who cleans the pathway from their horse's stable? Why I guess I am that girl. Never mind the grime in the house or the lack of kitchen prowess from where I am coming from, just give me a broom and put me in a stable and I will show you what I am about. Just call me "Suzy Home Maker!" or would that be "Barn Betty"?

"We are kinda hoarders, aren't we?" the kid noted, as we gathered some additional items we had gleaned from a clean out in our hay storage. "We are?" I was a little surprised, but then looked around at the piles that stacked up on every available surface in our home. And don't even get us started about the garage. "Why yes I suppose we might be considered that, ha ha!" I respond. "But check out my stable and my stable alley and you can really see what kind of a woman you are living with!" And yes, strange though it may seem, I am really not that bothered about the tidiness within my home, or whether I might be categorized as a hoarder or not by my know-it-all 19 year old. My stable is clean, my stable alley is clean and my water troughs are about as pristine as you might find. Oh and don't even get me started about how super my salt blocks might be considered!

Sometimes life is all about priorities and I think I have got my priorities super straight here on my ranch, within my stable and across the entire breath of the blissful land mass of our home we call "Solace." My animals are happy, we are happy. Who cares if the daylight blows our dust problem all out of proportion in our house? In the larger scheme of things, all is, ultimately, well.

The Animals Teach Us Everything & Other Short Tails

Published March 2014

Talking through our phones

"Hello, dear!" husband greeted me over our smart phones, as we are wont to do. We have some of our very best conversations over our smart phones I have noticed – quite often when I am busy doing something else as well. "Hello dear!" I replied and quite legally so, officer, on my Bluetooth device, as I indicated left and proceeded to the directed route, as per my navigation device "Martha," without whom I would certainly be able to get almost nowhere. Who uses maps these days? No one I know!

"There's a fabulous, complete set of Encyclopedias up for grabs here at the house where I'm working. Know anyone who would want it?" The mind drew a complete blank and almost a laugh. Why would you ever need an encyclopedia anymore? Anything you need at any time, you just 'Google'. It's even in the dictionary these days. "Google it!" We all do. The younger generation wouldn't have the knowledge, truthfully, to do anything else. I wonder what they'd say if we offered them a nice vintage set of encyclopedias? "LOL", as they would say. "Maybe time for a bonfire?"

Interesting, isn't it, how technology infiltrates our lives and sometimes canters ahead of it. "I'm taking some time away from Facebook," my friend declared. "I am becoming an addict." I can see how that happens. You wake up in the morning. Many of your friends are overseas, so they have been up at least 8 hours earlier than you. There has been significant time for them to post all kinds of juicy things. It is imperative that the FB gets checked before you even go out and feed the animals. Then, at lunchtime, wow a lot of time has passed. You had better check that Facebook and maybe even post that really cute photo of your dog under your blanket you took this morning. See if anyone will like it or comment on it. You 'Facebook' with your lunch, (note 'To FaceBook' is now a verb!) Then in the evening, before you sleep, it is imperative you check the feed and see what has been going on in the hours you have been gone – and naturally see if any one liked or commented on your cute dog photo from earlier in the day. Then, and only then, can you really rest until the next day. People enquired of my friend why she felt she was addicted and what she was planning to do while she was away – as if she really had gone into rehab for an indefinite period. She explained how much time she was spending away from her family and her 'other life,' all the things that weren't getting done, whilst she was busy chatting with those of us that weren't in that particular category and she left.

The next day, almost, she is back. "You're back!" I noticed, ever the sharpest tool in the shed! "Oh, not really," she whispered, if you can do that in social media. "I just had to post this really cute photo of my daughter and now I am leaving again." Addicted? Yes, maybe just a little bit.

You can sit in public places and just people-watch the

masses checking their phones, chatting on their blue tooth into the ether to someone, somewhere else and texting to St. Elsewhere as they walk. As we go about our lives right here, many of us are living our life elsewhere and that is very concerning. When I went to lunch with my daughter the other day, I made a point of not picking up the phone calls that came in, or checking any emails while we were waiting for our food. If I am with some one and my phone rings, that other person needs to be second in line, not first, and I think that that keeps things under control somewhat in the human scheme of things. "Be present in the moment," some one said and I do think there is something to that; especially in this world full of electronic intrusion and social platforms for everything except good old-fashioned face time, that maybe needs a little work now we are celebrating year 10 of 'Facebook', an institution that, the essence of which, for sure, is never going away. Husbands and wives, friends and ex-friends – they all feel comfortable talking to each other over the social media, no matter how private a matter it might be. The "world's a stage" concept seems to embolden people to speak their heart perhaps with a confidence they might not have one on one?

Though I do like to talk to my husband during the course of the day over our smart phones – crackle, crackle, crash – and I do confess I have commented in cheeky fashion once in a while on his 'Facebook' feed, nothing can beat a dinner table convo, eye to eye, or shoulder to shoulder, if we're in the stable, and that one-on-one connection that I hope doesn't ultimately disappear, because everyone's talking to each other through their phones and I'm sure that will never end.

As long as we can put these wonderful modern institutions in their proper place, limit our time and our attention to them, they should be able to keep their own happy place in our lives. If they are taking over your real life and making themselves the most significant thing you have, then it is certainly time to take a good hard look at your modern life, driven by technology and likely to remain so.

Published February 2014

The Animals Taught Me

Years ago, when I was waiting for my surgery – my mind plagued with awful scenarios of surgeries gone wrong, cancers spread all over the place and my life being cut cruelly short – I took my solace where I could. Very often that peace could be found with the animals.

I have a strong memory in my mind of lying on my back deck, after chemotherapy, feeling the sun on my body and listening to the birds singing. All around me were my 5 dogs. I knew I was safe and could rest easy. No one was coming close to Mama. She could rest in peace and never fear. That is the peace my animals give to me.

I have always been an animal lover. Julie, my black Lab-Retriever, features a lot in my early memories. Her big black presence could be found on every beach and in every back yard and wherever the children were; she was there too. She was such a constant and made all of us feel so safe. When my baby sister had her surgeries and she was bound up in a plaster cast, unable to move, Julie was there, right there by her side. Any one came through the gate to our back yard. Julie would circle and protect. She was our big old mama bear.

From a very early age – circa 5, according to the photos – I could be seen riding Steppie, a tiny little white Shetland pony with the attitude of a stallion. Every Sunday, my parents would take me over to the riding school where I grew up alongside Steppie, Gulliver, Morning Starlight and the others. It was such a magical time for me. When I was not at the riding stable, I could be seen "stabling" my own horses at home – Easter, Prince and others, my stable of hobby horses. They had their own stables in my fort at the end of the garden and I would ride them over jumps and play make-believe with them. Give something enough love and it becomes real; or so I see it now. At times, I would even let my sisters and my friends have a go. Another magical time!

My best childhood friend Isabel lived on a farm and her sister had a black horse called – yes, Blackie. She and I would take Blackie up and down the fields and lanes of their farm with her black and white collie dog called Susie. A charmed life indeed! But I never dared hope that I could have my own horse – that seemed much too far fetched.

On the occasion of my 7th birthday, I was fully expecting my own equine to move in with us. I had heard mumble-mumble in the house of grown ups, maybe buying the neighbor's land, maybe getting me a horse and I knew, I just knew, that they were going to make it happen for me They had to do it; it had to happen. I can remember the expectancy that I awoke with on my birthday, just tasting the horsey-mane of my new best friend in the whole wide world. And then it all came crashing down. My parents presented me with a – still beautiful – wooden rocking horse and explained that they were not able to buy the neighbor's land and they hoped I could love my rocking horse just the same. I can still taste the tears I tried to hide as I embraced my Moonshine, my beautiful wooden boy, who was to, very soon thereafter, become real and alive at night because I willed him to be.

Decades later and horses were no longer in my life, much as I still loved them from afar. My daughter was a horsey little thing with her weekly horse camps during the summer and she was a real natural. It was not until I was really down and really desperate, after my cancer diagnosis, that the stable door to the horses opened once again for me and I fell through it, as if thirsty from the desert. A retired cutting horse was lodging at the Hambey ranch for a while and my daughter had been given permission to take him out riding. What a lovely thing. She would trek across the fields after school, tack him up and ride him up and down the meadows and streams. If the special gift was not to be for me, then so amazing that it could be for my daughter; except that, oddly enough, the gift came packaged up for me too.

Sebastian, as I named him, after a lovely horse show from my childhood called "Belle and Sebastian," starring a glorious white horse, was a solid fellow of about 28 years old, when we first met him. He had been around a while and probably knew a thing or two about humans. I remember wrapping my arms around his neck and closing in for the horse hug, after my daughter had brought him back from a ride. I was particularly afraid, that day, of all that lay before me and all the unknowns that featured hugely in my every waking minute. Sebastian pushed back into me and gave me the most memorable horse hug of my whole existence. He knew I was in pain, he felt my pain, he took it on and he was able to help. To this day, I remember how that hug made me feel. He gave me a strange kind of love and hope that defies explanation. This exchange with Sebastian awoke something in me that I had not realized had been a volcano under the surface of my existence. The more I interacted with Sebastian, the more I knew I was going to have to find the way back home to my own horse.

Winston came to us by default. We rescued his roommates — the goats Charlie and Elvis — because they needed a home and we needed lawn mowers, to be truthful, to take down the immense brush in our back acreage. Winston — the grey, dappled, scarred horse - had been rescued from Mexico to Prunedale and still needed a forever home. For some reason, no one had wanted him, 'free' though he was. "We'll take him," my husband said and those words became forever etched in stone, in my mind, as the day the large memory gates re-opened for me and I allowed myself to, again, fall back madly in love with the equine world — a love affair that will bloom for always now, well after I am able to get my old body up on a horse and actually ride one.

It has been just a few short years since Winston Sebastian Churchill Mason Jensen came home to his forever home - our home, we call Solace. During that time we have overcome with love and care many of his issues from long ago and managed many of those that could not be overcome. We have taught him things and he has taught us many things right back. He has learned to trust us and to love his new life as he knows it. He is a lover and a comedian, an advocate for his own rights, but also a peace builder. He will snuggle with a kitten and then tell a large, boisterous dog who is boss and who needs to get the heck out of his stable. He is a one of a kind, and I shall always be grateful to him for rescuing me when I needed him most and giving me hope, when I had little left to muster. Even now, I can go to his side and take a huge horse hug from him. He will eye me with the calmness of a master and tell me everything is going to be alright. I cannot imagine my life without him, nor do I care to imagine. He helps keep me away from the dark side and look forward to only goodness and light. Every time I say goodnight to him, I cannot wait to see him again in the morning.

Like my other animals, it is as if he knows where he came from and knows where he lives now and he has the wisdom and the experience to know the difference. My rescue canines – each one of them – has stories to tell that would make you cringe and the scars to back up their stories. But the beauty and the clarity of their intense love and loyalty today tell a story all by itself. I shall always rescue and I shall never be surprised when my rescues rescue me right back. The animals do teach us everything, in my humble opinion.

Lucy Mason Jensen

Published February 2014

"The Attack of the Rooster

It was a sublime day in November. Those things should not go together, but sometimes in California, they do. My neighbor from across the street had asked if we would, kindly, feed and water their goats, while they were gone for the holiday. Cats and chickens would be fine, she noted, since they were on auto feeders. All sounded simple enough. Her goats were manageable – if a bit larger than my pygmies. What was another, smallish farm compared to mine? I strode across the street in my own little world to do my neighborlies. "Ah chickens!" I think to myself, about half way across. "Chickens equal fresh eggs and I do love eggs!" Now there is my payment for being neighborly. So I stroll out of the barn doors towards the chicken shed and there I nearly meet my maker. Out of nowhere, a black and grey, red-beaked manic thing flies towards me at lip-level all flapping wings. Initially I thought he had just approached me for a cuddle like all my animals do. It took me only a micro second - actually when he became airborne - to ascertain that he actually was attacking little me and not in a good way. I lifted my leg in self-defense- "get back, you pesky so-and-so!" I chided, or in a similar fashion. This wasn't enough. Again he flew at me and stabbed me in the arm. Here I am backing up away from the monster and towards the barn door and trying to defend myself. He then proceeds to hit me in the side. I am being beaten up by a rooster, what the heck! After about my forth pecking and several karate-style moves on my part – not elegant - I am able to exit the barn door, where I proceeded to breath deeply and finally have a little giggle at myself. I couldn't believe what I had just experienced. I rushed into my house, full of drama and fell, gasping, upon the full chest of my husband. "I have just been beaten up by a rooster!" I showed him the evidence of a large, evolving bruise on my arm. He couldn't believe it either. Our nice neighbors had never mentioned they had a bully boy living in their midst. Perhaps it was only me that he had taken such a dislike to!

The next day I take along the man of my house with his large stick in tow. Here I am, peeking through the barn door, while my warrior husband takes a fighting stance and raises said stick to the flapping grey mess. Not to be outdone by a 6'2, 240lb fighting man, the flapping mess started challenging him and met a rather large – if flat – foot up his bottom. And then he came back for more. "Oh yeh? Bring it on. BRING IT ON!" The man challenges back the rooster and there are times in your life, oh yes there are, when you wish you had brought along a video camera. Here, this ordinarily meek and mild man, also an animal lover, was in a boxing ring with a super-ornery rooster and it looked, from my perch behind the barn door, as if the man was winning. I have to say I did sense a little strut in the warrior stride of the all-conquering, as he boldly collected the eggs from the hen house, moved the stick one more time, threateningly, in the direction of the marginally-defeated rooster and strutted home on the balls of his feet, like a bit of a prize-fighting cockerel himself.

It was obviously the week of the chicken, or some of its close relatives in any case, as Thanksgiving befell us the same week as our fighting rooster encounter. I told my neighbor that her grey flapping mess had attacked me and she pronounced, without skipping a beat, that it was definitely time for chicken soup in her house. We cooked a big old bird at our home on turkey day and I do have to say it was particularly delicious this year. It could be because there was only a small group to feed and therefore the bird was smaller and more succulent, and everything was just that bit easier, or just that our taste for blood in our encounter with the fighting mess made the carnivores in us just a little bit more apparent come feast day. Whatever it was, turkey day was enjoyed for a number of reasons this year and for a few days after Thanksgiving itself, culminating in the most delicious turkey soup to clean out the gullet. Whether or not my neighbor came home and actually made chicken soup herself out of a certain ornery creature in her back yard, we may never know.

Continuing on the chicken theme of the week, I have to say that we "chickened" out yet again on the whole Black Friday fighting ring palava. There was a small minute and a bit, when husband and I actually thought we might, this one time, brave the madness for the lure of a rather large and handsome television that we were coveting, with its likely deep discounts, on Thanksgiving night or certainly the blush hours of Black Friday; but then the lure of gathering with the insane quickly passed us by and we knew we were not made for the pushings and shovings of all those blood thirsty roosters around a 60 inch Samsung. Just wasn't in our make-up – or at least this year. Next year, who knows? If we can go a few more rounds with the neighbor's rooster and get some serious practice under our belt, it could be that we are up for the challenge in the future. For now, I'll just read about the 'holiday' madness in the local papers and thank my lucky stars I don't currently need anything that much.

Published November 2016

The Boss

It was about the summer of 1998 when we started working together. I had taken a management job at the newspaper and she was one of our valuable crew. Initially, she was very suspicious of me; of management in general it seemed. She would avoid eye contact and call me 'ma'am' when spoken to, that made me feel very old. I think I had to ask her, in the end, to call me by my name. She was a bit of a rebel for sure, but obviously smart, with a story or two to tell. I love a challenge. I would ask her to come to my office and catch a slight eye roll or a disgruntled swing of her head. Nothing I could attribute to any kind of disrespect, just a bit of attitude mixed up with a reluctance for anyone to get into her space, let alone her head. Even back then she was a very efficient worker; versatile and very timely. It was rare she would call that she couldn't come in, even though she had two kids that she was raising by herself.

As a Manager, as in life, you should always treat people how you like to be treated. If you are kind, it comes back to you ten-fold. Little by little, I tried to break down the wall between us; between her and the world even. Under the tough shell, I found a very special person. I found out that her father had not been around in her life, that her relationship with her mother was a strained one; that she had had a pretty tough life so far. I discovered that she shared my birthday and our mothers shared theirs. "You only have one mother," I remember telling her. After I lost my mother in 2000, the message got repeated more often, as I urged her to mend any bridges with her mother while they still had time.

She left the newspaper shortly after I did in 2003 and, over the years, we would remember each other's birthdays and send the odd message here and there. I knew that she had secured herself a good County job and then, later, that she had married a good man. She had also mended the relationship with her mother and they now both worked in the same building and had a good mother-daughter bond. I felt proud when I heard that my little angry protégé had evolved to such a degree in life.

Then she told me they were looking for a home and asked if could I help them. Well, of course I could! What an honor to edge my *'Young One,'* as I used to call her, one step closer to home ownership, the largest purchase she'd ever make in a lifetime. "I tell everyone you're my boss," she told me. "Well, now you've had lots of bosses since me. How about just your friend?" I reply. "No," she said adamantly. "You will always be my boss." Sometimes it is the employees that teach the boss a thing or two about life, so I take the boss title with a smile.

As two major animal lovers, she started helping us with our South County Animal Rescue venture – fundraising, promoting, buying, selling – whatever it took. Even though she lives in Salinas and we do a lot of our work in South County; it's all about the animals, wherever they are. Nothing is too much trouble for her from selling caramel apples to getting hold of County information. This past weekend, she and her lovely husband and 5 of their 6 kids were at our fundraiser from early until late, helping out wherever we needed the help. I had to stop myself, once in a while, from becoming emotional. Success stories like this don't happen to all our young people as they should. As her friend, her near mother – her boss, if you like – I couldn't be more proud of the fabulous woman she has become and the lovely lives that she continues to nurture, both human and in the animal world. I look forward to many more years of watching her grow and flourish within the terrific framework of life she built for herself. Monica, you're awesome.

Published August 2016

The Half Date

When you have been together the better half of your adult life, it would not be a lie to say that the romance can fade just a bit, the pitter-patter acceleration of the heart-beat slow just a tad at the approaching footsteps of the beloved to your sphere of being, the all-consuming passion become more of a deep friendship somewhat akin to a cozy armchair with a great book by a blazing fire, where you feel really, really happy and fulfilled in life; but where you could also quickly fall asleep. In short, a long marriage is a profound and beautiful thing; but you do have to go searching for the fireworks and rekindle them, once in a while, in order for all the fizz to not fade entirely.

With that said, husband and I recognize all of those things and we do try to go out on a 'date' once in a while, an afternoon or early evening is good – we are old – where we spend quality time together, talk and engage like a normal couple wrapped up in the concept of just being together, him and I. We try to sit across a candle-lit table and talk about us and our feelings without the phones interrupting us, (well as the girl, I like to talk about us and our feelings. He will be a good boy and quietly listen.) We will break bread together, without any television interference, any dogs barking to come in or go out, or any teen insisting that they need something quite outside the parameters of our marital bliss, which quickly becomes the priority and will put any assumed 'marital bliss' back in the box where it had formerly resided.

During our 'Date' sessions, we will re-group a bit and talk about our next vacation or something really fun like fencing our property or building our barn or taking a couple of fun days together away from life, instead of our usual mundanities like "The toilet seat needs fixing again and I really wish you would listen to me when I ask you to do something and get on it right away." Or: "I'd really like for you to actually use the day planner I bought for you and intentionally placed on the work space where you couldn't miss it, instead of piling stuff on top of it in the office space I'd really like for you to also use. THIS WOULD SO HELP YOU BE BETTER ORGANIZED IN YOUR LIFE? WHY DON'T YOU LISTEN TO ME FOR ONCE????" (The caps are never good. That means that the tone is raised, the blood pressure is up and the irritation level is on the roof.) Or maybe, even, the quieter: "Maybe we could discuss those items in our shared lives that make us completely nuts about one another – and not in a good way …"

Living with another human being in a happy and peaceful state is an ongoing work in progress. Most people would agree with that.

And so it was that we planned to go on a date. A Friday seemed like a reasonable day to plan for such a thing, based on the fact that real estate people work most weekends. So, a Friday it was. We left late because there were calls and there were issues. We arrived at our lunch locale a little tardy and enjoyed a nice meal together, with a modicum of one-on-one engagement in between the phone calls and the texts. We did, however, miss the movie we had been planning on seeing as part of the date scenario. Move stage forward to another Friday, another planned date. We were going to enjoy a movie we had been wanting to see, a restaurant we had been wanting to visit – and we would still be home in time for the evening feed. For us, that would have been a perfect day, perfect date. Except for the fact that our work got in the way, once again, our times got shifted and there was to be no movie date. Also, the lunch date was not going to work out either, so we grabbed a quick sandwich on the way to a work appointment and we missed the film date entirely.

Headed back in the afternoon, the husband noted that we had enjoyed almost a "half date" that day, which could not amount truthfully to a full half of a date, but perhaps a small slice of date? "Oh, but at least we rode in the truck with each other!" I pointed out to him, my glass half full as ever. "And I didn't have to drive myself to all the places that I really didn't want to go to in the first place." We did not get to see the movie we had wanted to and we did not get to enjoy the lunch at the new restaurant we had planned to visit, but we returned home in better shape than we had left it. We had spent the day together and we had had some quality time along the way. Some days that is all you can ask for in the larger scheme of things and that is all you are going to get. Oh and our marriage gets to breathe another day.

Published March 2014

The heart of the animal rescuer

"You can't keep them all," he told me. He's been telling me that for the longest time. The husband; that is. Ever since our farm started expanding, in fact. I thought, over time, that I had become a pretty cool rescuer-type. You know the kind – they have the swagger of a foster parent, portraying cool efficiency at all times and being able to let go when necessary. It's a passion; an obsession; a job that you love. You have to love it. Whether you foster kids or animals – you are definitely not in it for the money or the professional accolades.

My first foster pup had been brought home by my daughter – bless her – apple doesn't fall too far from the tree and all that. After the poor baby had been cleaned up, groomed and fed, he was a real little love bug. We had him for several months under our foster care, until his forever Mom came from Aptos and took him home. I remember the lump in my throat when he left us. I knew he would only be with us for a little while and this was the best possible placement for him; but it was still hard. Down the road, a couple of small black chi mixes came to stay. They both needed surgeries in addition to everything else. We took care of them for a very long time and I figured they would probably never leave, but I didn't name them – better not to - they were always '*The pookies*' to us, for some unknown reason. And then they were leaving me, with only a 24 hour notice period to say goodbye and that was really hard too, but I managed.

Once we formed South County Animal Rescue – a group of animal-nut volunteers – I knew I was going to have to be Ms. Cool and Efficient Par Excellence. There were going to be many, many babies passing through our homes and our lives. It does help when you have a group and you work through the issues together. You have other people coaching you on being cool and efficient; even when you yourself know that's really not what you are.

Jaxxy - the border collie - was rescued from Prunedale. I first saw her on social media. She had been picked up on a highway median, starving and afraid. The foster family couldn't keep her and wanted to find a home for her. No one came looking for her. I convinced my husband that we were just fostering her until the perfect placement came along; but, deep down, I knew better. Year ago, I had fostered a crazy border collie. In essence, I had been her step mother, since her human was my daughter's boyfriend at the time. Then he couldn't take care of her anymore, he knew I adored her and I became her human for well over a year. Then he wanted her back. I was heart-broken. I had become so attached to this girl and thought we would never have to part. And so began my love affair with the breed.

Poor Jaxxy had been through far too much in her short life. We took her in to get spayed – she was pregnant. We couldn't figure out why she kept losing weight – she had parasites eating her up. Then she gave birth to 7 fabulous healthy babies and they take all the good stuff out of her; so then she gets ill again with mastitis and we have to rush her over to the 24 hour vet in Monterey for surgery. She had never had a chance to feel really good and enjoy her forever home in her first few months of being rescued. She had suffered so. But we persisted and gradually she recovered, as we kept topping her up with love and doing what was right by her.

For my part, I shall endeavor to work on the cool and efficient persona of an animal rescuer one set of paws at a time. If you love them, it's never going to be easy. But, as he keeps on reminding me, you can't keep them all. Nothing worth doing is easy; I know that. Jaxxy came through her trials in the end and is just the best and most ornery border collie in the world.

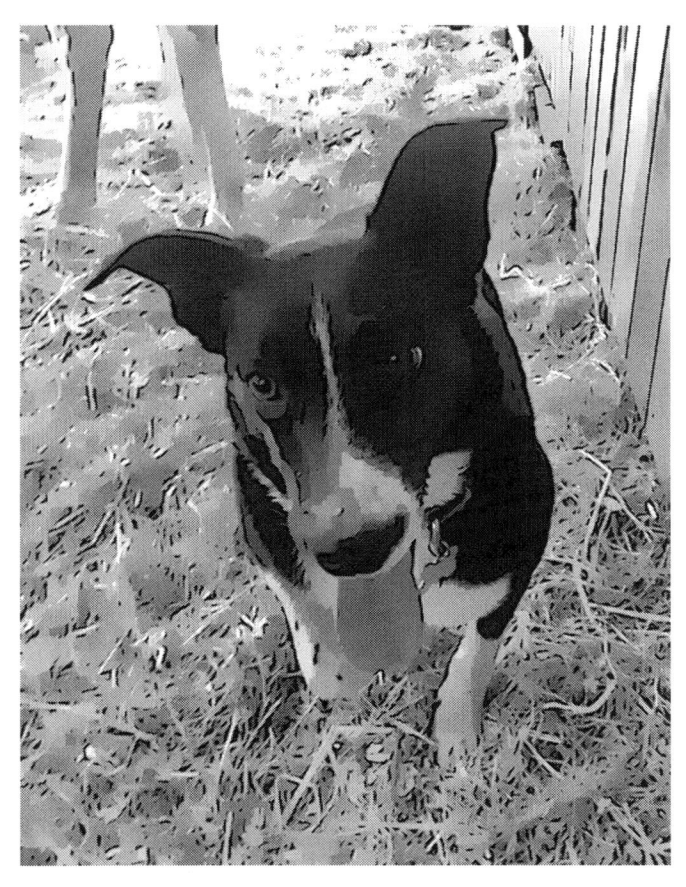

Published 2016

The Life of An Animal Rescuer

The life of an animal rescuer is filled with hills and dales, mountains and valleys. One minute you are happy-happy, because it looks as if one of the 'old inventory' is about to be adopted out to their forever home, or you just raised a boat load of unexpected money to fund your rescue kennels, their food or your web site. The next minute, you are racing to a rescue situation because an animal has been found hurt, or someone needs to immediately surrender a poor baby in need. It's a daily emotional roller coaster.

I'm likening my new unpaid position as similar to that of a law enforcement officer or maybe someone on the run from the law. Real estate is bad enough – you never know what the day is going to bring. Somedays things work out and you think to yourself 'I really do love my job'. Other days, you are tearing your hair out with frustration and wondering how on earth you are going to find the mortgage that month. Yes, valleys and dales with the odd mountain climb in the middle and sometimes great views along the way. So my life is now double time in the crazy department. I'm not just dealing with the unpredictabilities of real estate and those who float in her boat on any given day, I'm dealing with the animal world and all the colors that lie therein. It's an interesting mixture I tell you and not one that gives you much peace. But every now and then, if you stop and listen you can find it.

I found it the other day when one of our rescue puppies that I am fostering rested his head on my shoulder and held it there in a beautiful, trusting way for several moments. I found it when my crazy border collie woke me up to her cold nose on mine and I opened my eyes to her eyes and the deep love and trust that I found there. I grabbed a hold of the peace when our puppy TJ held on tight to me in the water and trusted me to bring him back to land safely. There was the witnessing of births of two litters of puppies who have been in my care ever since and the privilege to watch them grow and bloom and then move on to their forever homes. There are snippets of peace and harmony in all kinds of unusual places if you open up your eyes and your heart and stop for a moment to embrace them.

"You must love having all these puppies around!" she said. "This is my second litter this spring-summer – so 18 puppies in all! I'm actually quite tired!" I responded. But, truthfully, I am tired in a wonderful way; because these creatures have all grown up to be lovely, sweet, social animals and they have increased my puppy education and enhanced my life in indescribable ways. You cannot put a value on that. Looking back to the rescue of the Mama Jaxxy and the Mama Mollie and the beautiful litters they produced against the odds in our home, having been abandoned by their former owners and essentially thrown out with the garbage; what we have all managed to achieve is a very beautiful thing. I stand back and admire these lovely lives and it gives me the courage to carry on being a crazy animal rescuer and trying to save the vulnerable lives out there, one animal at a time.

The Animals Teach Us Everything & Other Short Tails

Published July 2016

The Llama Games

We missed the shear-circuit last year. Despite our best efforts, it was a confusing time to navigate, which then quickly passed us by. For those of you not in the know, llama-shear season is a very short one. Some folks said we would need drugs, others recommended a complicated chute-funneling situation, or a combo of the two. It was all a bit boggling for your first time llama-shear inductees. I felt bad. Poor Harold, Max and Sam had to tolerate some rather hefty warmth last summer in their enormous winter coats; but they didn't complain and seldom used the llama-land shade we provided for them in any case. This is the Central Coast, not the desert, after all.

The llama lady from Montana contacted me with oodles of time to spare this time around. She assured us that we needed no drugs, nor chutes come to think of it ... (fortunately husband had not yet started to construct the perfect llama chute he had been working on in his brain!) She arrived with a brace on her leg, a pair of tennis shoes and some very large and aggressive-looking panels she proceeded to lug around independently.

The llamas, meanwhile, had spent the entire night in llama land and were ready for liberty. There was many a break-out attempted while we endeavored to secure one in the trap and two outside – but all inside the perimeters of llama-land. It was a comic situation, really, if I had not been so intent on getting my llamas sheared and that item checked off my spring list. However, I could still not imagine how Lori from Montana was going to get this done. Max was the first – sweet Max – and he was really a very good boy from the pulley system of entrapment down to the worming shots. Harold Malcolm Democracy came next – less good – and very insistent on being done with all of this palava and wanting to immediately vacate llama land. Then came the piece de la resistance – Sam – who tried at every shear stroke to kick out at poor Lori. She conceded to him somewhat, leaving his legs pretty darn furry. But we had pretty much managed to get all three llamas sheared in just a few short hours. Then Win, my horse, eye-spied these weird skinny, camel-like creatures in his meadow and decided that some intruders had crossed the fence line and needed to be dealt with. It was the funniest thing, watching him race up and down the hills after these fleeing, long-necked creatures who couldn't believe how they could now feel the wind in their hair and breeze in their fur. It was one of those precious days you couldn't re-create if you wanted to. All is well now at Solace in llama land. The llamas are cool, the fur is more-or-less bagged and we can now pay attention to other more pressing matters such as our inadvertently pregnant cat and foster dog …

The Animals Teach Us Everything & Other Short Tails

Published July 2016

The Nickers of Solace

The older we get, the more we know suffering. It is the same for all of us. We lose, we lose, and we lose – if only, on occasion, our sense of humor and often our tranquility and feeling of well-being, and, as the years go by, all of the other stuff too. I recall so clearly my grandma telling me that it is better to have loved and lost than never to have loved at all. And this was a lady who had lost all of her husbands and siblings and was ready to go herself.

This week I put my self on time out; in some respects

to maintain my sanity and stop the cascade of loss that was eating me up and making me just a tad neurotic. Life can have you up on a jagged cliff on the edge of the world, on occasion, and it is then that you realize that you need to rescue yourself first before you might be in a position to help the others. During those times, when you have isolated yourself from the world, it can be the simpler things in the world that will give you the most comfort. Pause and you will see, you will hear and feel the comfort of the world breathing all around you. Just inhale, exhale and listen and you will know what I mean.

Standing at the water trough in the middle of the meadow, accompanied by only my own raw thoughts of a morning, I am greeted by a dark green and maroon humming bird flapping and flitting around just me, without even a flower in sight to drink. He just whizzed around me, magically making me think of happier things in happier times, and then he was off – up and over the stable and back to flower land, in our front yard, where the living was easy. Why did he come and see me in the meadow? What was his business there? There was no food there for him. A few days later, I am at the same water trough, slow-watching the green water circulate and fill to the top and there I am greeted by a cool grey dove with the prettiest eyes. She fluttered around me also and then flew off to join her mate on the fence. The watering trough is where I can have some of my darkest thoughts, yet my most beautiful visits, at least of late. It's as if our resident birds know that I need a bit extra solace these days. I now stroll down the meadow in the early morning light wondering who will be there to greet me and how I'll feel when they get here.

Another day, I watch and wonder at the tiny yellow breasted sweethearts, for want of knowing their actual breed, splashing and playing in the bird bath without a care in the world. It gave me comfort that they were the same little birds who were nesting in our cypress grove and creating a new family for themselves not so long ago. Again, it is the small things that can bring you out of yourself and back to life, back to living and all we know that we have today. Who knows about tomorrow; I most certainly don't.

The warm nickers of my horse and my daughter's horse do it to me every time. Whether in the early morning, or during a late night visit with a cool carrot in hand, you will hear a heavenly rumble, an equine purr, a horse's chuckle of glee, if you like, as you surprise them and they surprise you back immediately. I never tire of their chortle, nor their noisy smile. Sometimes it has an impatient edge to it – when I am late, for example, with Winston's breakfast and he is trying to give me some "Hurry up with that, will you?" attitude. Or it has some deep love attached, for instance, when I surprise The Bear at night in his pen and he is nickering me his happiness and his love back to the point he can bring tears to my eyes and get rewarded with a huge horse hug. It is at those times that I can feel most at peace and most in love with my world. It is then I forget about the other stuff, by-pass the grief and the reality and ascend to plains I'd rather be, where nothing aches, nothing nags and everything is at peace. I inhale the grass-scented, soft-muzzle kisses of my most dear equine friends and I gain courage to plan for the best, hope for the best and be as kind as possible to all around me while I am busy planning and hoping. I rescue the lady bug from the water, I help the bee out of the trough and I make sure the birds all have plenty of food and water all around. I will do all of that, hoping that they will stay close and be safe and guarded in my care. If I do it for them, perhaps the universe will do it for my nearest and dearest, so far away, but so close to my heart that it hurts sometimes. "Be kind to one another," I hear the voice say and I try to be kind, generous even, where and when I can. The feral cats behind my office – they now know neither hunger nor thirst. The bees in our front yard have safety and water. The birds – they have a playground seldom seen anywhere in the world. And my other beasts – from horses, to llamas, to turtle, fish, goats, dogs and cats – they are the most spoiled bunch of creatures I ever laid eyes on. If you can spoil with love and comfort, then, this bunch, they are spoiled through and through. Surely, in the way of the universe, it all has to count for something? Strange thoughts go through a person when they are standing at the watering trough of a morning hoping for a sign that everything is going to be okay.

Lucy Mason Jensen

The Pack Horse

I am renowned for my travel habits. And, sadly, not in a good way. I have steadfast memories – as do my oldest friends, unfortunately – of the time, aged 18, that I dragged the largest case known to man - with no wheels, let me tell you - from London, on and off trains, through the Paris train and metro system, in the rush hour - where said case broke its strap I do recall, to hysterical laughter from my accompanying 'friends' - and then onwards to Florence in Italy, where, I'm pretty sure, I burned said dragged and thrashed luggage on the funeral pyre of bad choices. My friends – yes that crowd - they can still laugh, really loudly, about that particular adventure and, amazingly enough, they are still my friends.

I never seem to learn. I always have the 'rainy day' theory when I travel and it's incorrigible. "What if it is hot? What if it's cold? What if it's wet?" (Certainly likely in the UK; less so in other places around the globe!) I also feel the need to bear gifts for folks, in addition, when I travel from place to place. I cannot have the "less is more" attitude of imagining I can buy stuff where I'm going, if things get really rough in the luggage department. Oh no. My family is accustomed to me arriving on their doorsteps with cases I can't actually manage up their stairs. However, people can change in this department; let me tell you; for example, in the luggage department, not in many other ways. And yes, in that department, they can appear to change.

I knew, at the outset of this particular adventure, that I would be on and off trains where I was headed, with likely no assistance, so I had better be a little light handed. Can't count on "cavalier" these days, can you, and I'm not quite old enough for the formal kind of "Those needing assistance please remain in your seats!"

I would be headed to the depths of the Cotswolds in South West England, when I landed in old Blighty. My dear friends always pick me up from the airport, so no worries there; but when I left my first abode and moved on to locale number 2, I would be setting myself on the train with my cumbersome luggage in tow. So here you have your first dilemma, when you are mature and thinking ahead, as I do try and do a little more these days. When you know better, you do better; or, that's the theory, so they say.

I took a bragging photo of my small pink case alongside my son's monster case, before we left home, since he was traveling alongside me and I would be leaving him behind in Europe. I sent it over to my friend. "Guess which case is mine?" I challenged my friend – one of the Parisian crowd, in case you're wondering. Of course she guessed wrong. 36 years of friendship had taught her well. But she was in error in this particular instance. "NO WAYYYYY!" she squealed when the truth was revealed. "Yup, way," I tell her smiling from ear to ear. "I have turned over a new leaf. I'm traveling light". She was unusually speechless and a bit disbelieving; though still prepared to be impressed, as the best of friends are.

When she picked me up from the airport, serve to say I had a bit of a kick in my step. "Traveling light, yeh! "I sing along, "and it feels so good." I don't think the song goes that way, but that was the one that got sung to her, as we headed out of the airport, one small pink case being proudly schlepped behind.

And then, somewhere along the way, something happened. I'm going to blame my hostess entirely for what ensued. "Do you want to stop by the charity shop?" she ventured, as we drove home from the airport. "It's only open on Saturday, so that would be today only." Well, of course, she had me there. Never mind the fact that I had just got off a long-haul flight and was grubby and situated in another time zone entirely. Of course, we must stop! Stop we must! I always have to stop by a charity shop; it's part of my make up. Love the designer labels at just a snippet of the price and the excitement of the chase. So there began my immediate decline into the realm of having too much luggage for one small pink bag and I had barely been on the land mass for an hour. Character is fate, for sure, and mine really messes me up sometimes.

The following day I sank even lower into decline, as I had much more than I could carry in the bag from the day before and we were visiting more charity shops. "I have your case!" she said brightly, producing an extra piece of storage on wheels. She had borrowed it to return to the UK from the States with all the extra stuff she needed to schlep from my house back to hers. And this is what we do. We always have a traveling case of some description between us – one that spends time at one house or another, our ocean apart – and there is never a chiding word between us, or a comment about how the small pink bag had immediately bred and multiplied, before we could say 'charity shop'. But we always get a good laugh out of it, that's for sure. So now I was a traveler with two small-ish bags. The one small pink number had already multiplied within a few short hours.

Moving forward from my train ride, with two small-ish bags, to my father's house in London. "I have some gifts for you to take to your sister in Turkey," he ventures. Ok, no surprise there. But then I eye-spy the pile he is pointing at and I swallow just a bit. "Um, "I say quietly. "I had only planned to take along one small bag." Then my middle sister calls and she has a plan for me too. "I'm sending presents over for you to take to Turkey," she tells me. "They should arrive before you leave."

"But I …" I ventured meekly in the face of all this expectation that I would be carrying the family Christmas over to Turkey – and here it was only October. And now we had an issue. Two small cases equals one reasonable sized case. But lo and behold – two small cases equals super-challenge, when getting on and off trains on the way to the airport. Hm. Instead of fighting the masses and insisting they go the normal way of the Royal Mail, I broach the subject of "Super Monster Case," that entered the country in the possession of my son, now just a large city mass away from me.

"Oh, the Boy might be able to lend us that case and then the problem is solved," Somehow those words came tumbling out of my mouth before I could bite my tongue and stop them falling off the tongue. And there the problem was solved. Son sweetly traveled all the way across the city with The Monster Case in tow, so that I could borrow it to schlep piles of packages over the seas to sis. I then packed "Christmas" inside said M.C. and staggered off on the train, wishing this were only a documentary about the ways of the world and the disappearance of chivalry in our society, not what was really happening to me. I will say this – if you are dragging an enormous suitcase on and off trains in this modern day world, no one, really, no one offers to help you; not even if you are sighing and spouting like a elderly humpback whale. It was quite a pitiful sight.

Me and M.C somehow made it to Antalya, Turkey. "That is a very big case!" said my brother-in-law, helpfully, when he lifted M.C into the truck. "Yes," I noted, wearily, with just a touch of martyrdom smeared across my brow. "I have brought Christmas to my sister." And there we had it. I had dragged this pack horse across Europe, I was the pack horse – let's face it – that dragged these packages across the land mass; but the expedition was successful; we had made it, the 'Eagle Had Landed' and sister was going to hide everything from herself until Christmas Day to make it all super special when the day came.

"I can't believe you brought all of this over with you, sis!" she observed, as I carried the copious packages over to her storage cupboard. "Enjoy it," I said quietly, grinding my teeth. "This will never, I repeat never, happen again."

And so the moral of the pack horse story is a simple one. Always keep your mouth shut, when other people have plans for you. The odds are the plans aren't great ones. If you open said mouth to make a helpful suggestion, you are likely to spend the next few days sorely regretting your foolishness. Yes. This was a true story which will never repeat itself in my lifetime. The End.

The story of the wolf and the full moon

There is something about a full moon that can remind mankind that they are just miniscule spits on the planet. They are nothing and everything else all around them is everything. I get that feeling, once in a while; sometimes when I am before a full moon and I am in the dusk of the day and in awe of the majesty of the moon. This month's "honey moon" has been no exception; in fact she has reminded me of that flick where Jim Carrey has the power to grab a hold of the moon and pull her closer to him and his lady and make her appear even more super large and impressive than she already is.

"Wo, wow, look!" and other descriptive words from the world of the comics, we exclaimed, as we watched the honey moon zoom her way up and over the Gabilan Range and into our view shed. She was fast coming up and she was formidable once she was here. "Magic" was another word used. And "awesome" another!

But some people believe that funny things happen around the time of a full moon and it sure has been a "funny" week, mix-matched with strange and unusual occurrences that just wouldn't weather the conversion to paper in their examination and analysis; but I'll give it a go. Then when you bring wolves into the equation, you have quite the mystic fairy tale that needs to be told.

Two weeks ago or thereabouts, our neighbor's husky girl – quite the wolf looking thing – attacked Elvis, or pygmy goats. It was a pretty understandable thing at the time, since our neighbors had thought that our goats would be super lawn mowers for their ever growing brush and we thought it would be a perfect feeding scenario too. We dragged our goats over there to their yard and the peaceful scene soon turned to a melee, when the two husky dogs turned on the goats and attached to the throat and back leg of our smaller pygmy. It took a second to register what was happening before we flew down the hill to the rescue and got the poor paralyzed goat out of the jaws of the mini wolf, finding him dripping with blood from the jugular and back leg and frozen with fear. At the time, we imagined that it was a territorial thing; the goat was in the husky's territory and therefore we had poorly anticipated her reaction to that invasion. It made perfect sense.

Then, on the cusp of the milk moon reaching her full potential, we hear our dog Tucker barking his "all is not well" bark, in the early hours of the morning, followed by the plaintive wail of an animal in distress. A goat wail, to be precise. It is barely daylight and we fly up and out of bed and witness the neighbors' huskies in our goats' pen and the female in the process of mauling the other goat, Charlie. They had crawled under our shared fence and bee-lined over to the home of our goats to continue their attack from several days prior. Now this was a certain kind of war we weren't about to tolerate. Husband grabbed the shovel and I grabbed leashes, anxious to reach the, by this time, cowering huskies before husband got there with a shovel. It was a tense time and, to add to it, super early. I hadn't even had my first cup of coffee. I grabbed the male and headed over to wake up the neighbor. The female shot under the fence, her face covered in our goat's blood. "It happened again," I whispered, as the neighbor answered her door in her nightgown. "They went in and savaged our goats." And there we had it —a new word - to savage. (When you knowingly go back and cause more destruction.) It could be a modern day gang term, if you want to go there. But it was what happened on that day, without a doubt.

I rushed back and applied my trusty cleansing tool of rubbing alcohol to my goat's neck and leg wounds. He ate a few vanilla crème cookies and made me feel hopeful that nothing major had happened to him. He was breathing heavily though and not putting his body weight on his back leg. "What on earth?" Why would such a, seemingly, calm and loving dog turn into a vicious killer? My neighbor and I went online to see what we could find. "Huskies? Oh yes," my friend told me in no uncertain terms. "I had so many problems with my huskie and livestock. Oh and especially around a full moon," she told me. And there we had it. The story of the husky and the full moon. You just cannot make this stuff up. Some times nature and magic just combine and give you a short story that cannot be fully explained. I will also never understand why the goats failed to fight back. God gave them horns – when they are under attack, then why don't they use them? I have seen them threaten a forward collie once in a while, when she was in the herding mode. Why not when their very lives are at risk. My friend tells me that the husky has a technique of stealthily moving towards her prey and not pouncing until she is right where she wants to be. Our goats are familiar with friendly dogs in their backyard and have never had to be afraid of them.

From this time forth, the female husky would be forever limited to the confines of her house or leash. Once they have had the taste of blood, all the bets are off, and she would most likely find a way to maneuver her way across our fortified fence. The neighbors were mortified and immediately ordered muzzles and the electric fence-collar combination. "You have the right to shoot and kill anything attacking your livestock!" one of my Facebook friends announced in no uncertain manner. I am not the killing type. I just want me and my brood to be left in peace. My feeling is that that will happen this time. But I shall be watching, especially around the time of the next full moon. Strange things seem to happen then.

Published February 2017

Throwing out the Garbage

"The pups were found starving at the top of Bryant Canyon," she said. "I went up to rescue them and one of them didn't even get up as I approached. I could see it was nearly over for him. He no longer cared anymore. He just wanted to die." Someone had dumped a couple of innocent dogs in the middle of nowhere and left them to fend for themselves in the wild – inconceivably, with no food or water - or simply discarded as irrelevant to become a quick coyote meal out in the wilderness. How do some people live with themselves? Of course, that is not remotely an okay thing to do. We, as a civilized society, need to make animal dumping a serious crime. We need to educate people that animal-dumping is not an acceptable practice in any shape or form. Just as you can leave a newborn at a hospital or a fire station, perhaps you should be able to do the same thing with animals you can no longer care for. Fortunately, a caring citizen witnessed their plight and called the local animal rescue – us – and lives were able to be saved, no thanks to the callous former owners. I do hope they worry about what happened to those poor, defenseless pups.

I'm glad to be able to say that the Soledad mountain dogs look as if they will make it. They are already gaining weight and recovering from their ordeal out in the big beyond, thanks to a concerned phone call and the compassionate nature of South County Animal Rescue Champions. I would love to look their dumper in the eye and ask them how they could do such a thing and what makes them feel that animals are just disposable items. We, as a society, have, obviously, not done enough to protect the innocent and educate people as to what is correct behavior. This continues to sadden me enormously.

I drive down Metz Road, the Gateway to the Pinnacles and my personal gateway to town. Today's bounty includes a broken mattress, discarded furniture of various shapes and sizes, bags of old clothes and more. More disposable items that people didn't want and didn't want to deal with. More garbage that folks decided they had easier dump on the scenic 'Gateway to the Pinnacles,' where the tourists could enjoy the view of all this trash, than take their sorry load over to the dump where they would be charged a small fee for their civic responsibility. How do people do that? A tad further down the road, there are a few empty pizza boxes waiting for whoever cleans up that piece of roadway to equally deal with. I, simultaneously, noticed a couple of out of town Priuses cruising towards the Pinnacles turn off and wondered what they made of our small town, rich with poorly patched tagging areas and piles of discarded trash on the side of the road. If they were business owners, I'm sure they wouldn't want to locate here; if they were possible future homeowners, they would equally wonder how indicative of the local society are the piles of trash.

Sometimes I just despair. Then I look into the eyes

of my most recent rescue dog and I see the love and the gratitude. I receive all kinds of donations from kind people for our upcoming rummage sale and I feel the community support and the generous effect that caring for animals can have on people. And I am then reminded that the world is a melting pot of good, bad and indifferent people. When the indifferent people behave in an indifferent way, perhaps it is time to load a couple of cameras along the roadways where they commit their illegal dumping acts. Maybe it is time to hit them in their pocket book and remind them of the laws of the land and the decency of a civilized society. I don't think that would be a bad thing for anyone. I, for one, would be hugely in favor. Let's also get working on an ordinance to make animal-dumping a crime, if it's not already. Who's with me?

Published February 2016

The Winner of the Beauty Contest

Rev, also known as Revlon, would win every beauty contest, if there were ever one of those in his category. He was quiet, dignified and elegant – if you can, rightfully, say that about a male – also sweet, kind and adventurous in his own way. I'd have to say he was one of a kind. Bring out the carrots, apples, broccoli, cauliflower, nuts or the like – and Rev would be right there, saying "Sure. I'll try it! Let me try it first!" Never mind the oats or sugar beet; he would be first in line. "I'll give that a go! Try me first!"

I have to say he was somewhat of a trailblazer in his own right. He had no interest in fighting after food either, never pushing, shoving or – god forbid – spitting if he did not get his own way, he was the peace builder of his species and then some. In all the time we had together, I never saw him even go towards the mannerism of spitting, yet alone actually spitting! That was just how he was. He was quite the special dude of llamas; it does have to be said. And don't even get me started about how good looking he was; boy, was he. He was tall and very, very fluffy white, like a big, pouffy, special cloud, with soft, large brown eyes and long batting eyelashes that could coo you at every turn. All he had to do was look at me and I was manna in his hooves; he just had that kind of power. I really did see him as the king of them all in his quiet, but commanding manner.

Then, one day he was sitting up on the hill in the meadow by himself. He was not racing up and down, chasing the grasses or playing with me as I filled up the water troughs. I was concerned and took him over his own personal food and treat pile for the morning. Everyone has their off mornings, I told myself, and Rev is most certainly entitled to his. However, in the evening, he was still perched up on the hill and I became a little concerned. Our llamas like to follow the food, race up and down hills for lovely fresh grasses; they do not sit on the hill waiting for us to deliver said fresh grass to them. But here I was, for the second evening in a row, doing just that.

"Rev?" I said to just him, sitting down on the ground

beside him. "What is going on, baby Boy?" It was still not quite dark, so I could still see him and he me. I stroked his long, woolly neck and he nudged me just a little. "Come on. Boy," I told him. "Can't be that bad, can it?" The next day, true to form, he was down at the water trough and drinking as if his life depended on it. "Yes, Rev!" I tell him. "There is my boy, back and fighting!" And I really believed it. When you see an animal thirsty as he was and standing up and fighting for his life, as he seemed to be doing, you go, "yes, boy, that's the way, go for the touchdown". Gosh I was happy that day; he was rallying like you always want them to.

But the next morning, he was back on the hill and not looking so good. I went and sat with him, stroking his long woolly neck. "Bud, we went backwards?" I couldn't understand the progress we had made the day before and the now forlorn aspect we both seemed to be viewing. I brought him along some dried apple and fresh carrots – both firm faves – and he didn't want either one of them. I was worried. I tried to make him drink some water. That wasn't happening either. We really had gone backwards; this was not good.

That evening I took him out some treats as he sat on the hill. "Rev!" I called to him, as I strolled up the meadow towards his spot. He didn't want his treats, or his hay, or his water. I felt that chilly finger of doom touch upon the pair of us, as we sat upon the hill and I realized, in that moment, that there was nothing more to be done. Almost in that same split second, the alpha male Harold Malcolm

Democracy came over and laid down on Rev as he sat upon the ground, making a strange noise I had never heard before. He leaned down low and simply pushed his neck to the ground as if to quash any air that might issue forth. I screamed at Harold, leapt up, jumped on him, pushed him, pulled at his tail – did whatever I could do to get a 400lb animal to stop killing his brother. But still he pushed and laid his body over the poor sick llama. In despair, I ran up and retrieved a broom and some water from the house. When I arrived back to the hillside, the other llama Max was lying on Rev, also pushing down against his windpipe, as if on a mercy mission for their falling brother. I couldn't argue otherwise, except that I had never heard of it. Never heard of it; but I saw it that night.

We scurried the healthy llamas into their own penned area, so that Rev could be in his own peaceful space without fear. Maybe, alone, he could rally again? The next morning, when I woke up in my bed, I could see him lying on the hill. I could also see that he had peacefully passed on in the night, right in his own special spot on the hill. Looking back at that night, we could only wonder if this whole llama ritual was something from out of our world that we weren't supposed to witness and aren't supposed to challenge. Llama experts we questioned had not seen this before and it seems we were, somehow, the first. Did his brothers know that he wasn't going to be able to recover from his ailment and they couldn't stand to see him suffer further? We'll never know for sure; but I know what I saw. We went to him in the morning and told him again that we loved him and would miss him and keep him at Solace for always which seemed the right thing to do.

The other llamas seemed unsettled the day that Rev passed. It seemed that they still looked for him and wondered where he was. It certainly seemed as if their thoughts for him were only of concern and love and not any type of animosity. Maybe the ritual we had witnessed the previous night had honestly been a mercy mission we were not supposed to see and nothing more. The animals teach us everything; certainly in my world they do.

We shall always remember Rev, as the boy who always seemed as he should have been a girl, with his soft good looks, big brown eyes and long eyelashes, not to mention his sweet, kind disposition that melted your heart. We shall always hold him up high as the sweet, adorable dude who still had so much more to give us, his humans, as well as his llama brothers. In his short time with them, we are sure he also taught them a thing or two.

This story is dedicated to the lovely memory of "Rev" Revlon Jensen, a true gentleman of the llamas and the sweetest soul. He will always be missed.

Published February 2016

THE ANIMALS TEACH US:
Hope, Courage, Promise, Love

These tales were published in the South County Newspapers 2017-2019

A dog named Spirit

The owners called the rescue to surrender their chi baby. They were sad but they couldn't really take care of her, they said. Come to find out, some time ago, the chi had been run over in their driveway by falling fire logs from a pick-up truck and she was paralyzed in her back legs. They had let her scoot around and recover herself over time, but now she was developing sores on her belly and it was more than they could manage. You get all kinds of painful situations to deal with in our line of work. They told us they couldn't afford to treat her or euthanize her. We took her to our vet and asked if she still had quality of life, or if the kindest thing was to put her little soul to sleep. She wasn't in pain any longer, she managed to get around just fine. She had a spectacular appetite for a little dog with just a few remaining teeth. None of us wanted to make that type of judgement call.

However, the vet surprised us all by saying that the little girl did have quality of life and wasn't suffering; so she got to come home with us and continue to live. We named her Spirit. She found early love in a foster home where she maneuvered her body deftly with the use of a scoot bag and then some wheels later on, but mostly she just loved to shunt her way around, getting up to quite a speed. I discovered that when I left the gate ajar to go and get something and found that she could honestly catch up with a fast walking human if she wanted to. Her little back legs have, over time, adjusted to being a support for her belly. She is not in any pain and she seems to genuinely love life and adore people. Her first foster gave her up to a second foster who decided to keep her. She named her Lolita and would take her to the park to make new friends. Lolita likes a nice bit of sausage or chicken in her dinner and some one to give her lots of loves and cuddles.

Then her mama fell on some hard times and needed a spot for Lolita to rest her head, while she figured out some new accommodations. "She doesn't need much," she told me. So Spirit came back to Puppyland and landed the tough job of a supervisor to three sickly caged cats. She would watch them through the cage and put her black nose through the bars as if to say. "We are a funny lot, aren't we. But we are friends and friends are good." I'd open the gate in the morning and here she would come at speed, rushing over on her belly to greet me and see what kind of treat I might have for her today. She loves life, there's no doubt about that. She also loves it when I put a warm blanket in her igloo and slip her a little piece of cheese.

My friend's daughter is coming to stay from England and she cannot wait to meet Spirit and the three sicky kitties in her care. She is special needs herself and will spend many hours, there's no doubt, just sitting by the cage, or in the cage, holding and loving on the animals she loves so dearly, without judgment. I wonder whether she will really notice the lack of mobility in Spirit's back legs, or will just accept her for who she is and what a special little character she is in all of our lives. I am certain that she will fall in love with her just the same way we all do.

Who knew that a disabled chi would have such a profound effect on humans? She teaches us to value what we have, cherish what we can and smile every day, no matter what the hurdles might be in our way.

I'm so glad we checked in with our vet to see what the prognosis might be for Spirit. It was well over 2 years ago that we did that and she seems to go from strength to strength. Her love for life shows no bounds and I feel inspired by her every day.

Published March 2018

A simpler life

The more difficult I see the world become around me, the more I want to pursue the simpler things in life. I aim to stay away from the awful news in the world and instead watch the dragonfly swoop over the pond and back again. I plan to avoid politics of any kind - it increasingly sickens my stomach and hurts my heart - and instead I choose to talk to my turtle when he swims over in my direction for his breakfast. I call his name – Gilroy – and tell him how good-looking he is when he pops up nearby and how his slider stripes are the wonder of the turtle world. I fill up water troughs like a maniac that's going to run out of water. I watch my abandoned kitten try to feed from his surrogate mother and thank the universe for letting me rescue his lovely self and hers also. I crave the company of my dogs – all 8 of them with their issues and scars and bruises galore – from the minute I start prepping their breakfast in the morning to heart-warming whoops and howls of delight – to when I lay them down to sleep at night in their various beds around and inside our home. I take time to watch my wild dog smile when she greets her beloved friend in the morning and how she cannot help display her happiness and delight when she sees him all over again. Hopefully, one day, I will get her inside so that they can sleep together and then she will know true bliss.

When I am forced to go out into the working world - without which we would be kibble-less – I find extraordinary patience with humans, I have gleaned from all of my quiet alone time, so that I can do my work and then I rush home again after work to be again smothered by the simple love of the animals and their needs. They are not proud or vain, greedy or self-oriented. They love me much more than they love themselves. I listen to them breathe and talk in their special way to me and each other. I tell them to be nice to one another when one or other gets a little huffy and they seem to understand me. I hug the ones I am able to and reach out to the one I am not. One day she will let me hug her; I'm sure of that. I talk to the cats and do the same with them. Some of them are not especially fond of humans either and watch me from a wary distance while, all the time, knowing that I will be back later with more food and loves and knowing they should trust me more than they do.

This morning a tiny baby hummingbird hung on the feeder for a long drink of nectar, her paper wings flapping like crazy. I stopped in my tracks and held my breath, lest she be startled by any movement at all. I was entranced by her dance and happy to give up a few seconds from my day to indulge in her magic. And I think these small steps back to the natural world have to be good for us multi-tasking humans. We are such complex creatures, living in an accelerating and complicated world of immediacy that has many spiraling out of control. I plan on taking the country road, as much as possible at this stage in my life - the slow lane, the pathway through the woods and avoid, where I can, the freeways of the universe, where the noise and bustle is not a good noise and many, many people are getting hurt.

Everything is so fast these days. I'm sounding like

an old person longing for the good old days. But I watch people literally speeding on the freeway, as if they were on their way to a fire. Some are tail-gating, texting, applying make-up – they have no regard for their lives or the lives of others. Accidents are frequent nowadays and often tragic. Our expectancies are that everything be quick and gratifying. Why cook a nice meal if you can just grab a quick sandwich in the drive-through and eat it on the way back to work? Why slow down a bit and enjoy the mountains, if you can spend an extra five minutes on Facebook before leaving for work and then not see the mountains or the morning at all. We are all late, we are all rushing, many of us are discontented or addicted and it is a horrible vision of mankind in my eyes – this rushing, gobbling, racing spiral of madness that seems to be too much of the modern world we live in.

We cannot change the world nor the progress of technology; nor people's will to stay in the fast lane and live as close to the edge as possible. We can change the way we maneuver our own personal way through the world. We can aim to leave it a kinder, softer place than when we came in. Our footprints should be only quiet ones full of love. We should care for the helpless and love the needy. Take care of the animals and those not able to care for themselves. Help the elderly, be kind to the scarred and do no damage where at all possible. I have learned many of my footprints in recent years through my life with the animals. I would recommend this pathway to anyone looking for a less brutal lifestyle and a stepping stone off the ladder to insanity.

Published August 2017

Always Look On the Bright Side

The older we get, the more my old friends and I – all ladies of a certain age in our 50's, (the new 40's I'll have you know) … - try to seize the day, 'carpe diem', do things we would never have dreamed of being achievable in our 20's or even 30's, when we were quite ambitious babes, out there and ready to set the world on fire – in one way or another. For myself, I used to be a very 'Type A' person - in my working life at least. I took my work far too seriously. I could have been one of those folks on whose tombstone would be written 'She Worked Very Hard' …..but that is no longer the case!

Thankfully for me and all in my circle, I'd say; after my illness I returned to the real art of living and, with a new lease on life, learned how to do it right the second time around – sometimes to the point these days that I exhaust even myself.

"I need to have things to look forward to," I bemoaned to the pair of them, both friends for nearly 40 years now. "I need to book a stay in my place by the sea…" For those of you, thinking that this might be a weekend trip to Marina, or even a quick sojourn down to Shell Beach, no I was talking about my place by the sea where I was born, the East Coast of England. No sooner had I bemoaned my present lack of reasons to be cheerful, than our resident travel agent had researched the available houses online and picked a few out for review. "Do we want the cheaper one in the back streets?" Of course we don't. "Do we need a sea view and a sea wall to sit on right in front of our palace with the sea view? Of course we do. And so the seaside mansion has been booked and I have happy, gleaming thoughts ahead of me to guide me through any pitfalls of life in the coming months. You might say that I have dragged my friends with me into this new art of real living, since they have little choice these days, when I get the bit between my teeth ... and, truth be told, I know they love it as much as I do.

Nowadays I wrap my work around my life in a much more healthy way than before. Naturally the portability of a self-employed person these days means that I can write a real estate contract from my 12th floor bedroom in the hotel on Union Square, or deal with tricky end of contract issues, as I'm headed South on the freeway to spend a night somewhere else. I don't actually have to be in my office to do my work and I am so grateful for that, being more of a gypsy than a 9-5er.

One of my old friends was flying over to stay. We always start her visit with a few nights in San Fran, as we have done for years. We do a little shopping, eat some nice food, visit galleries, make tea and catch up. It's always a blissful time. As we strolled down from Union Square to Market in the lovely winter sunshine, we heard loud and cheerful reggae music blasting through the streets. We looked around for the street band, or the record store pounding out the flavor of the day. "Wait, it's coming from the wheel chair!" She proceeded to laugh out loud! Across the street, an elderly, wizened white man in a wheel chair was zooming down the street, blasting out his music and rocking out in his chair as he whizzed along. We burst out laughing and ran after him, videoing this beautiful slice of life before us. "Always make lemonade from the lemons!" she said. "Always look on the bright side," I say. It was the most delightful encounter that will stay with us for those rainy days when we forget both of those positive attitudes towards life.

And then came. "How about we only stay 2 nights this time instead of the 3?" She broached a shortening of our City trip. Hmmm. If she was really considering cutting short her coveted stay at our hotel, then she really must be a bit short of cash; and she would never let me cover the additional last night, so I reluctantly agreed to slash our stay from 3 nights to two. The day we were leaving, the weather was foul. Chilly, wet, dank grey. It would have been the perfect day to snuggle up in our hotel room with steaming cups of tea, cookies and the daily papers. But we didn't heed Mother Nature's warning signals and we took off through the storm anyway, taking 6 hours to get home from our white-knuckle adventure, via the San Jose airport, for some reason, on the random search for a gas station.

"Maybe we should spend my last night in San Fran," she suggested, after we were home and recovered. "It is such an awful drive and all ... Should we try and find a cheaper hotel this time?" I smiled to myself, knowing that, if we were to spend another night up in the Bay, we were not going to try and find a cheaper hotel. We were going to seize the day, stay at the place we loved and make up for the 3rd night we should never have given up in the first place.

The wheelchair-reggae-rock star came back around, almost bowled us over in his chair and reminded us that life is super brief. We need to always make lemonade out of our lemons in enormous jugs that brim over the top and spill to the floor. We need to always look on the bright side of our trials and tribulations and monies we might need for night number three. And we need to do that for as long as we can.

Published January 2018

Bacon is a Beast

It's not easy attempting to trim down in this world. For my generation, not only do you have the fat-holding tendencies of The Menopause to deal with; but temptation is lurking around every corner you find yourself. "Do you want to have lunch? How do Cheesy Enchiladas sound to you? Extra sour cream and guacamole?" "Shall I bring the dessert?" "Do you have enough wine?" And so the challenges go on. Dieting is a planet full of minefields.

I am officially old. My doctor suggested that I work towards lessening my cholesterol – the bad kind – getting the blood pressure down and shifting a few pounds of unnecessary weight i.e fat baggage, that I had allowed to accumulate over the years. (I still don't know where this belly fat came from. Such an insulting and unexpected guest that showed up to the party.) Slimming down the 30 pounds or so that I really need would take a village to accomplish – I knew this and I made it very clear to my room mates – the husband and mother-in-law.

"I'm starting the 5:2 again," I announce to Husband, also the Chef in the house. (The 5:2 being a program I had great success with in the past. You highly restrict the calories for 2 days to 500 a day and then eat carefully, but normally, the other 5.) In the past, I shifted a lot of weight this way. I wouldn't say that my metabolism started, at that point, processing like an Olympian, hope though I might; but I certainly moved some fat this way in a pretty painless fashion. I cannot 'do' regular diets like some can - the bars, the shakes, the tedium that just make me crave a cheeseburger and fries like no other thing. Plus they are super boring. The 5:2 is not a normal thing, so it is not boring — plus there are no expenditures required and no serious planning — just a family that works together towards the same end — a healthier, more vibrant human being.

"Want some bacon?" he asks, as I almost fall over the threshold to the kitchen in, what we will just call, a *baconic* swoon. Of all the smells in the world, bacon is the most convincing and the most evil. Think you are turning vegetarian? Smell some bacon sizzling in the pan! Want to try and make today a diet day of fruits and veggies only? Get the bacon going! (How do you like it, crispy or not?) Want to try and attempt to make today a 5:2 day? Oh just have husband throw those sizzling rashers in the frying pan and you tell him that today you are just having fruit and soup and he can just enjoy his bacon all by himself. You don't need it and you don't want it. Except that is not what happened. "HOW DARE YOU SABOTAGE ME AND MY DIET BY MAKING BACON? YOU KNOW I AM TRYING TO SLIM DOWN, THAT TODAY IS A 5:2 DAY AND HERE YOU ARE BREAKING ALL OF MY PLANS AND RESOLUTIONS BY MAKING BACON?" Yes, you would have thought he had committed some heinous crime in his culinary skills and efforts to put some weight on his mother. How dare he? I flew out of the door in a massive fury. I would not eat bacon, I would not allow my plan to be sabotaged by that most pervasive and enticing scent.

Move day forward to an evening meeting – another 5:2 day plan. I would drink only decaf coffee. No matter what anyone else ordered – whether it be super nachos or bacon-cheeseburgers – I would stay on track with my decaf coffee and I would not digress. There would be some delicious chicken soup waiting at home for my saintly self. I doubted I could manage this extreme test of my will. Around me, others order Super Nachos and Fried Chicken Salad, burgers and the like. "Just Decaf," I hear the voice of the Queen of Fat BootCamp say to the waitress. "Nothing else?" She replies, "Just the coffee?" Oh I came close, I came so close to slamming into my Diet Will with a bacon cheeseburger, but no. I just sipped quietly on the decaf and focused on my meeting. That was a rare thing. I think I told most of my friends and anyone who would listen about my huge accomplishment against the beast of bacon and other evil choices.

And then it was back to Sunday, the official bacon day in our house. Husband peeks around the corner. "Is today a 5:2 day, darling?" He enquires meekly. "No, Sunday is never a 5:2 day, dear!" I respond and he beams widely as he heartily puts the bacon on to cook. Oh how we enjoyed that bacon together! I can still hear Oprah calling out to the diet world congregation that anyone who ate real bacon was kidding themselves, but how can you not? Life is only so long and I'm hoping that, a bacon binge once a week, will not throw my whole diet and cholesterol and blood pressure reduction plan down the tubes. Let's face it, we don't all get the same allotment of bacon opportunities and, if I live another 20 years, that will be only be another 1000 times or so that I am able to sit down with bacon and feel the love. I don't think that's too much to ask. Baconholics unite! What else can we do?

Published 2019

Bricks for Feet

"Looks like you have bunions," middle sister said helpfully, as she peered down at the swelling plates on the end of my legs. "You mean that nasty big-toe attitude that is headed the wrong way away from the foot. That is a bunion?" I respond. "I thought a bunion was like a corn." Sister looked down at the brick-like mess at the bottom of my legs and shook her head. "No, those are some bad bunions and you had better get them seen to. They are not going to get better on their own." Come to find out, middle-sister had been frequenting a foot doc for some decades and counting, and was way ahead of me in her foot recovery measures. "It's genetic, you know," she added, helpfully. She had caught them before they were way out of control. Of course, I had missed that memo.

I spent the rest of the summer happily sporting my splayed-out bricks in a pair of nicely-cushioned flip-flops. I convinced myself I didn't need to visit with a foot doctor; I just needed larger shoes. And so, I bought the larger shoes - also stole some from my daughter - and imagined all was well in my world with my larger foot size – width and length ways, resembling a brick. Band-aids became my friends, a part of my weekly shopping list.

I would gaze wistfully at the stunning Manolo-lookalikes

in my shoe closet with their elegant heel and foot-slimming stylishness. I'd touch my divine winter boots with the tassles and the clunky heels, the willowy summer sandals and all. As a shoe-holic, I started to be very afraid for my foot future. But I was just going to power through it, as you do when you're not ready for the unadulterated truth quite yet.

However, the water aerobic exercise that I enjoy so much during the summer wasn't working so well for me either. Every time my feet would pound on the bottom of the swimming pool, a pain would issue through the soles, so I stopped that. My feet were, strangely, super sensitive. I stopped wearing my pretty summer sandals also; they hurt. It was either flip flops or wide trainers or extra-large cowboy boots – there was my choice. I was headed into foot hell, which, for a former shoe-holic, is a pretty dark place to be. How on earth was I going to live out the rest of my days – in a pair of slippers?

I made my first appointment in my whole life with the podiatrist. "What seems to be the problem?" he asked cheerfully, grabbing a hold of the swollen meat on the side of my foot. "Oh yes, bunions! You are about 3 years late." "What?" He went on to explain that, right around 50, all the ladies come in with problem bunions after a lifetime of lousy foot-wear. And I was no exception. We all kept him in the manner to which he had become accustomed. "You're welcome," I said, cheerily. I expected that he would counsel me a little on wearing better shoes, give me a nicely efficient foot emery board and some yummy cream for the scaly parts and send me on my merry way to work on my bunions. But no. Apparently, it's not that easy in the bunion world.

"Surgery is the best fix," he tells me. "We straighten out the wayward big toe and encourage it to get in line where it was before. If you need both feet fixed – as you naturally do – it is a 2-3-month recovery per foot," 2-3 months per foot? Who has that kind of time? I was crushed. It was also about $4000 per foot, so about as reasonable as the 2-3-month recovery time, which obviously wasn't going to happen this side of retirement.

As I caressed my bunions with foot cream that night and vowed to baby those ugly lumps until I could fix them, I realized that I had spent my whole life unwittingly cramming these precious parts of my body into the most beautiful of shoes and now I was paying the price. As in most parts of life, there is a price to pay. For a shoe addict, the price was going to be huge.

I broke the news to my friend – also a shoe-holic, that there would be no more tustling with whether to buy 8 or 9 pairs of inappropriate delights in the shoe aisles at Ross or DSW. I was going to have to reform my former ways, No, our shoe lives would have to stay in more the extra-wide Birkenstock aisle, than the 4 inch sexy babies we had sported in yester-year. But I wasn't going to cry about my bunions, no not me. I was going to slide these puppies into my extra wide fur boots and go about my business. I have also ordered a rather fetching set of bunion massagers that may be fodder for another funny story. In short, the longer we live, the more the parts of our bodies are going to get a bit worn down, or in my case splayed out. My parts started deteriorating years ago and I was just too busy to notice. Bad, bad girl. Bad, bad bunions. Now I have arrived at the point of no return and surgery is my only option; I shall just have to pay more attention, as I should have been doing all these years, and touch only the beautiful shoes that now belong on the feet of the beautiful people – something I thought I once was. Well, my feet at least.

Published December 2016

The Bucket Bruise

It seemed innocent enough – the bruise on my side. It even kind of matched the other plentiful ranch bruises I could identify all over my body, which were caused by throwing my heavy saddle onto my horse's back, pushing my wheelbarrow – Lola - with one hand and dragging a heavy water hose in the other hand, carrying weighty buckets of orchard hay against my body, chasing after dogs, lifting up cats, picking up heavy feed box lids, tustling with goats and llamas. You name it. There was a whole myriad of reasons why I should have a blue, yellow, green and purple bruise on my side. But then along came the accompanying lump.

For anyone who has had cancer in their lives, when 'The Lump' shows up, that is when you get more than a little nervous in your present day life and your plates start shifting. It's the time when you regress in your mental progression towards a happy, healthy life cancer-free and immediately start putting yourself back in the oncologist's office and prepping yourself for the chemo lab with all of her various gifts. In my case, I stopped sleeping as well and started stressing about what I imagined to be my lot in the coming days.

Many of my cancer friends had already been

re-diagnosed. There is something about the 3 year mark that clangs a bell and the little scratchy pests come out of the woodwork and back into your life, I've noticed. Did I have to prepare myself for that all over again; because, if I did, I did not want it to be the enormous shocker that it was the first time around! I wanted to be Miss Prepared with my suitcase already packed for surgery and my bed on the 5th floor at Salinas Valley Memorial already pre-booked with my name on it. Thank goodness my husband had just got his ASHI home inspection certification to add another string to his bow, in case I am out for the count for a few months again and unable to contribute to our household's needs! Here I was already planning our household budget and how stretched it might get all over again. Your brain can go to kingdom come and back, when you locate 'The Lump' and it doesn't seem to be going anywhere anytime soon.

"Stop poking at it," the husband told me. "You are going to make it more swollen!" "Just go to the stupid doctor!" my wise baby sister told me with her 'been there done that' tone. "The onc will at least be able to stop the wondering." I told myself not to even go there with the lump until the day before my visit with the oncologist. I left it alone to its own devices; I did not go near it or even give it the mildest of pushes or prods. The day before my appointment I willed it to be gone, I wished it to be gone; but, lo and behold, it was not. It was the same; the bruise around it had just lessened.

In the recesses of my blurry memory, I do remember

my oncologist telling me, circa three years ago, that a side gift from the particular potion of chemotherapy that I had just undergone could, occasionally, very occasionally, be a reoccurrence in the form of leukemia. "And how would that manifest itself?" I recall enquiring, Miss Curiosity all of a sudden. "Quite often it can show itself through the skin," he replied. "In ways that you might not imagine!" I may be dreaming up this whole conversation in the 'See Nightmare' room within my memory vault, courtesy of extremely strong drugs that I was probably taking at the time of this dialogue, but, in any case, this snippet from the past stayed with me as I examined my weird area of purple, blue, yellow and green blush with a prominent lump beneath the skin. "In ways that you might not imagine!" His words came back to me, echoing in the mind of the hypochondriac I had obviously become.

"I have leukemia!" I self-diagnosed, recalling my buddy Rudy in the chemo lab who was being treated for leukemia with a hefty dose of arsenic – I kid you not - while I was being infused with my own personal potion.

Since my kid was in her first week of her CNA training and, surely, on her way to becoming one of the Central Coast's most qualified nurses, I figured she might be of some medical help here and together we perused her sizeable anatomical text books. "Mum, there are no organs underneath where your lump is," she concluded, almost, borderline making a medical diagnosis. "It's probably just a bruise." Yes, a bruise. It's probably just a bruise. We went with that for the time being.

All the edges were smoothed over by the Super-Xanax dose I took the morning I went to see my oncologist through a door which would not, ever, pass by the chemo lab and throw me into panic attack mode. "Hmmm," said my oncologist as he prodded my still-present lump on my side. "I do not think this is anything to be worried about. But come back in a week and we will see if you need to go and have an ultrasound." Oh no, not the waiting game again. Can't you just stick a needle in the darned thing and tell me what is going on? I will have to book for the ultrasound, show up for the ultrasound, wait for the results of the ultrasound and then, most likely, go through the exact same list of agonies for the biopsy that would, inevitably ensue? Aaah, don't know if I can go through all of that again.

The week later came and I had the stomach flu. No one believed me. "Running away from it, sis, is not going to make it go away!" my baby sis was not having a bit of it. "You didn't go?" Another friend persisted. "When is the rescheduled appointment?" All of a sudden, all of them had me back in the 'C' circle, back in the chemo chair and back in the world where I never wanted to be in the first place. "I'll go, people, chill, I'll go," I told them all and especially myself.

In the meantime, I wondered if the way I carried the heavy buckets of orchard hay on my hip up and down hills twice a day to Llama-Land might, possibly, have had any bearing on this sudden lump situation that was causing all of us so much grief. Could it be? Ever the self-diagnoser,

I switched my feed bucket from my right side to my left side and kept on schlepping up and down dem hills. Sure enough, an evil bruise started growing and breeding on that side of my body in all its Technicolor glory. Aha, we had found the culprit, the source of the bruising and the head aches. It was a bucket bruise, a small testimonial to a ranch girl just doing her chores like ranch girls do; but then forcing her to remember that she was a cancer survivor all over again and putting her through her paces. Some places you will just go back to again, without ever wanting to.

In the meantime, I will keep my onc. appointment in the coming days so that he can also tell me that my areas of concern were just bucket bruises. His office must be full of mental cases like myself, forever self-diagnosing themselves and already pre-seating themselves in his chemo lab without a cancer cell in sight.

Published 2018

Changing the Lens

My sister was a brave soul. She had Lasik surgery before it was really even a thing. She had it when she was less than 40 and the surgery was performed in Turkey. Even braver than you think. Just before she died, her eyes were starting to need a little something to see her through the day – lol - but that wasn't a bad run of it – 8 years – without having to deal with eye issues, glasses, contacts …. I don't have that kind of courage. I looked into it and the whole lack of proper anesthesia creeped me out so much that I could investigate no more. When you are a real wimp like me, it takes serious drugs to even get you to the dentist. I digress.

To be truthful, I don't mind my glasses – 'face furniture', as I call them. If you have more than one pair, you can use them like accessories to go with your shoes, boots, outfit in general. Today is a Ralph Lauren day, today I've got my tiger blacks on – it had better be Toni Burch … and then there's my daily drivers – the Ray Bans and so on. It can get a little pricey, if you like all the name brands, but mostly I've got used to the fact that my eyesight is not good these days and I can't pretend it is. I see souls wandering around the world outside with spex on their heads, peering at the prices in the grocery store, forgetting their glasses are on their heads … and then, realizing, it's the wrong pair and they have to go digging for the other ones. "Oh, these are my driving glasses, these are for reading and these ... well I can't remember!' No, I can't be doing with all of that stuff; life is chaotic enough.

My friend in England tells me she is going to get contact lenses. "Oh yes, my other sister has worn those for years!" I respond, encouragingly. Her husband had cruised through the training and enactment of contact lens insertion and now it was her turn. How hard could it be? "I failed it," she told me with some attitude after her 1st attempt. She and I usually fail things the first time – driving test, math class and so on. It is only fitting that we also fail the contact lens class together, but I couldn't imagine how difficult it might be. Now there's a thought, lightbulb goes on. I will get contacts too, so that, once in a while, when I'm trying to be a bit babe-alicious, I could just pop in the contacts, smile at my babe reflection in the mirror with slightly better makeup than usual and zoom off, no face furniture required. How marvelous it would be to be able to put my make up on and see what I'm doing, without just relying on memory and not in a good way!

I make the appointment and off I go. First of all, they make you watch a video. Ok, got that. Then the young thing comes in and shows me the basic prep of how to get tiny slippery, almost invisible bits of jelly out of a container, onto the end of your finger and then perfectly position them onto the eyeball. Oh dear me. I dropped the invisible jelly, then I tore it, then I turned it upside down and then, my crowning glory, I lost it in my eye. Young thing sighed deeply. "Oh well, I can see you won't be going home with contact lenses today; let me go and get the doctor ..." I had failed the class. If my eyes had not been already burning from the floating piece of prickly jelly lost in St Elsewhere, I would have had a good cry. The nice doctor came in and extracted the piece of jelly from my now streaming eyes and told me that 'contacting' is not as easy as it looks. "Well, no kidding, Einstein!" I almost called my friend, who had also failed the class, for commiseration. But, it would have been the middle of the night her time and she would not have appreciated it; even though misery does like a companion.

I nearly didn't go back to the optician for my second class; but it was a different person this time, so I thought what the heck. This one was patient and thoughtful, unlike the Young Thing from before. He seemed to acknowledge that old dogs can take a while to learn new tricks. We tried and we tried again. Then, I did it, I really did it. I was so proud of myself. Right and left eye. Took a while, but I could honestly see a little modicum of technique emerging from all the floundering and dropping and sighing.

I try again at home when I am getting ready to go to go out and do an open house. Not. One breaks, the other falls down the sink. My eyes are getting red and streamy again. You can't get upset with these darn annoying things either, because they seem to just disappear, evaporate into thin air, as if they never existed in the first place. I talk to another friend of mine. I tell her I failed Contact Lens School. "Me too!" she exclaimed in sheer delight. We were now a class of 3. Oh we were so happy we had had that conversation. The Class of 2019 in Contact Lensing. We were 0 for 3.

Will I go back to school, will I lean in for a Contact Lens Class Part 3 and put myself through the demoralization of failure once more, or will I just clean up my designer glasses and accept that sometimes you cannot teach an old dog new tricks and this dog needs to just suck it up and keep wearing her glasses, as she has been for years. I mean, what is the alternative, Lasik surgery? Oh heck, I could not imagine going to that class. The jury, on contact lensing, is still out.

Published 2019

Everyone needs at least one animal

For many of us – animals have been an important part of our therapy throughout our lives. They have shared joy, given delight and laughter and dried many a tear in their determination to be everything to you, their human. (Unless your main animal is a cat, however. They are more self-absorbed and make it all about them.) I love the animals' honesty and simplicity of sorts – their extreme loyalty and lack of judgement, their pure hearts. In my world, a house is not a home without being surrounded by various kinds of animals – and I know I shall be forever around them.

They are my sanctuary and my happy place. I feel calm and capable around them. When I was ill and the axels of my life turned inside out, it was the animals that brought me back around to living without fear or desperation. From cats and kittens to goats, dogs, turtles, birds, llamas and my magical horse called Winston .... they gave me back my quality of life in a sense; but in a, strangely, much richer way than before. Not only did I still have animals in my life, I went on to rescue animals and help them onto better lives, as they had assisted me back on the pathway to mine. My love became a quest and grew from there into a mission that I shall likely never quit. It is a circle of gratitude I'm still trying to understand. There is all measure of examples where animals heal – from the parrots at Serenity Park to the dogs of SCAR. It has been proven time and time again that animals can help fix humans and vice versa.

Our animal rescue became recently involved in the possibility of a very special dog training program and, from there, we were asked about K9 therapy dogs and whether we could provide them. We decided that this was a service we needed to accommodate. The patients in question had, previously, enjoyed the benefit of a therapy dog who had died and morale and behavior had significantly declined from thereon. For one reason or another, they had never been able to get another one. Now we were going to be able to bring a dog or two back into their lives, we were very curious about how we would be received. "Oh, I remember Winston, the therapy dog. He died though." "I haven't petted a dog since Winston died. Will you come every week? Will you come back? I miss Winston." These patients of the hard knocks in life talked about their old therapy dog Winston, as they cradled my dog Tucker's head in their hands and I didn't worry for his safety – they were so gentle with him and grateful for his presence. Some wrapped their arms around his neck, some just smiled and watched his every move, took his paw, scratched his belly. All responded to him in a positive way, even if they didn't wish to engage with him this particular time. One patient told me ... "Next time, I will talk to him. Next time." And I saw that as progress.

"What's his name, how old is he? Will you come back next week?" They asked over and over. "Thank you for bringing him, thank you for taking time out of your week to bring him to us. Can I pet him again? I wish he could stay here with us." Tucker, my big old rescue Border Collie-McNab, had never had so much attention, not even when he visited the rehab center for the elderly and that was quite the captive audience. Everyone here wanted to feel him, touch him, give him a treat – he lit up each pod that he visited and his body swayed with positive feeling and pride as he, as I told him, went 'to work'.

"I haven't petted a dog in 13 years". "I haven't seen a dog in 18 years." "I haven't touched a dog in 24 years…." Whatever their problems and their issues with the outside world, they all seemed to remember the last time they had done such a simple thing as touch a dog, the last time they had felt the warmth of an animal's body, seen the happy wag of the tail and the big, unjudging smile on the dog's face. "He's so happy," said one patient, stroking Tucker's head and giving him a small piece of jerky. "Yes, he is happy to see you," I replied. "Happy to see me? No one is happy to see me," the patient remarked, eyes cast downwards. "Well Tucker is. He loves everyone," I said and I witnessed a glimmer of a smile in return.

There were some valuable dialogues I soaked in that day, as we made our rounds with some of the scarred of society and watched how an animal can transform a day, lift a mood and give someone a bit of happiness and hope of an afternoon, necessary components of the human condition. "I like petting him," this was a younger patient. "I've been going through a lot recently and he helps me feel calm." I felt almost euphoric.

As we left the patients for the day and returned to our regular lives, I was left with many voices in my head, a certain amount of aching in my heart, but also a sense of joy that my Tucker had lifted some spirits today and would be doing so indefinitely, every week, as long as he was invited to go visit. Everyone needs an animal in their lives – I am even more convinced of that than I was before. To see the desperate and the downtrodden respond in such a warm and loving way to my big old rescue dog gave my soul an indescribable feeling of peace. Sometimes, it is along the darker corridors, that the purpose of your journey becomes clear.

The Animals Teach Us Everything & Other Short Tails

Published 2018

Fences & Feelings

Like most married couples – if the truth were known – everyone has to work at the healthiness of their union and, in our house, we are no exception. Often times we can literally pass like ships in the night, or not even then really, if we are honest. Truthfully, we can skip several days without a proper conversation or a peck on the lips in greeting. Like a lot of people, life is full-to-the-brim hectic and we don't have time to check in that much with one another. We know we are good, we think we are good. We are good, aren't we?

But, in the back of my mind, I will always remember my father telling me, "Marriage is like a plant. Pull it up by the roots and see how quickly it dies." I can see that same analogy applying to a plant that you leave in the corner and forget to water. For sure, you will have the same result. So I try to make sure that doesn't happen to our union; that we check in with each other once in a while, even if it's only a car ride to go somewhere, a quick breakfast chat across the table from one another, whilst en route to someplace else, or a conversation sans electronic interference in the form of television, mobile phones and so on. In my opinion, this 'sound check' is vital to the flowing life artery of a thriving family.

So it was our day to check in. We had a bunch of errands to run during the day, culminating in the reading of a chapter of my book at the 'Central Coast Writer's Club' at the end of the afternoon. I don't expect anyone I know to sit through a reading of my book, least of all my family who has, truthfully, suffered through more book signings than they would care to attend; but if they want to go along, I'm not going to forbid it. And he said he wanted to go. We might even sell a book or two along the way, I thought in positive mode.

The morning started off swimmingly - only about 30

minutes off our proposed schedule – so good for a sort-of day off. We had been discussing, recently, the plan for the next portion of fence building on our property. It is a piece of land we have owned for about 10 years now, but somehow, have never had the extra money to be able to properly fence; so we can only pass over, through or on with caution, making sure our pack of dogs don't get a rabbit scent or the trail of a coyote and flee at break neck speed across Metz Road and in front of who knows what might be driving along it. Consequently, ours is a parcel that I covet, not only because it is spacious and beautiful with exquisite river peeks and breathtaking views of the patchwork quilt of the Salinas Valley below, but also because my horse and I love to trail up and down the hills and valleys of the land enjoying the freedom and the view, until, that is, one or other of my motley canine crew decide to pad too close to the road and then it becomes a stress fest and not relaxing at all. Hence the fence plan and what we are doing to fix all of this! We have been working on this fence plan with renewed zest recently, hoping to be able to complete phase two over the course of the winter.

"It's nice we have this time together," husband noted as we cruised off down the hill together on our quasi date-day. "We can spend time talking about our Fxxxxx". He caught me off guard. "Our feelings?" I responded with astonishment. I'm sure that was what I heard. "Feelings?" he laughs. "No, silly, our fencing!" And we both roared with laughter, as we had yet another 'Men are from Mars, Women just hear what they want to hear' moment. But it made for a ripe and humorous start to a lovely day and gave me food for thought. If we can miss each other's meaning or intention so completely and succinctly and we are actually sitting side-by-side, how rife would it be if we were to miss said thing not side by side or in close physical proximity? I'm thinking that this happens all the time in human relationships.

My friend tells me that she and her husband are divorcing after being together for over 20 years. "Can I ask what happened?" I have to ask, I just can't believe it. They had always seemed so much pieces of the same puzzle, when the rest of us were falling apart. "We just stopped communicating," she responded, "and it was a swift downhill run from there." And there I had it. You have to keep trying to stop the ship-in-the night scenario from crashing into port and make time for a significant connection with your significant other, while you still have the opportunity. We make time to go to work, don't we? We make time to get our hair and nails done and to take Ziggy to the vet? We find time to take our children to their activities and their school? Why don't we make more time for our marriage? For sure, this particular aspect of the busy homestead gets taken for granted. After a certain period of time, the honeymoon blush has faded to a daily routine, which, without wake ups and reminders, can quickly cascade into a 'blah blah' existence of bills and obligations and nothing fun if you are not careful. Note to self and the married world at large: you have to continue to make it fun. You have to laugh together and connect in meaningful ways in order for your plant to continue to grow. Otherwise, as my father duly noted many moons ago, it will die and it will most likely be gone for always.

Whether you talk to your spouse about fences, or you talk about feelings; it really doesn't matter; just talk. That will be the beginning the middle and the other part of your healthy relationship that has a chance of blooming and blossoming, well after the blessed fence is built. As long as you are communicating, there is a substantial hope and expectation that your union will not become just another statistic, but a standard for your children to follow and your friends to admire.

Published 2017

Finding her legs

We were all glad, in the animal rescue world, when the law changed about being allowed to chain up a dog. To the civilized animal lover, that was an inconceivable thought in any case; but in backyards the world over this cruel practice has been witnessed over and over, as if it were a normal, everyday practice. No more in my backyard, at least.

We got the call that a large German Shepherd was chained up in the yard. Her owners had been warned by animal control that that was an illegal practice. The individual confessed that he would have just put her out on the street and let her go, but that she was micro-chipped and would have been picked up and linked to him. It was going to be $200 to release the dog to animal control and he didn't want to pay. South County Animal Rescue came along in the form of Champion Maria, who gave him food for the starving girl whose ribs were protruding in an ugly painful way. These were not poor people. She was only young, yet downtrodden from her life of neglect. I agreed to bring her home to Solace, since it's very hard to find fosters for any dogs, let alone a large young Shepherd.

Fortunately for her former owner, I took my peace-loving husband along with me to pick her up. "What's her name?" I asked the man. He had to look at the vet paper to be able to remember. That hurt my heart. "She's hungry," I told him in my best Spanish, as I poured her out some food. "She has no water…" I wanted to deck him to the ground so badly at that particular moment, as I looked at the empty food dish and the small amount of dirty water in the bottom of a bucket. "WHAT IS WRONG WITH SOME PEOPLE?" I could feel tears burning at the back of my eyes. Her collar was bolted on – you could barely get a finger underneath it – and that hurt my heart too. We managed to get her in the truck, without her even giving a backwards blink to the man who didn't know her name. She stretched out in relaxed fashion between the front seats and looked around her, as if to say. "Whoa, I didn't know there was all this fascinating world out there beyond my chain!"

She ate and drank like a Queen that first night in Puppyland, after we had cut off her bolted collar and let her walk around, such as she had never been able to do from the end of her short chain. The next day I introduced her to my pack and witnessed her try to stretch out her legs and run with the other dogs. It was as if her back legs didn't really work properly at first; but soon she got in her stride – if a bit dorkily – and thundered up and down the hills, leading by the front paws and near dragging the hind legs. This time I had good tears, as I watched her frolic with a pack like a normal, if a bit disabled, dog and try to assert herself as top dog, as only a young shepherd might endeavor to do.

We called her Maria, after Maria our animal rescuer, who took the time to do a well-check and ensure that a swift rescue was made. She has a way to go, our canine Maria, in that she needs to learn her manners and not be quite such a bull in a china shop; but she remains amazingly unscathed from her former grim-filled life and just exerts joy and love with every bounce. If anything, she doesn't want the humans to leave her – ever – and tried to leave out of the gate with us every time. But she gets lots of walks these days and plenty of good quality food and water. Having been deprived of water so entirely before she came here, she is a water-seeker and loves to have lots of buckets to splash in and her own personal paddling pool to play around in. She is an absolute water hog, wherever she goes, and it is a delight to behold.

Animal rescue has days when you think you can't do it anymore; but watching Maria find her legs and be able to run up and down the hills has given me a happy heart that cannot be measured.

P.S. In time, Maria's forever family found her and she is now living the happy life she serves in King City.

Published October 2017

Happy Birthday, my Beautiful Border Collie

Social media works wonderfully for dogs, I've noticed. Whether it is the posting of a lost or found dog, or the need to immediately launch a rescue effort because of a pressing need and a ticking clock at a local pound, dogs and their cute furry faces do very well in the new social media world we have at our fingertips. And my dogs and my life are no exception.

I first saw her with bowed head and sunken rear – the classic abused pose in a canine – photographed inside a metal cage. Her chocolate brown eyes were so sad. "FOUND ON THE MEDIAN OF ELKHORN BOULEVARD," the posting read, that someone from the Prunedale area had shared – another super feature of social media. "ANYONE MISSING A BEAUTIFUL FEMALE BORDER COLLIE?" I held my breath. I wasn't missing one exactly, but I would certainly like to have one again in my life. The border collie Allie, who had stolen my heart and who lived with me for about 2 or 3 years, had been rightfully returned to her original owner some time ago, when the boyfriend-in-question split up with my daughter, left his dog in my custody and then approached me years later and told me he couldn't live without her. (The dog, not my daughter!) After a failed foster-share effort, I then proceeded to give her back to her rightful owner, as you would in the cosmic scheme of things. I shed many a tear over that most amazing of amazing border collies. So, a few years down the road, my heart remained a little sore and bruised from that loss. Was I missing a border collie? Perhaps I was.

I approached the stranger who had posted the dog – again, another lovely feature of social media – I was easily able to contact her. I told her who I was and that I would be most interested in rescuing the border collie, if her owner didn't show up. She had already done her hold time and no one had showed for her. I kept sneaking back to the page where the pup was posted and looking deeply into her beautiful brown eyes. I did not believe her owner would ever come for her – I believed she had been dumped on the Boulevard and had a lot of stress-ridden stories to tell from her journey out there in the mean, dark wilderness.

And then I got busy with life, as I was preparing for a trip, and didn't sneak so many peeks at her photo. The morning I am leaving, the lady contacts me. "We can no longer keep the border collie. We have 3 of our own and my husband is getting way too attached!" Oh my; I could hardly stand myself. I wished I were not leaving that day, so that I would have time to situate the pup and her new family members, but the lady was adamant. The dog needed to leave today. En route to the air bus, my husband agreed to make the stop to pick her up – doggie angel that he is – and soon she was in our care. She was safe, out of the road, not having to fend for herself anymore, nor being put into the cold pound situation. She was going to be able to recover at Solace and then we would see what would be next. Deep down, I knew that she would be staying with us, but I needed to see how the blend went with the rest of the pack. Besides, husband doesn't always need to know the full story right away. It's mostly better if he is allowed to fall in love first.

The love part took a little while. "Great, just great!" he texted me as I am prepping to fly away to foreign lands. "She puked all over the truck, escaped over the 5 ft. fence and then tore up the garage and garage door."

"Oh dear," I respond meekly. "Thank you, dear. Thank you so much! Love you!" But, by the time I got home, she had her feet firmly under the table, so to speak. She was sleeping in the house, sitting on his lap in his chair and the pair of them were completely in love. He had even named her; always a good sign. And then I allowed myself to also fall deeply in love with this super smart young lady. She had obviously been through the wars – it looked as if she had been thrown out of a truck by the old injuries she had sustained on her legs. She was full of worms and parasites from eating dirt and drinking polluted water. She was pregnant and starved. She had many, many health issues – come to find out – that took her a long time to come back from. But she was amazing. 7 healthy puppies later, a nasty case of mastitis and consequent surgery, deep worming and parasite treatments, plus, later, a spay, and she has gone from strength to strength. She adores all of us – but me especially these days. She loves balls even more than anything else in the world, and she is always exhilarated by the challenge of the chase up and down hills and up and down again. Her agility is something to behold. When she lays down next to my bed at night and I hear her heave a deep and satisfied sigh, as she curls up to sleep herself, I know that I have truly arrived at a place I wanted to be in life and my soul can be at peace. I rescued my own border collie this time; and this time she gets to stay.

Jaxxy Girl just celebrated her 1st year of life at Solace. We think she may have forgotten she ever had another life, unless of course you try and take her for a ride in the car.

The Animals Teach Us Everything & Other Short Tails

Published February 2017

Hope springs eternal

Some weeks you feel so immersed in sadness and world catastrophe that words fail you. Some days you could not even say whether you had seen the sun or not, your mood is so dark. Sometimes you feel so heavy and burdened with worry that you can barely wait until the end of the day so you can close your eyes to darkness and away from reality. Those are not good days or weeks. Many of those feelings are catapulted towards us because of things beyond our control that make us sad, worried, stressed. The modern world can be a tough, unrewarding place at times.

But since my illness, I do try to see the bright where I can, the sun behind the clouds, the stars in the night sky, the spring-green of the grassy meadow. Heavy of heart after work one day, I took my dogs out on the land. They tore up the hill, thrilled that that we were out walking and looking for balls. The greeting of the neighbor dogs heralded a huge gallop down one hill and up the other, making me laugh as it always does. Looking down at my feet, there were so many different types of wild flowers, I had to look more closely to examine their beauty. The raspberry color of one, the lilac and bright yellow of others, nestled so stunningly in front of the bright green back drop. The air was sweet, puffy white clouds above wafting through azure skies, occasionally near a scent of sea salt from beyond the Lucia range, wind rushing through the grasses creating an elegant dance. We stopped at the top of the hill and rested on my red bench. I had a compilation of 24 paws around me, all adoring. We sat in quiet contentment. They were panting like hot dogs do and I was watching the Salinas river winding its way north, feeding our rich valley with her gifts. Then the train came shunting through and I wondered where the people were going and why they chose to travel that way. The wonderful noise of the conductor's horn echoed through the valley as they approached town and then they were gone, until the next time. 10.30am and 6pm daily – with some others sometimes in between. It's nice to have things you can count on, however small.

I look around my garden at the sunflowers shooting up from the bird seed offerings the birds allowed to grow. The blossom on the fruit trees promises some generous summer presents and the California poppies sway in the breeze, as they decorate the soil. Doves coo around the olive trees and swoop from tree to tree. I hope they nest here again this year. Little sparrows hop around my 'Peace Tree' that contributes to the yard and I remind myself to sprinkle gifts there too, so those little munchkins know that I saw them too. A sign next to my olive tree, 'Enjoy the Journey' reminds that this is all we have, that we know for sure, and we need to take the time to enjoy it; turn from the darkness to the light and embrace the multitudes of free gifts in our viewshed, where we can. My statue of Saint Francis guards the last resting place of our dear tabby cat Joey and reminds me of the fleetingness of life; also that we should always be kind, especially to those less fortunate – and to the animals, of course.

I go to my Secret Garden and call for the turtles. You know it is spring time, when you call them and their heads pop up. During the winter, that is seldom the case. Gilroy, Thursday Solo and our newest member of the pond club, Turkey, (bought to me on Thanksgiving Day), all lifted their little faces, popped open their mouths and gobbled up their breakfast. They basked for a little while and then took off under water, powering away with glee. I was reminded that Turkey is likely a female and we may be looking at some little turtlelettes, if we are very fortunate. The gifts of spring can be found everywhere, if you take off your dark glasses and allow the richness of new budding life to come in through your window and help you breathe through the darkness and push through to the light. I think this is also called hope. May it spring eternal.

Published April 16, 2018

Laughing At the Old Man

My poor friend was in bed with a bad back. "Had a busy week?" she asked, thirsty for news outside of her sick bed. "Ack, too busy!" I squealed in return and went on to tell her about my week for the next 30 minutes. Well, she did ask! First, we had our largest fundraiser of the year for the animal rescue - 'Pinot For Paws' – a resounding success. Next it was off to the Central Valley for the Celebration of Life for my friend's mother – and all the interesting adventures that come along with that sort of occasion, not to mention the central valley heats that will sucker-punch you in a micro-second. (Note to self – do not step on the pool concrete in the heat of the day with your naked foot!) Back home again in the more forgiving airs of Monterey County, I did some work, laundry, groceries, animal-related duties. Just relating my traveler tales from the last few days made me completely exhausted all over again. Gosh, how does anyone have time to read a book anymore, let alone finish the book they are supposed to be working on, or write a story for their weekly column! It's Father's Day weekend and I hadn't even unpacked. Thank goodness, our son canceled his Sunday visit, or I would have had closets packed with dirty laundry and unpacked bags.

Our daughter made it home though – two days prior to Father's Day. And she made it with a plan. A long time ago, she hatched a plot to purchase her dad a new recliner for his 'area,' as we call it. This 'area' is a very shabby corner of the family room where he works on his home inspection reports, where he snacks, eats and watches tv. Also sleeps. He pretty much has roots in that corner of the room; even the odd mouse has been known to hang out back there, safely in the knowledge that there will always be things to eat and no danger of any cats entering that toxic zone. When the kids come to visit, they always sink into the nasty old chair, maybe as a sort of primal effort to smell the skin of their father again all over themselves. I would never sit there – it was completely disgusting, as far as I was concerned; but he loved it. The more people would criticize his nasty chair, the more he would beam lovingly and stretch out almost flat with his arms above his head in contented fashion. Even his mother expressed concern that he was increasingly spending the night in the darn thing, but what could you do. It was a sort of indescribable love for a super gross object that completely flawed me, but pretty much ensured I got the whole of the Cal King bed most nights to myself.

"How am I going to get him out of the chair?" my daughter hissed at me, noting that the new chair would be arriving in 30 minutes. "Just tell him!" I whispered back. We peeked around the corner at this human root vegetable, not looking as if he were going anywhere for the foreseeable future. I slink over, helpfully, towards his corner. "Francoise has something to tell you, dear!" I broached. He sat up sharply, or as much as you can in a recliner with no springs. "Well", he said, just a little more boisterous than usual, glaring at her left hand. "That can only be one of two things." We laughed. "Noooo, dad!" Francoise tittered. "My brothers and I have bought you a new chair for Father's Day and it's arriving in 22 minutes; so you need to get out of this one!" To our amusement, he didn't seem remotely relieved; more alarmed, if anything.

The beautiful new dark brown leather recliner arrived. We made him go to his man cave outside, while it was being set up in the corner and made to look entirely splendid and welcoming. Eventually he was allowed back in to feast his eyes on his new chair, his new clean space, his new working area. He sat down awkwardly, frowning. "Do you like it, dad?' Francoise broached. Not being, perhaps, the most gracious receiver of gifts on the planet, I was so ready for the "Yeah, it's nice," response, using the flash of my eyes for tools. "Yes, darling, it's lovely" … He struggled in response, still frowning.

All ready to get the old cesspit chair out of my house and to its proper funeral and final resting place at the local dump, the old man duped my efforts and, instead, steered the ship away from the trash pile and towards the man cave, where he proceeded to set it up. "Perfect!" he announces. "I can sit out here as well and do my inspection reports!" Oh my, how we laughed.

The next morning I get up and the beautiful new chair is on dirty old bricks in our family room, so that it is tilted back at the same angle of the old one. "What the ...?" I choke. "It's just not quite right, dear!" He counters quickly. "Needs wearing in, or something ..." and, mumbling, off he goes to the man cave to relax in the old stinky one we had done our best to remove, for the collective good, from the household.

We cannot get upset with him, as I relayed cautiously to his rather upset daughter. In 20-years' time, the new chair will be just as 'perfect' as the disgusting one now out there in the man cave for the cats to pee on. We just have to accept that he is a stubborn old beast who likes it how he likes it. His mother agreed, noting that he probably got that quality from her. Somehow, I couldn't find argument with that.

Published Father's Day 2019

Lucy Saving Lucy

My neighbor contacted me and said there was a dog standing in the middle of Metz Road just down from our house. It was dark, cold and wet. Of course. The beginning of the perfect drama. My other neighbor told me they had seen the pup that morning too. Well, heck. This is what we do. Off I go down the road at night, abandoning my car by the gate because I didn't want to scare the poor baby any more than she already was. I had warm chicken in my pocket from my dinner. That is, ordinarily, a shoe-in for animal rescuers. I find my way along the muddy banks of the road, diving further into the marsh every time a car came by and internally laughing at myself for wearing my fur boots to go on a wet and muddy rescue. And around the corner and down the slope I went and there she was, just standing in the middle of the road. A car would come by and she'd barely flinch from her stance. She was waiting right there, I thought, for whoever had abandoned her. We see that quite a lot in our line of volunteer work. The dog will just wait and wait forever. It's heartbreaking. I started my dog-cooing noises, holding the warm chicken out in the open, so she could smell it. No, she just kept moving further and further away. A nice CHP officer came by and tried to help me and then frightened pup just took off into the vineyard. "You'd better get out of the road, lady," he suggested nicely. I had a terrible night thinking of the poor baby, alone and scared in that freezing dank darkness, miles from home.

The next morning I see a dog posted on FaceBook that looks very similar to the one I had been pursuing the previous night. 'Lost from downtown Soledad,' it read. My, she would have traveled quite the distance if that was the same dog, I pondered. Then my neighbor notifies me again. "She's back in the road!" And off I go again, this time with better footwear and provisions to be there for the long haul. I would not return without this pup. And there she was in the middle of the road. I could see it was the same dog from the posting that morning. I messaged the family and parked myself on a side road with my treats, doggie wet food, water, blanket and more. Folks, seeing me sitting on the ground next to my tire, seemingly having some kind of random picnic, did not stop to see if I needed any help. And then one lady stopped."I've been trying to catch her too," the lady said, surrounded by a chorus of small barkings in her red car. It seemed as if a lot of us had. And there she was, coming closer and closer to me. I made my sweet doggie sounds and watched her. Some of my very best animal rescue work is done when I am sitting down on my bottom. She sat down, not too far away. She was exhausted. Maybe I would be able to get close enough to call the number on her collar. I could see there was one. I gradually approached her on my knees, a bowl of wet food in hand. She let me. I sat next to her so I could see the number and dialed it. "I have your dog," I said to the lady at the end of the line. "I have Lucy," because that was the dog's name. I put my hand under her collar, so she couldn't take off and sat with her in the mud. She sighed deeply as I nuzzled her pretty head. It's days like these that make up for some of the more painful days in rescue work. As her Mama rounded the corner, her ears pricked up. She recognized her car and started to wag her tail. Mama was beside herself with happiness and had a good cry. Naughty Lucy had pushed out a window screen at their house downtown and gone off on a little adventure. And then she couldn't remember her way home. It made me so happy to tell all the worried folks in Facebook and Dog- Loving Land that Lucy was safely reunited with her mama Brenda.

And so, that was the week that was; a ridiculously emotional and demanding mix of peaks and furrows that had nothing to do with my paid work, (which was going pretty well, fortunately!) The week was one when Lucy saved Lucy and then, as we know in animal-lover land, she rescued her right back.

Published 2019

Ode to the Fastest Dog on the ranch

Fate nearly kept us apart. It was many moons ago and our daughter was a mere nine years or so young at the time. My husband and I had finally conceded that, yes, in the countryside, it is imperative that, as a normal family, you have at least one dog; so we had set about the huge task of trying to find that perfect canine for our 'perfect' family. Of course, it becomes quickly apparent, when you start looking, that there are lots of perfect specimens out there from the canine world to be embraced into a family unit. It is just mostly the humans who are royally sucky; but that is another subject entirely.

So off we went to the Salinas Animal Shelter. And there he was; the perfect specimen. He had been found off the freeway at Gonzales at about 3 months old. He was small, but not too small; a gorgeous rich ginger-sorrel color with the sweetest chocolate brown eyes and silky-soft ears known to man or beast. He was perfect for us. The only problem was that he had already been promised to some one else. We put our names up on the list as his second choice humans and went off to lunch, hoping for the best. The best came our way and he became ours. Several years down the road, it is still clear to me that human beings could learn a lot from my alpha dog. That much I do know.

Baxter or 'Buddy,' as he became fondly known to those closest to him, has had to get accustomed to a constant flux of change in our household over the years. Whether it was the addition of cats, goats, other dogs, llamas, other dogs, other cats, horses, other horses, or — can you hardly believe it — yet more dogs, Bud learned to take everything in his stride. He was never jealous or fazed by a new arrival. If a new pup showed up on the scene and needed to burn off some of his pent up energy, Bud was ready to take him on and give him a good work out, bouncing around like a two year old and teaching the pup some nice oral manners. Need to learn how to handle the equine component of the ranch? He was on that. Need to know how to maneuver your way around a 400lb llama running at full pelt? Yeh, he could do that too. He was always the great chameleon of the flock, the constant welcoming-mat for all the waifs and strays that needed a good meal and a peaceful place to lay their head at our home we call 'Solace'. He totally understood that aspect of our home and never gave us any grief over the lack of dog bowls, the constant competition in the petting zone or the need to share the love. I have always felt he could teach the human race more than a thing or two about how to live and how to be.

As time went by and his hips became a little stiffer and his muzzle a little more salt and pepper, his personality remained the constant all the way around. He knew his place; he was the Alpha, the main man, the rock star and the most civilized of the flock, no matter what. He knew how to train the pups, love on the kittens, mix with the goats, hang with the llamas, run with a horse and, boy, oh boy, could he run. He was, is and will, most likely, always be the fastest dog on the ranch. He has the most tremendous, effortless stride that, at full pace, is like watching a greyhound on the race track in pure, glorious speed acceleration. Throw the scent of a squirrel a quarter mile down the road or the scamper of an accelerating rabbit way down where, Baxter would be on it and very often would end up retrieving said munchkin. Who knows what kind of breed is wont to do that, but Bud could do that and he was a breed unto himself.

Then one day he was quiet, he was distracted and he was definitely not himself. Like an old man, he did not want to get up and out of the chair, he did not want to come inside to rest or eat, he just wanted to sit like a statue and just be still in his own zone. I went out to see him and he did not remember me. He moved his head at strange angles here and there, as if it hurt him. He wanted to lay it down, but it did not lay well. He got up and fell over, swayed from side to side as if drunk. We cried and kissed on him, we told him what he meant to us and that we were not ready to let him go. It was a painful and difficult day, the day we thought we were saying goodbye to our Bud, our Alpha, the fastest dog on the ranch.

But, apparently, he wasn't ready to go either. He took some fluids from the vet, some steroids and some pain pills for his mega head ache over the course of an entire day. He let us cry on him and worry about him all day long, and then he just came home, stumbling just a little and not quite where he was just two days ago, but more himself than we had hoped for. He perked up at the sound of his name and gave me a little wag as I picked him up to take him home, almost telling me wryly, "Well, it's about time, Mother! Where have you been all day?"

So here we are in no man's land, not knowing if our beautiful Baxter has days, months or many more years to live. He may be super sick, or he may just be taking a time out and be back to normal tomorrow and the day after with a vengeance and an appetite to match. We can only wait and hope that this was just a blip along the way of what has been a truly wonderful, healthy life for him.

In the meantime, I am reminded of the fragility of all of life and how, from one day to the next, you can never anticipate how your plates will shift and how all your best made plans can go from rock to sand in a heart beat. My family and I went through that today with our beloved Alpha and the wake up call we received may keep us alert for some time to come. Life is a delicate gift in all of its shapes and forms. Never miss a chance to tell your loved ones how much they mean to you and what it is going to mean to you when they are gone. You never know if today is going to be that day.

Baxter 'Buddy' Jensen, forever the fastest dog on the ranch, passed away peacefully at home April 18, 2019. Always kind. Always loved.

Sophie & The Cockroaches

This was a very long time ago. One Halloween. My daughter and her friend wanted to go trick-a-treating by themselves and they were all of 8 years old, so alone was not going to be happening. But we, the parental unit, agreed to stalk them from house to house in our VW van and, that way, they could act as if they were alone, but with a creepy adult shadow following behind. That was acceptable to them. Plus they could dump out their candy buckets when they got too full; also a useful service.

We were parked near the new homes at the time, formerly known as Snob Hill. I noticed a car drive past, pause at the curb and then swing a u-turn away from the homes. It had dumped something on the curb. At first, I thought it was a child. I leapt out of the van and over to the shivering bundle, that turned out to be a skinny yellow chi-pom mix, trembling with cold and fear. I picked her up – she was boney and terrified. "Poor baby," I show her to my husband and we were instantly smitten. "Other people get candy on Halloween, you come home with a dog…" Or so the popular myth goes.

And so Sophie Halloween Jensen came to live with us and became the smallest dog I had ever been around. She was a glorious golden yellow color when clean, which was not very often, since she was quite the scallywag and loved to roll in dirt the minute she was clean. The vet thought she had been used as a breeding machine and then, when she dried up, so did their use for her. She was quite nervous of people in the early days, but loved her best friend Baxter - our first rescue dog - and always sought out refuge at his side.

She loved to run with the horses in the vineyard, her little legs drumming a hundred miles an hour to keep up, so that you could hardly see them. Seldom would she accept a ride in the golf cart and rest her tiny self. She just loved to run with the big dogs, and, truthfully, she was always the boss of them. She had no fear and the sharpest little screechy bark, when any of them thought that they could maneuver their way over to her bowl. Even in later years, when she was deaf and blind, she still knew when something was nearing her food dish and would immediately issue her warning screech. She was the smartest little thing.

One time, my daughter and I were exercising our two horses and the dogs in the vineyard, as we did quite often. Suddenly my daughter turns around and witnesses Sophie being picked up by the jaws of a coyote, which proceeded to run off with her. My daughter kicked up her horse and they took off in furious pursuit. Even from a distance, I could see that Sophie's little body was limp and I feared the very worst. Terrified by all the hoopla behind him, the horse hooves approaching and the other dogs barking, the coyote dropped little Sophie and took off down the vineyard rows. To my enormous surprise, Sophie picked herself up and started running for home. I couldn't believe it. I took off after her and found her back at the house with a small gash on her back. We were all in such shock and the light was fading fast. Husband pulled out his needle and thread and sewed her up; as you do. The next day she was as right as rain. This was when the 'Sophie and Cockroach' myth was born. 'At the end of the world', so the story went … 'There will be the cockroaches … and there will be Sophie.' We have still never heard of a dog being carried in a coyote's jaws with its razor sharp teeth and living to tell the story, as it were.

She kept on living with her tiny body and huge appetite, not to mention attitude. People told me they had heard of chi mixes living to be about 25 and they reckoned she was around 23. Even deaf and blind, she still seemed to have quality of life. When Baxter died, however, she had no sleeping mate. We should have known. She disappeared one day and we found her at dusk, walking in circles down below in llama land, a place she hadn't visited in years. She was disoriented and covered in strange bugs. I bathed her and gave her some salami and cheese – her favorite. A few days later, she went missing again and husband caught sight of her headed down to llama land again, as if she had chosen her spot to pass and she was going there again, this time uninterrupted. He picked her up and she died in his arms. The reign of Sophie Halloween Jensen, one of folklore in these parts, had come to an end. But we will always remember her amazingly feisty self and pledge to live by the lessons she taught us. 1. Bark big, even if you're not. 2. Eat well. Always. 3. When necessary, play dead.

We buried her right next to Baxter in Puppyland. Interestingly, like old married couples, they passed away well within a month of each other. She would have liked that a lot. He was always her chosen one; now they would be together forever.

Sophie passed away peacefully in her Dad's arms on May 21, 2019.

The Equitation Safety Guide & Other Cautionary Tales

"I don't want you to take this the wrong way, Lu," my father cautioned at our weekly Facetime call, "but I am sending you a book called *The Equitation Safety Guide*, actually written by a Dane, but very good apparently …" I assured Father that I was a safety girl, that I was always open to refresher courses around my horse and we left it at that. Imagining the book was targeted at English riders, who knew it all anyway, I imagined it would be good story material; I just didn't imagine to what extent.

It had been a funny old week – one that you never knew what time or day it was – a week without structure. My daughter had gone in for surgery on the Monday and had been at home requiring my care ever since. I had adopted a rather unfamiliar nursing cap during the day, accomplishing little of my own work, as the hours blended into days and I couldn't really say what I had completed at all. The main thing was that the kid was going from strength to strength.

It was a glorious Sunday afternoon and the house was napping. I hadn't taken my horse out for too long. It was the perfect time. He took about an hour to saddle up, because he had other ideas about the whole riding thing. Always the stubborn mule, I battled on, determined to have my time with him. One thing I had ignored from my years as a safety girl. You do not ride your horse when he is in dire need of hoof trimming. Yeah, I knew that.

It was then happy, frisky clip-clop down the hill with me singing to him, then a little lift to go trotting along the meadow and then ker-plunk he took a major trip, almost down to the ground and the singer on his back went cascading over his shoulder, somehow scraping the top of my hands as I went and bashing the other side of my chin. What a mess. Poor Winston just stood there like something out of a cartoon, as I watched my hand swell like a balloon, gushing with blood. Heck. Win and I walked up the hill together, I took off his bridle and went in the house. Daughter was still napping. "I need a nurse, I need you!" I gasped dramatically, watching my hand take on a horror-flick resemblance. Within minutes, the house was awake and my family were covering me with ice packs and treating my wounds.

"You just couldn't handle letting me be the patient for the whole week, could you Mum," my daughter noted, almost not joking. I was a horrible mess for the ensuing days and in buckets of pain, having taken off several layers of skin, aka a 3rd degree burn. At the end of this insane week of doctor visits up the ying-yang and oodles of self pity spitting out of every orifice, my *Equitation Safety Guide* arrives smugly in the mail, as if to say – "We figured you really needed this, so here we are ..." Some things you just cannot make up.

Published November 2017

Lucy Mason Jensen

Published November 2017

The Fastest Dog on the Ranch

If friends call and ask me what I'm doing and I respond 'cleaning,' they know there's something up. When I grieve, I clean. Not that I'm a complete schmuck the rest of the time, but there is never the fervor nor intensity that comes with a grief clean. "What are you doing for Easter?" they ask. The answer: cleaning. My goodness, this has been a difficult month. I could not think of going out for Easter, or doing anything special. Heck no – it was going to be a cleaning day.

He was rescued about 18 years ago from the freeway at Gonzales and taken to the County Shelter. We had decided that we were country people now and needed a dog to match our two cats. Off we went. We saw him and had a nice visit. He had rich brown eyes and a rusty coat. "Some one has a hold on him," they tell us. "Oh no, we already wanted him so much!" We went off to lunch a bit disappointed and then received the call that the hold wasn't going to be able to follow through and would we like him. Would we! We called him Baxter – always 'Buddy' when he was a good boy. He was the most mellow chap, even as a youngster. Though he went through the usual puppy stages of shoe-eating – mine – and so on, any time we brought a new character to the ranch, he was so fine and accepting, whether it be cat, dog or whatever. Newcomers flocked to him because he had no envy or jealousy of his humans – he always acted as if there was room for everyone; even when it meant giving up his bed or bowl.

In recent years we had developed quite the rescue ranch of odd characters and Buddy loved them all. He liked nothing more than to race around after the squirrels – quite the hunter in his day – and look for creatures – rabbits, squirrels or whatever - that hid in the metal pipes on the land. He adored to run with the horses in the vineyard and had quite the stride on him. We called him the fastest dog on the ranch – but he loved being around his humans most of all and longed to be by their side, wherever they were.

Years passed, as they do rather quickly in the animal kingdom and his muzzle went grey, his step slowed a little – though he could still show the young whippersnappers who was boss when necessary. When there were fires behind our houses, we prepared to evacuate our possessions and smalls in the VW van. We were locked and loaded and ready to go at a moment's notice; though the call never actually came. Baxter was so high on anxiety at the time, he wouldn't come out of the van for two days. If we were going to be leaving, then so was he.

A couple of years ago, he had some kind of stroke or seizure. We rushed him to the vet, fearing the absolute worst. I called, expecting devasting news. "Oh he's fine now," they told me cheerily. "We just gave him some fluids and he's as right as rain." In recent months, he had large lumps and bumps all over his body and he was stone deaf. He still had a superb appetite and knew exactly what was going on in his world. "It's getting close," my husband warned me, giving a nod in his direction as Buddy struggled to get comfortable – up and down, in and out. I could not imagine making the call to the vet that it was time and then taking him into their office, knowing he would not be coming out again.

We go away for a few days and leave him in the care of my sister-in-law. The call comes in. 'Baxter died.' He just lay down peacefully in the sun and went to sleep, in the perfect Buddy way. No fuss or upset, or vet appointments necessary. He was ready, he was tired; and so off he went.

He was buried with full canine honors and a large t-bone. The others looked for him and I couldn't, for the life of me, remember just how many bowls I might need at feeding time. Yet again, we were all a bit of a mess at Solace; our plates had shifted once more. "The heavens shine a little brighter with you there, Buddy Boy," my friend told him. "Always kind. Always loved." I told him.

We'll miss the original alpha, our squirrel hunter, always the fastest dog on the ranch. But I'm sure I'll catch the occasional sight of his rusty-colored body streaking down the hillside after a foolish squirrel, or flying through the vineyard rows after a jack rabbit. I have a feeling he wouldn't want to travel too far from home in the larger scheme of things. He was very comfortable here and we loved having him.

Baxter 'Buddy' Jensen died on April 18, 2019. He just lay down on the step in the sun and went to sleep.

Published April 2019

The Happy Book

Reading the work of a London columnist this weekend and her woes about 'non-specific unhappiness and anxiety' in this crazy modern world of ours, also her pledge to think of only happy things despite grim newscast after newscast, gave me food for thought. One friend brought me a 'Happy Book' recently to record all my reasons to be cheerful. Another bought me sparking gold stars and lovely white horse stickers to cheer myself along and stick into my happy book when I have done a really good job of being happy and content with my lot.... (Am I over-using the word 'happy'?) So far, I have managed half a gold star and one white horse. My happy book is borderline gloomsville. What to do? I resolved – this week at least – that I would steal the advice of the London columnist and compile a feast of happiness, a positive plethora of cheer – or as she puts it, rather more eloquently, 'a list of good things in the world.' And that I would share that cheer with other gloomy-folk, who are avoiding the current day's news and sticking their heads as deep into the sand as they can ...('There simply isn't enough sand for all the heads that want to be hidden in it ..' she says. Hear, hear! As they are wont to say in the British Parliament ...) Maybe between us and the ocean between us, not to mention land mass, we will start a movement.

Today is Father's Day. I am so grateful for the wonderful Father I have in my life – a thoughtful, caring man who is always there for all of us. I am also hugely happy that he continues to live life on his own terms and as he wills in his own home. He knows when we need cheering and he acts accordingly. A gold star for him. I am also thrilled to be able to say that I married the best father in the world – the father and husband who puts his family first always and who stops time for all of us, no matter what.

Other wonderful things to report in this happy story is the amount of water our fair State received this winter – no small thing. Though it is hard to remember that particular deluge now in late June when the hills are corn colored again and the ground parched, the river is still visible and flowing through our abundant valley and I am so delighted about that.

I have the best friends in the world – who can say that? This should warrant lots of sparkly stickers in my happy book. My friends in England are always just a text and a giggle away – occasionally even a video or photo – that we entertain each other with. We are consistently planning our next adventure together and it is always so much fun. My friends here are just around the corner. This weekend I spent an amazing day at the Monterey Pop Festival with a very dear friend from about 26 years ago. We were honoring the Summer of Love from 50 years ago, no less, at this year's festival and saluting the break-out event for Hendrix, Joplin, Redding and more in a marvelous scene of peace and joy – and that was indeed a pleasure to behold. Though we were shade-jumping much of the time, I went to soak in the atmosphere, enjoy the old photos and the film footage and I just did just that. Plus, I caught up with my buddy – always a good thing. A gold star goes in the book for her and her substantial involvement in the event and the marvelous souvenir photo book she created from the 1967 festival. Even the original event photographer Fred Arellano commented to me that she was a marvelous woman without whom this tribute to the Summer of Love would not have happened. And this made me proud just to call myself her friend.

I also have the best animals in the whole world. Those of you who know me know how many seats in my heart are reserved for just the animals. Some of them wouldn't win any beauty contests, but their souls and hearts are pure and I just adore them. I'm pretty lucky to be able to brag that they love me right back and every day I cannot wait to see all of them again. Gold stars all round, plus one large white horse sticker.

When we switch off from the world outside a bit, we give ourselves the opportunity to be at peace and take stock of all the good stuff around us. Turn off the phone and read only the happy columnists in the papers – like this one. Don't watch the news, don't dwell on the negative and make a point of sweeping the worries under the rug for a while. This has to be good for us; has to nurture our aching hearts and souls and have us digging for the pretty gold and silver stickers and the white horses to put in our happy book. If you don't have a happy book yet, get one. If you have one and it's not working for you, write down everything you love about your life, buy yourself some extra special stickers and then get yourself a pet. They are the best therapy you can find and you will never be lonely or sad again. Also, you will be providing a home for a needy animal. Gold stars all round.

Lucy Mason Jensen

Published Summer of 2017

The Lady Bucket

It all starts innocently enough – because I love her and we have been friends for over 40 years and she knows how much she and I will love it when we are together again; we just have to make it happen, as we seem to several times a year these days. "When are you coming? You haven't been over here in a while? What seems to be the problem?" Truth be told, I really do enjoy her company and we laugh the entire time we are together, just as we did when we were naughty teenagers back in the home country. It's hard living away from your peeps and not being a part of their every day; but that is the price you pay for location-location, because they live over there and you live all the way over here and we are just not a 'let's get together for the weekend' kinda distance apart. Let's face it – forever friends are the family you choose, so you make it happen - period. Finally, she admitted it had been too long and she was coming over. "Just for a week," she said. "Oh," I respond, enthusiastically. "You can get a lot done in a week!" (I was laughing at the time.)

Some friends will come over and tell you that you have too much crud in your house and you need to really 'Feng Shui' it, or whatever the current trend is, in order not to become a hoarder. Others won't stay with you because you are so messy and your animals have taken over the house – yes, the original 'Animal House' – and they like a nice white fabric couch in their place, blah blah. And then there are the old friends who will come over and, without judgement, happily clean out your cupboards, vacuum your floors, or sweep up your ranch after a long and muddy winter. I'm so happy to say I have those kind of friends and I love it when they come over on vacation – I mean, on work duty.

"I can't wait to start doing the housekeeping," she says before the plane has even taken off from the ground on her end of the planet. She means the outdoor type of housekeeping; the stable sweeping, poop collecting – of various different kinds – the dusting and sweeping of decks and alleys, the weed-wacking of various areas of the property … she does it all and I am happy to let her do it. "Where's my Lady Bucket?" she asks me, as soon as she arrives, after a 10 hour plus flight, pale with jet-lag. What she's looking for is a bucket full of useful tools that she has purchased at least twice to my certain knowledge and that she needs to do her work at our ranch we call Solace. I link her up with her bucket and off she goes. That is the kind of friend you need on a ranch. Early in the morning and she is up, tweeting with the birds. She is sweeping and dusting and cleaning the stables. Later on I holler at her from the stable that I need help and she runs to help me extract winter fur off my poor old horse who doesn't shed of his own accord these days. It is all good and we have a marvelous time. The day before she is leaving, she is up with the birds, playing with the power tools again and weed-wacking the rather shaggy and overgrown areas of our gardens. "Can't you stay a bit longer?" I whine. "There's so much more work to be done …" "Maybe you can come back again this year and stay a little longer? We will feed and water you …" She smiles, knowing she would love to stay longer or come back soon, but she does have other items in her life to attend to like a husband, family, cog, life. "What the heck!" My normally taciturn husband exclaims. "She has cleared all these pathways and now it's raining again! We need her to come back when it stops raining." Oh dear me. Katie-Girl, we really don't take you for granted; we just love it when you come to stay and take such pleasure in all those life-enhancing things that give us pleasure too when you do them. Your room awaits with clean sheets, by the way. The fridge is also full. When did you say you are you coming back?

Published March 2019

The Vineyard Dog

Social media can be quite the bear at times; but for animal rescue it can be useful. It's one of the main ways we find fosters and adopters for the fur babies that cross the paths of South County Animal Rescue.

"Some one needs to come and rescue this baby," the post came over with a picture of a very skinny Catahoula hound dog. "We are in the Oasis Vineyard off Jolon Road. The dog has been here for several days." It was Saturday. The post was shared. Dog lovers, such as myself, were tagged in the post. This is how *FaceBook* can work at its best.

I thought about the poor, starving dog all day. Couldn't stand the thought of him all alone in the vineyard anymore. He had obviously stayed around the area where the vineyard workers were and they likely didn't work on a Sunday, so he would get no food and water that day. They probably gave him a few scraps from their lunch pails, but never a proper meal. And what about water? It's pretty barren out there. Thirst is the worst. I couldn't stand it.

In our line of work, it is mostly, "Some one needs to go and rescue .." Sometimes it is…. "I am going to rescue – can you help me," but that is rarely the case. The some one was going to need to be one of us.

It was Saturday. Husband and I had accepted an invitation to go to a birthday party that evening. I couldn't stop thinking about that poor baby. Despite the fact that I was looking forward to the party, I know where my priorities lay and so would the hostess, also an animal lover. We left prepared with dog food and water, hot dogs and treats. I hoped to be able to bring him home tonight and stop his long stay out in the desert all alone. It was approaching dusk when we made it to Oasis Vineyards out in the middle of nowhere. Acre upon acre of vineyards. We called him, we walked and whistled. We looked in water culverts and near the farm machinery. The light was fading. I started to feel a bit sick to my stomach. Mountain lions, coyotes, who knows what must roam around those remote vineyards. That poor baby. Another Champ had been out there too – and another and another. It did warm my heart that so many people were out there in the middle of nowhere looking for the abandoned vineyard dog.

I didn't sleep at all well that night. I awoke to social media telling me that the dog was with the farmworkers again. Everyone was all a-flurry. The Champ from the night before was on his way down there in a second. "I have him, I have him!" I couldn't believe it when the messages and photos starting coming through. Our vineyard dog was in the car and looking all around him – right after he drank a bowl of water and ate some kibble. If a thought bubble could have sprouted out of his head, it would have said, "Oh my, things are really looking up!" He gave his rescuer kisses all the way home.

And then he came to Solace and he bounced up and down, smiling all the way. "He looks like The Joker!" my husband noted, and yes he does indeed. Such a happy fellow with a wonderful, full-face smile. The fieldworkers named him 'Bailey' which is a good, solid name, but he's also known as 'Joker' in our house. He had a nice, clean bed in an open kennel, a large area of Puppyland to play around in, a swimming pool of his own, fresh water, fresh kibble and treats. He slept like a king that night without a peep. Then he had to leave again to go to County for his stray hold. Those were tough days, thinking of him feeling all abandoned again, but in a different situation. He was soon back though, after no one claimed him, which we knew they wouldn't. I wonder if those wicked folks cast a thought his way, had a small hope that someone nice would pick him up and save him from certain death. This is what we do. We pick up the pieces from awful humans and we make things whole again, one small piece at a time.

It will take Bailey a little while to gain weight and health and stop being afraid, but he's so full of pure abundant love that, with the right family, he will live the best life ever. I'm so glad we skipped most of the party to go and look for him and that other wonderful people did the same. This animal rescue gig does take a village, saving one precious life at a time. We thank you all for the help.

Published June 2018

To begin somewhere towards the end

It became a subject of much urgency, the last time I saw my father, that I get to know his last wishes. When I asked him, I could see a look of concern come over his face, as if he hadn't got quite that far yet – well, obviously not – but that he had not yet decided, or given the subject much thought and would likely have left that rather large decision to the care and perception of his last two surviving daughters.

I'm so glad we had the conversation, because it opened

doors to treasured memories that would likely have left the planet with him. At the time, I also enquired about his early years in Aldeburgh, the town where we grew up, his early days with Mum and the cottage where we spent every weekend and holiday. He put his thoughts together in a swift gush of decision and wrote a piece for my sister and I, illustrated with evocative photographs.

"I expect to be cremated at Golder's Green in London and Lucy intends to share my ashes with sister Mary. She would then divide hers between Aldeburgh, she said, and, at my suggestion, the Pacific where they would join Una's ashes (Lucy and Mary's mother). We did not discuss what she would do with the Aldeburgh lot, but now I have decided. Of all the places on the River Alde for which I have particularly fond memories it is Iken and there I wish my ashes to be poured into the river, please' …

The memories came flooding back. Back then, we co-owned a 'fishing' boat – or rather picnic boat – called Gossip. Father had tired of any of his girls, including his wife, wanting to join him in his sailing boat and 'settled' for the more family-oriented style chug boat, where we could all have fun on the water together. We would board Gossip and cruise down the river from Aldeburgh to Iken – a small bay tucked away behind the Tunstall forest where we would picnic on the sand – my mother's sandwiches were something to behold – play in the water, swing on the tree rope over the water and play 'Swallows and Amazons' on the deserted old boat that was stuck in the mud there. Often our friends/neighbors would drive around to meet us, or some would come with us on the boat. My old friend Lizzie and I were the bosses of the 'Swallows and Amazons' and our long-suffering siblings, the underlings, who were normally in line for extreme punishments for just breathing. I wanted to immediately dig up the old photos and have a good laugh. If Dad had not relayed that particular cluster of memories from the past, I would have likely made the decision for him and a portion of him would not have ended up poured into the River Alde at Iken.

 I told my old friends about this, including my old friend Lizzie, and since we were all going to be meeting up at Aldeburgh for a few days in the coming month, we decided we would also pay a pilgrimage to our old picnic spot at Iken. It has been many, many years since I was there and I hope my memory serves me well. We will be renting kayaks for our river adventure and it will likely generate more fabulous memories and lots of laughs along the way. In the meantime, we are re-reading 'Swallows & Amazons' and remembering who was who in our 'naughty girls on the river' fantasy life.

 The moral of this story is to ask the questions, know the truths and then be at peace. I urged my friends, with our parents all of a certain age and some already passed, to ask them about their last wishes. I feel so comforted now that I know what my dad wants and where. Not to say I am looking forward to his last ceremonies, but at least we will be performing them with his blessing and his cheerful memories all around us. We have all had a lot of fun recently thinking about the old times and those to come. I highly recommend that you have this dialogue with your nearest and dearest as well. It gives you a grounding and comfort that silence will not.

Published 2019

Valentine Vacuums

It was heart day the world over. My husband had left the house early, leaving one of his amazing cartoons behind as my V-Day card. (Move stage back to the previous day ..."Honey, is it Valentine's Day today?" With his voice going up at the end, riddled with premature anxiety.) My daughter's boyfriend had messaged me that morning that he wanted to sneak in and bring her a gift before she woke up. I laughed at that, knowing that he would have to get through the welcoming committee – her resident Queensland – before he had any chance of stepping a foot in her room. (As predicted, his sneak-attack was promptly destroyed by barking dogs and the cover was promptly blown, but she super-appreciated the thought - plus the flowers, gift cards and teddy bear!)

Being more of a 'let's buy the chocolate for half-price the day after Valentines kinda gal', I was going to do my 'daughterlies' and visit my Mother-in-law for Valentines. Honey and I were not going to be standing in line at restaurants together to celebrate heart day and he certainly wasn't going to be sending me any overpriced flowers. Yes, we have been together that long.

Mother-in-law has a love of hamburgers and so we were going to head out for lunch and enjoy a burger together.

"I also need some jeans," she noted. I had an immediate flashback to the jean-buying days of yore. I was about 13 and Mother and I were going jean shopping. I couldn't ever make up my mind, so we would walk the mile plus each way up and down the main downtown shopping mecca of Oxford Street in London, trying on all measure of shapes and sizes of jeans. And then I would realize that the first ones I tried - or nearly the first, maybe - were the ones I really wanted – and then the dilemma - where were they and how would we find them again amidst the parades of jean shops? I remember her clearly telling me, after that day, that she loved me dearly, but could no longer go jean-shopping with me and she didn't. All of that flashed through my mind, at the words 'jean shopping'; but surely my sweet M-I-L would not be even close to a reflection of my 13-year old self?

About 10-15 pairs later and the reflective image was firmly imprinted on my brain; but we did eventually adopt a rather successful system of her sitting down and me pulling the jeans off the legs and feet, as we worked our way through the various sizes and styles at the store. I almost recommended that we try the children's department, tiny as she is these days – but then we found the winning pair and I ran off to find its twin, so that we could leave the store before dark, boasting two brand new coveted pairs of jeans that actually fit her. "Wait, did you want to look at the vacuums?" I enquired tentatively, as we were headed to the check-out. She had mentioned that she still liked to vacuum her house, but that she found her machine very heavy. "Oh problem, no problem !" I say, as we cruise back away from the cashier. We are in the land of vacuum cleaners also. And there she was before us – a light and simple beauty. No silly, difficult hoses and gadgets designed for the brain of a male engineer and a gadget aficionado. No, this grey and lime-green machine was the queen of vacuums. We tried the floor model and both decided that this was the bees knees, so to speak. "Wait, I need one of these too!" I suddenly remembered how much I hated my vacuum and never used it because of that. It had all of the irritating qualities listed above and I would hardly ever even plug the blessed thing in, let alone use it.

And there we were on Valentine's Day, shopping for vacuums. I joked with the cashier about possibly being able to secure the 'buy one, get one free' option for the jeans and the vacuum cleaners - she wasn't amused - and off we went with our goodies. I bought myself a vacuum for Valentines and I couldn't be happier.

For those of you out there who purchased, for your beloved, the most expensive red roses that you will ever buy the whole entire year on February 14, maybe the item they truly wanted is on the other side of the store. Maybe they really needed a new pair of jeans – or perhaps a vacuum? In our house we normally buy ourselves the things we really need and want – because that is so much easier – plus there is always the half-price candy sales the day after the holiday to add a little icing to our cake. I like to take advantage of that too and stun my beloved with late purchases of the chocolate he so loves. He knows he's my Valentine; he doesn't mind if the gift is late.

Lucy Mason Jensen

Published February 2017

Sir Winston White Horse and all the love he gave

Lucy Mason Jensen

The Animals Teach Us Everything & Other Short Tails

I rushed home after a 10 hour flight from Europe with an 8 hour time difference. He was in his stable; something was wrong. He didn't want the salted caramel biscuits I had toted home from across the world. He looked so much older. His eyes were hooded and flanks shrunken in. His back was curved and I could see his ribs. Something was very, very wrong with my gorgeous boy. The next morning, I gave him a good groom and tried to encourage him to eat. Something was wrong with his mouth and his head was swollen. Emergency vet time. They came over quickly and, hoping there was something in the way that limited his ability to eat, they sedated him and put on the jaw openers to see what might be the issue. The vet showed me the massive tumor on his inside cheek and another one on his tongue. 'Let's hope it's not melanoma," she tells me all matter-of-fact and I find it hard to hold back the tears. How could this happen in such a short period of time? I leave for a week and then I come back to this? They made him comfortable and promised me blood test results by the end of the day. That would be the telling thing, we all knew that. He tried to nibble on the grass and the senior grain he loved, but it was obvious he was in some considerable discomfort. "Oh Win," I signed, feeling the foreboding crawl of grieving anxiety take over me like a dark cloud of gloom. I sang him his favorite songs – 'Edelweiss' from The Sound of Music and 'On the Street where you live' from My Fair Lady. He loved his music so much – it would send him into a dreamlike trance. Someone in his former life had sung to him and been kind. I kissed his soft muzzle and told him that he would always be king of the hill, forever my bestest boy, my first and only horse, my best friend. He nickered softly, as if to say, 'I know, Mum. I love you too, but I'm tired. You need to let me go."

The results came back and they were not good at all. His liver was failing, everything was tumbling, spiraling down. He likely had lymphoma as well as all the other stuff. The emergency vet told me she recommended we put him to sleep. I spoke to Win's own vet and couldn't help bawling down the phone to her - (that, I'm sure, was really helpful after a long day's work!) She knew how much I loved him, how ours was not an 'ordinary' horse-rider relationship. "Let's take it day by day," she tells me. "Maybe he will rally some with the medication. That can happen." I cheered, imagining that we would get a few more days together to go back through all the memories, to imprint further our love and trust of one another.

Early the next morning, there was further decline and he was starting to suffer. I knew what I had to do; not a call you ever want to make. They came quickly and soon my beautiful noble steed, my Winning Boy, was lying on the ground, his legs in running position, his face peaceful and serene in the warm morning sun. I sang him his beloved songs once again, kissed his sweet muzzle and told him he would always live with me, always be at Solace, the place where he found his forever home steeped in love and security 8 short years ago. I would take him back to his favorite beach where he liked to roll after a good ride and I would be sure and put him down on his luscious 'basin,' now rich with spring grasses – a place where he would have been headed next week, when we opened the gates to the 7 acres, rich with spring grasses. Winston Sebastian Churchill Mason Jensen would be cremated, soon to return home again forever. That was the only way I could think of letting him out of my sight.

The outpouring of love and grief from across the world flooded in. Winston had been the wonder horse to so many people. Who knew that a big old rescue horse could inspire such a response? It made my heart so full.

The day Winston's spirit left his body and cantered to live inside my heart for always, we received a call that an injured dog was on the road just down from our house.

Off we went, despite our grief and my flowing tears. He had been abandoned with a fractured leg and left to fend for himself. The poor sweet boy was so happy someone stopped to pick him up. I gave him some treats and he kissed me all the way to the vet's office. We immediately called him Winston and will be pulling him from County this week to nurse him back to good health at Solace, before he finds his forever family that will never give up on him; one that will adore him, just as we adored our Winston. The circle of life has some interesting curves along the way.

Our hearts are tender and aching, but they are full. All the animals at Solace felt enormous loss this week and showed their sadness and respect in different ways. Thanks to all of you who reached out to our family during these difficult days.

The Animals Teach Us Everything & Other Short Tails

Winston passed away peacefully on the morning of April 2, 2019 at Solace, a place where he learned, among other things, love.

THANKS!

Must go out to all who helped me with this epic adventure that seemed to go on rather too long! From my family who tolerated me taking little 'writing breaks' to my baby sister Rosie who kept telling me to just get it done...and all of you in between who supported and cheered and coached me through the more arduous tasks of writing and editing, I thank you.

Enormous hugs and slobbery kisses must go out to all the rescue characters that inspired this tome. You hold gigantic places in my heart and you will for always. I like to think that you made me a better person for our lives having crossed.

This collection of random 'tails' from South County Newspaper publications dated 2011-2019 is dedicated to all my lovely friends and family, without whom I'd be a nutcase, to my darling Baby Sister Rosie who helped steer my ship for as long as she could, and to all the spirits of Solace that live on in my heart making me a very rich woman.

Printed in Great Britain
by Amazon